DATE DUE

DC 6 '98			
DE 18 '99			

DEMCO 38-296

Making Muslim Space
in North America and Europe

COMPARATIVE STUDIES ON MUSLIM SOCIETIES
GENERAL EDITOR, BARBARA D. METCALF

Making Muslim Space
in North America and Europe

EDITED BY
Barbara Daly Metcalf

UNIVERSITY OF CALIFORNIA PRESS
Berkeley   Los Angeles   London

University of California Press
Berkeley and Los Angeles, California

University of California Press, Ltd.
London, England

© 1996 by
The Regents of the University of California

Library of Congress Cataloging-in-Publication Data

Making Muslim space in North America and Europe / edited by Barbara Daly Metcalf.
       p.   cm.—(Comparative studies on Muslim societies ; 22)
    Includes bibliographical references (p.   ) and index.
    ISBN 0-520-20403-4 (alk. paper).—ISBN 0-520-20404-2 (pbk. : alk. paper)
    1. Muslims—North America.   2. Muslims—Europe.   I. Metcalf,
    Barbara Daly, 1941–   . II. Series.
    BP67.A1M34   1996
    297'.3—dc20   95-43429

Printed in the United States of America
9 8 7 6 5 4 3 2 1

CONTENTS

PART II • CLAIMING SPACE IN THE LARGER COMMUNITY

ILLUSTRATIONS

PREFACE AND ACKNOWLEDGMENTS

This volume has emerged from a project of the Joint Committee on the Comparative Studies of Muslim Societies, a committee of the American Council of Learned Societies and the Social Science Research Council.[1] Over a number of years, the committee initiated several workshops and conferences intended to elucidate the experiences and institutions that various Muslim societies shared. One perspective that shaped several meetings was that of studying societies in contexts likely to produce new emphases and interpretations of Islamic symbols and institutions and, in some cases, self-conscious articulation of those changes. Travel, migration, and the experience of living in plural societies were among those contexts.[2] Like many people currently engaged in cultural studies, we deliberately moved away from an approach that had sought (what were often illusory) "pure" societies or texts as an object of study in favor of contexts of heterogeneity and change, the "borderlands" that could be seen as "sites of creative cultural production" (Rosaldo 1989: 208).

Muslims in North America and Europe have typically experienced cultural displacement, whether through migration to a largely non-Muslim area or, in the case of many African-American Muslims, through conversion, that places them in the kind of borderland likely to illuminate cultural processes. As a way of understanding Muslim cultural practices in this new arena, the essays of this volume utilize the theme of "space." They examine the use of space, claims on space, the architecture of built forms, and conceptualizations of space.

This volume, in short, offers a picture of Muslim life quite different from the political, or "fanatical," one often presented in the media and, indeed, in many scholarly works. Even an article written to enhance "Muslim-Christian understanding" speaks of the "hundreds of thousands of Muslims who have *invaded* [my emphasis] Western Europe at an increasing rate" (Ferre 1985). Some Muslims have challenged these anxieties: the president of the Islamic Society of North America, for example, who urged that Muslims be viewed as a community "of solutions, not a constituency of problems" (*New York Times,* September 3, 1990); or M. Arezki Dahmani, the president of France Plus, who, in a much-quoted phrase, has urged that immigrants be viewed as "une chance pour la France comme la France est une chance pour eux" (*Le Monde,* July 31, 1991). However regarded, what is incontestable is that all our societies are increasingly plural, and that we need to understand that pluralism from the perspective of all the participants.

The volume begins with a focus on everyday life, above all on the "sacred words and sanctioned practice" discussed in the introduction below, which are often not readily visible to outsiders. This emphasis continues into the second part of the book, but now in a context of interaction, often contestation, with the larger society. This approach directs us to central themes in Muslim cultural life, to the matrix within which cultural change is negotiated, to the behaviors that sustain cultural reproduction, and to significant commonalities among Muslims in areas scattered across the globe.

Muslims in North America and Europe embrace a great range of peoples, from migrants from old Muslim areas to recent converts, who may be industrial laborers, highly educated professionals, students, or others. Without wishing away the deprivation, racism, and prejudice that are realities for many, these essays emphasize the cultural strength, creativity, and inventiveness that are equally real. The focus on space directs us to real people in real settings and at the same time lets us glimpse something of imagined places as well: new Medinas, new Toubas, new Karbalas, and possibilities that range from Alevistan to a Muslim Europe. As nation-states lose some of their role as a totalizing force in their citizens' lives, new boundaries and new kinds of consciousness clearly now emerge: these Muslim populations offer one concrete example of these changes.

Our hope is that this volume—even in the aftermath of the Rushdie affair, beginning in 1988, and the bombing of the World Trade Center in 1993—will provide some fresh, nonstereotypical ways of thinking about Islam and, more specifically, of thinking about Muslims, who, in an infinite variety of ways, enlarge the global space of which we are all part.

It is a pleasure to thank many people who have contributed to this volume. Thanks above all to the ACLS/SSRC and, through them, to the Ford Foundation, which provided support to the joint committee. At the SSRC, David Szanton served as midwife, or maybe progenitor, to the committee when it was launched in 1984 and continued as staff to the committee through its first half-dozen years. No one played a greater role than he, both in practical terms and in vision, in sustaining the committee over these years, and his faith in this project, for example, was crucial. Since this project, one might argue, was his last with the council before he moved on to Berkeley, we wish the volume to be dedicated to him and his exemplary role in international studies.

William Roff and Lila Abu-Lughod, as successive chairs of the committee, played similarly invaluable roles. Bill in particular was responsible for convening a one-day workshop (September 18, 1988) that focused on African-American Muslims, one of the building blocks on which this project was built. Thanks to Al Hajj Muzaffar Ahmad Zafar, Aminah Beverly McCloud, Dawadu Haneef Abeng, Kamal Hasan Ali, Mark Brown, Muhammad Abd Al-Rahman, and Yusuf Nuruddin for their participation on that occasion. Committee meetings organized by Gilles Kepel in Paris (December 1987) and John Eade in London (June 1990) gave us opportunities to visit Muslim sites and neighborhoods in those cities. Committee members held two one-day workshops specifically to plan for this conference, joined on both occasions by David Lelyveld and on the second by Talal Asad and Aslam Syed, in addition to Akbar Muhammad, Beverly McCloud, Gulzar Haider, and Susan Slyomovics, who offered oral presentations of their work.

From November 1–4, 1990, we held the final conference of the project. Our thanks for additional support for that meeting to the Aga Khan Trust for Culture, and particularly to Hasan Uddin Khan and Ahmet O. Evin. Special thanks too to the Middle East Center at Harvard and its director, William Graham, also a member of the joint committee, who were our excellent hosts. Additional commentators and paper presenters, beyond those included in the volume, were Lila Abu-Lughod, Ali Asani, Felice Dassetto, Oleg Grabar, Heidi Larson, David Lelyveld, Roy Mottahedeh, Azim Nanji, and William Roff, whose presentations and comments inform what is offered here.

NOTES

1. Members of the Joint Committee in 1990–91 included William R. Roff (Emeritus, Columbia University), chair; Lila Abu-Lughod (New York University), Richard Bulliett (Columbia University), Christian Decobert (Institut Français d'Archaelogie Orientale, Cairo), Ali Hilal Dessouki (University of Cairo), William Graham (Harvard University), Muhammad Khalid Masud (Islamic Research Institute, Islamabad), Barbara D. Metcalf (University of California, Davis), and M. Nazif Shahrani (Indiana University).

2. A first fruit of these meetings has been published, with papers organized around the themes of doctrines of travel; travel accounts; pilgrims and migrants; and saints, scholars, and travel (Eickelman and Piscatori 1990). Additional volumes are forthcoming: one on *fatwas, Islamic Legal Interpretation: Muftis and their*

Fatwas, edited by David Powers, Brinkley Messick, and Khalid Masud (Harvard University Press); a second on the Tablighi Jamaʿat (based on a conference held at the Royal Commonwealth Society, London, June 1990), being edited by Khalid Masud; and a third on transnational *daʿwa* organizations based on a conference organized by James Piscatori (Aberystwyth, October 1992).

WORKS CITED

Eickelman, Dale F., and James Piscatori, eds. 1990. *Muslim Travellers: Pilgrimage, Migration, and the Religious Imagination.* London: Routledge; Berkeley: University of California Press.

Ferre, A. January 1985. "The Role of Migration in the Expansion of the Muslim Faith." In *Encounter: Documents for Muslim-Christian Understanding.* No. 111. Rome: Pontifico istituto di studi arabi e d'islamistica.

Riding, Alan. 1991. "France Sees Integration as Answer to View of Immigrants as 'Taking Over.' " *New York Times,* March 24.

Rosaldo, Renato. 1989. *Culture and Truth: The Remaking of Social Analysis.* Boston: Beacon Press.

TOWARD ISLAMIC ENGLISH?
A Note on Transliteration

Notes on transliteration typically explain such issues as the differences among the Arabic, Persian, and Urdu alphabets; the conventions used for the equivalences of the original letters; and the presence or absence of diacritical marks. In this case, as I began to review the essays, I automatically assumed I would be changing a typical transliteration such as *taleem* (education) into *taʿlim* and trying to decide whether to include the appropriate macron over the final *i*.

As I read on, however, I suddenly realized that such change would be misguided. We were dealing with what could be called an emergent "Islamic English," in which certain words, and even certain spellings, were coming into the language. If "(PBUH)," the initials of the words rendering the Arabic blessing as "Peace be upon him," was now widely used after the Prophet's name in English-language publications from Malaysia to Karachi to South Africa to Bradford to Philadelphia, why *should* an orientalist enthusiasm presume a "correction" like a spelling out of the Arabic or a computer-generated Arabic glyph? A range of Arabic words are now acquiring a familiar presence in English publications, and they should, one might suggest, be spelled as Muslims currently spell them, and even be left as English terms—that is, not signaled as foreign by routine italicization.

The issue of English terms in Arabic was raised in the mid 1980s by the late Ismaʿil Raji al Faruqi, himself an immigrant to North America, in a short book whose title I use above, with the addition of a question mark: *Toward Islamic English* (1986). The book was printed in the United States, but the copyright page lists distributors in Britain and Saudi Arabia, reminding us of the transnational network created by English-language publications. Islamic bookshops in Washington, D.C., Durban, London, and Karachi will, for example, likely carry the same range of English books produced by English-speaking Muslims throughout the world, as illustrated for example, in figure 1. A Muslim writing on an Islamic subject in English might well read and cite books and scholars in all these places (see, e.g., Samiullah 1982: 71).

Faruqi's goal was to foster the inclusion into English of a wide range of Arabic terms that were, in his view, untranslatable and would enrich and enlarge English and other languages. Thus, for example, Urdu, a language based on Sanskrit, was enriched by Arabic words, which become the vehicles of a "new vision and new spiritual sensitivities" (al Faruqi 1986: 13). Faruqi pointed out, for example, how misleading it was to translate *salat* or *namaz* as "prayer," since that term makes no distinction between the requisite, chronologically appointed, salat and the spontaneous supplication of *du'a*. Al Faruqi included some thirty pages of words, provided in Arabic script, correctly transliterated and properly defined, to serve as an initial pool of words meant to be regarded as English vocabulary. By adhering to the old cosmopolitanism of Arabic, one would contribute to the new cosmopolitanism of English.

The issue of Islamic English goes beyond lexical items to what can seem a stretching and pulling of English. Thus the language of African-American Muslims at times seems neither equivalent to other Muslim languages nor familiar in English—people speak of "giving shahahdas," for example, rather than something like "pronouncing the attestation of faith that signals conversion." It is the former expression we need to hear. English, to be sure, has limitations. Thus, a pamphlet published in London by the Islamic Information Bureau (n.d.) notes that "The use of the masculine terms 'He' or 'Him' is a grammatical necessity and does not mean that God is masculine." Presumably the pamphlet's authors join hands with non-Muslim proponents of "inclusive language" to influence liturgical and theological writing style.

Whatever Muslims may think of him, Salman Rushdie, perhaps more than any of the other creative bicultural writers in English today, has laid an exuberant, euphoric claim to English as his own, mixing in Hindi-Urdu terms and references with no apology or explanation, punning across languages as those who hear English from the distance of bilingualism most successfully do. Witty and "trendy" English is evident in some British Muslim publications, for example, *MuslimWise* and *Trends,* the latter particularly directed to young people. English has long ceased to be just an English language; for generations, now, it has, for example, been an Indian, African, and Caribbean language as well.

Religious leaders such as Abdulaziz Sachedina argue, moreover, that it is crucial to use English to reach the young (Schubel, this volume). Azim Nanji, himself of Sindhi and Gujarati background via East Africa to Can-

Figure 1. Ta Ha Publishers' catalogue, illustrating a sample of their extensive list of English-language books.

ada, Oklahoma, and Florida, carrying English with him all the way, pointed out at our conference that English is today one of the most widely spoken languages among Muslims in the world. It is being shaped, moreover, not only by the literary elite but by the ordinary voices we hear in the pages below.

There is, apparently, some objection to "Islamic English" on the part of highly assimilated American Muslims, for example, who hope to make Islam seem familiar to non-Muslims. Thus they would always prefer such usages as "God" in preference to "Allah" when speaking English. They stand in marked contrast to African-American Muslims, who, particularly in the past twenty years, have used Arabic terms extensively in everyday

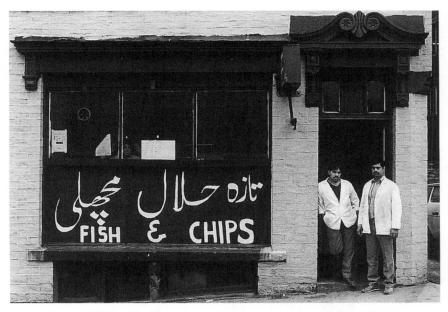

Figure 2. Assur Rehman's fish-and-chips shop, Cornwall Road, Manningham, Bradford, England. Bradford Historical Research Unit, *Destination Bradford*, cover photo. Photograph by Tim Smith.

conversation, presumably because they want to emphasize differences (Haddad and Lummus 1987: 161, 174; Dannin and McCloud, this volume). Figure 2 illustrates a sign that offers both familiarity and (admittedly only to insiders) difference. English-reading customers see the familiar "Fish & Chips," while Urdu readers are assured that the fish is *taza,* fresh, and *halal,* ritually pure.

A subject for further exploration is what happens to old Muslim languages—Arabic, Urdu, Wolof, Persian, and so forth—in the diaspora. In Britain, for example, Urdu has spread to people who did not know it previously; it is the lingua franca of religious teaching, of the many daily newspapers, of teachers in the state schools, of signs in public places, such as libraries. Subcontinental Urdu poets travel to Britain and North America for poetry meetings, and some intellectuals, like the London-based Z. A. Shakeb, predict that an Urdu renaissance will take place precisely in the diaspora.

To return to English, in this volume, we have imposed some consistency in transliteration to aid the reader and have eliminated the capitalization of religious terms that Muslim writers often use. Proper names suggest the phonetic transliterations that abound. Arabic terms are only italicized on first use in an essay. We thus make our own contribution toward the project of an "Islamic English." English is, of course, not alone: "Un mot nouveau entre dans notre vocabulaire: *le hidjeb* [the veil]," noted *Le Nouvel Observateur* (October 26–November 1, 1987), doubtless with typical French anxiety about linguistic purity. It is, one can be sure, not the last to so enter.

BDM

WORKS CITED

Bradford Heritage Recording Unit. 1986–87. Oral histories, catalogue, and transcripts. Bradford Public Library, Bradford, England. Cited as BHRU.

al Faruqi, Isma'il Raji. 1986. *Toward Islamic English.* Ann Arbor, Mich.: New Era Publications.

Haddad, Yvonne Yazbeck, and Adair T. Lummis. 1987. *Islamic Values in the United States.* New York: Oxford University Press.

Islamic Information Bureau. *Islam: Some Basic Facts.* London, n.d.

Samiullah, Muhammad. 1982. *Muslims in Alien Society: Some Important Problems with Solution in the Light of Islam.* Lahore: Islamic Publications.

Introduction

Sacred Words, Sanctioned Practice, New Communities

Barbara D. Metcalf

DIASPORA MUSLIMS AND "SPACE"

The essays in this volume explore aspects of the religious life of the new Muslim communities in North America and Europe, communities largely made up of immigrants and their offspring, and, in the case of African-Americans, converts.[1] In the United States and Canada, the immigrant Muslim populations have been dominated by professionals and have formed a relatively small proportion of the population, probably some three to four million people. The African-American population, probably at most about one million, while including some members who are among the educated and steadily employed, often represent the less privileged, not least the prison population discussed in one essay below. On the whole, political concerns about a Muslim presence have been muted in North America, the one exception being the alarm about Muslims at the time of the bombing of the World Trade Center in 1993.

In France and Britain, by contrast, and to some degree in Germany, largely working-class Muslim populations have been a major issue in public life. In France, Islam is regularly described as the "second largest religion," after Catholicism, its adherents numbering some four to five million. The Muslim populations in Britain and Germany, although fewer than in France, are more visible than in North America, in part because of their more concentrated settlements, and have also been much discussed in public life. These populations also vary in their countries of origin. Muslim immigrants from the Indian subcontinent (including India, Pakistan, and Bangladesh) have predominated in the populations in B itain itself and in Canada. Muslim immigrants in France have been largely from North Africa and, to a lesser degree, French West Africa; those in Germany, from Turkey. A recent estimate puts the number of Muslims in Western Europe, the

United States, and Australia at more than twenty million (Robinson forth-coming).

Many Muslim migrants came originally as industrial workers, beginning in the 1950s; by the early 1970s, many began to settle with their families. Since then, not only have many Muslims been attempting to sustain and reproduce distinctive cultural values in a non-Muslim setting, they have also, in many cases, been doing so in the company of fellow Muslims whose practices originated in homelands different from theirs. These diaspora Muslims now find themselves in countries that vary demographically, eco-nomically, and juridically. Despite this variety, their shared experiences have produced some commonalities in their engagement with the Islamic tradition and their modalities of creating late-twentieth-century communi-ties. They have, moreover, not negotiated such issues in isolation: Muslims today are tied together globally through a range of institutions and media that further suggest the appropriateness of studying this "diaspora" as a single phenomenon. There are, of course, new Muslim communities out-side North America and Europe—in Australia, for example. And "old" communities, as will be clear in many of the essays below, are engaged in many of the same processes as the new. Nonetheless, the particularities set up by the new Muslim presence in the "West" seemed to us sufficient to justify its study on its own.

As for singling out the "Muslim" identity of these groups, we do so, of course, without assuming that anyone labeled Muslim focuses wholly on Islamic cultural expressions in place of all other loyalties. For some, other networks, such as class or professional organizations, have proven more important. This has at times, for example, been the case with groups rang-ing from embattled "blacks" in Britain to wealthy professional or business groups among Iranians in Los Angeles. Some researchers have used sur-veys to show a marked falling away from religious practice among second-generation Muslims in France.[2] Typically, those we study live in a web of loyalties and networks that may well take on different emphases in differ-ent contexts and at different times, and that typically change in the very processes of social and political life. A Muslim identity has, however, been important and has entered into public life at both local and national levels.

To explore the cultural life of these populations, we have chosen to focus on the theme of "space." Many of these Muslims have themselves moved physically from one geographic area to another, and they, their offspring, and converts as well often have a vivid sense of "displacement," both physical and cultural. Each essay, to varying degrees, explores issues of space in the multiple senses of that word, seeking to delineate the "social space" of networks and identities created as individuals interact in new contexts, as well as the "cultural space" that emerges in a wide variety of ways as Muslims interact with one another and with the larger community.

In some cases that interaction entails "physical space": the very right of residence, the erection of community buildings, the processions that mark an urban area. The emphasis on space allows us to explore Muslim cultural practices beyond the articulations of elites to the everyday practices of ordinary people. And this focus guides us to values and to (dis)unities that define moral and social life.[3]

Simplest to identify are visual clues to the presence of Muslims: people distinguished by beards or head coverings, for example, and the ever-increasing array of objects distributed by Islamic shops and catalogues: posters, hangings, mugs, bumper stickers, key chains, jewelry, and so forth—a modest "commoditization" of Islam. Similarly, the outsider may look for built or altered environments—homes, mosques, shops, neighborhoods—that seem "Muslim." But "Islamic architecture" proves to have complex meanings. Certain Middle Eastern architectural styles are often, to be sure, taken by the larger population as quintessentially Muslim—an unfortunate stereotyping, as Gulzar Haider argues below, in which arches and domes were enthusiastically used in the United States as shorthand for self-indulgence, luxury, even decadence, in gambling casinos, movie halls, and the like.

It is all the more ironic, therefore, that Muslims in Europe and America today have turned in many cases to such conventional styles. Thus, in one American college town, the Muslim Students' Association recently worked with picture books and a local restaurant designer to plan what the architect called "the prettiest traditional mosque on the East Coast" (*Raleigh News and Observer,* January 3, 1989)—one that could, quite simply, have been set down anywhere.[4] Yet clearly, if one reviews Islamic architecture throughout history, no such single style emerges, to the point where the art historian Oleg Grabar has proposed that "traditional Islamic culture identified itself through means other than visual," and certainly not by conventions of architectural form (Grabar 1983: 29).

In light of Grabar's cautionary comments on architecture, the visual—although easiest to apprehend, and privileged in European thought—should not be taken as primary. Virtually every essay here emphasizes that it is ritual and sanctioned practice that is prior and that creates "Muslim space," which thus does not require any juridically claimed territory or formally consecrated or architecturally specific space. The essays, moreover, describe people whose personal and community lives may be engaged at multiple sites on different continents, or even people who seem to transcend sites completely, caught up in global movements of proselytization and trade, so that they essentially exclude the outside world to carry with them a world of ritual, relationships, and symbols that creates some variety of Muslim space wherever they are present.

This new space, one might suggest, is largely created by humble "postmodernists" creating their own cartographies and living the new globalization implicitly as they travel and interact with one another (Rouse 1991). But there are also intellectuals, such as the late Ismail al Faruqi, Seyyid Husain Nasr, and many others, who challenge narratives that objectify diaspora Muslims as the proletarians or underclass of late capitalism, disadvantaged Third World migrants in need of modernity, or materialist professionals contributing to the brain drain. Instead, invoking the powerful Islamic concepts of *hijra* (migration, "hegira") and *da'wa* (mission, invitation), they see themselves as providentially poised to both challenge and render service to the "West" through the defense and spread of Islam. Muslims, inhabiting their own imagined space, thus become subjects in a cosmic history of their own making, far greater than the narrow histories of Marxism or nationalism handed to them.

WORDS IN THE ISLAMIC TRADITION

What constitutes a Muslim space? We might well expect to find characteristic Muslim patterns in a context like this where people have experienced the kind of cultural displacement, whether through migration to a largely non-Muslim area or, in the case of many African-American Muslims, through conversion, that places them in the kind of "borderland" likely to illuminate cultural processes and characteristic practices. Muslims are Muslim precisely in the sense that they are people who, across time and place, engage with what Talal Asad (1986) calls "a discursive tradition" created by interaction with sacred texts and with the history of that interaction.

A central theme that emerges in these essays is the individual and corporate recitation, display, and transmission of sacred words as a focus of Muslim worship and of moral behavior. Over and over, in context after context, we find elaborations of practice—in the very specific sense of ritual centered on sacred words—coupled with attempts to organize everyday life in the light of those words. If there is a recurrent visual clue to a Muslim presence in these multiple settings, it is above all those Arabic words, whether as documents—calligraphy on paper, objects, and buildings—or as talismans. The Arabic script alone has served historically as a constant visually perceived symbol of Islam (Grabar 1983: 29), often supplemented today by the images of the holy shrines at Mecca and Medina.

For a Muslim to feel at home or for a non-Muslim to recognize a Muslim space, the presence of certain spoken and written Arabic words is most telling. Even when they arrive in unknown places, familiar Arabic dicta greet Muslims from Arabia to China, from Detroit to Mali: "Bi'smi'llah" (In the name of Allah), "Al-hamdu'llah" (Praise to Allah), "Insha'llah" (If

Allah wills). Now that Islamic symbols have become so much a part of public space, the Arabic name of Allah and other phrases leap out from billboards or vehicle decorations (Starrett 1992: 1–4). The photographs of calligraphy in a Muslim home in Canada and an African-American Muslim home in Philadelphia, below (figs. 10 and 14), depict a use of sacred words widespread among Muslims everywhere (Qureshi, McCloud, this volume). Public processions display moving "texts," not in some abstract sense, but on the placards that are carried (Slyomovics, Schubel, Werbner, this volume).

And beyond the words, one encounters shared practice. The linkage between sacred word and practice is clear. Clifford Geertz has elaborated this point by noting that Islamic buildings are primarily spaces where the faithful engage with sacred words, whether in prayer (the mosque), education (the *madrasa*), or meditation (the *khanaqah*).[5] Grabar, even while seeking to analyze a specific design feature of a class of mosques (the placement of tiled panels in mosques of Safavid Iran), again resorts, albeit tentatively, to the priority of practice:

> In the Masjid-i Shah's main dome seems to me to be an extraordinary attempt at symbolizing the Revelation not as the static and learned order of a Gothic portal or of a Byzantine church but as the dynamic and sensuous illumination of a faithful praying. The symbolism of the decoration is not inherent to the design but is the result of man's prescribed action in the building. (Grabar 1983: 30)

In chapter 1, Gulzar Haider describes his own most recent designs as ones that circle back to this kind of inspiration.

That these enduring themes are evident, indeed thrown into high relief, in the context of today's diaspora Muslims validates the emphasis on the importance of studying "border" populations, those living in contact with other peoples, for understanding enduring characteristic processes and themes. At the same time, and equally gratifying, it links what are often the most humble of communities, deprived of material resources and marginalized in relation to the surrounding cultures, to the great historic periods, studied by scholars like Grabar and constituting the pride of all Muslims, of the classical past.

These themes of the preeminence of sacred words and normatively enjoined practices as the core of cultural elaboration, transformation, and reproduction are evident in the entire collection of essays presented here, both those in the first section, which emphasize interaction among Muslims, and those in the second, which turn to interactions with the larger society.

MAKING A SPACE FOR EVERYDAY RITUAL AND PRACTICE

Part 1 of this book looks particularly at Word-centered ritual and Word-sanctioned practice in the context of Muslims interacting with one another and not oriented to the larger community. The difficulty of maintaining this distinction is signaled by chapter 7, the first essay in Part 2, on imprisoned African-American Muslims, who, one might argue, are merely engaged in the same kind of inner-focused activities as Muslims in their Canadian or Philadelphia homes, in French foyers, and in community mosques, the subjects of other essays in Part 1. Imprisoned Muslims, however, engage in continuous negotiation with prison officials to allow the ritual practices—which, after all, define such basic daily matters as schedule, food, and dress—they seek to follow among themselves.

A significant dimension of this practice in these new contexts is the utter "portability" of Islamic ritual. As Akbar Muhammad, himself rooted in the American Muslim experience, has emphasized, Muslim ritual requires no "sacred place." There is no formula of consecration or deconsecration of a site of worship, and historically mosque sites have been used, not only for praying, but for everything from doing business to levying troops (oral comments, May 13, 1990). That it is the activity that defines a place is nicely illustrated by an anecdote told by Heidi Larson based on conversations with Muslim children in Southall, London, who spoke often of going to the mosque for Qur'an study. The "mosque" proved to be an Anglican church, which made space available to Muslims for children's education. Similarly, among Americans, the term *mosque* can be used of a group of people uniting for worship, rather than of a building. Surveys of American Muslims have, moreover, shown little correlation between conceptions of "being a good Muslim" and mosque attendance (Haddad and Lummis 1987: 27, 35).[6] This interpretation of the relative insignficance of the physical mosque resonates with normative Muslim resistance to sacralizing any object and thus risking *shirk* (polytheism). That mosque buildings may become deeply significant in certain historical contexts, including those discussed in Part 2 here, is of course equally the case. But for ritual, it is the practice, not the mosque, that matters.

The essays show how these enduring themes are recreated and reimagined in new settings. An outsider might think that ritual and sanctioned practices among migrants are merely a clinging to the past, continuing the cultural practices of the communities they have left behind. This impression is heightened by the presence of "imported" religious leaders and of ghettoes or neighborhoods—rue Jean-Pierre Timbaud in Paris, Brick Lane in London, Manningham in Bradford, Kreuzburg in Berlin—that seem to reproduce the home country. One manifestation of the assumption of continuity has been the European television programs meant to provide education about immigrant rituals and celebrations by filming those rituals in the home country.[7] German television, for example, prepared programs on 'Id al-Fitr and the Prophet's birthday filmed in North Africa (*Arabia,* November 1984).[8] Such an approach, as has been effectively argued in relation to similar filming of the Caribbean Carnival as a presumed way of understanding such rituals in Britain, assumes a fossilization of practice and fails, above all, to see the new meanings such practices take on in a new environment. Carnival in London's Notting Hill, for example, is clearly linked to the sociological position of the immigrant black population (Diawara 1990). We cannot assume that the old and new cultures are fixed, and that change results from pieces being added and subtracted. Instead, new cultural and institutional expressions are being created using the symbols and institutions of the received tradition.

What then is new? One significant change is the very fact of such representations as television programs, and, even more, of Muslims' own initiatives that define, "objectify," and represent "Islam." This "objectification" (Eickelman 1989) has been advanced, not only in America and Europe but in lands of origin as well, by modern education, the media, and by Islamic movements. "Objectification" entails self-examination, judging others, and judging oneself. The sense of contrast—contrast with a past or contrast with the rest of society—is at the heart of a self-consciousness that shapes religious style. "I'm always aware that I'm a Muslim, that when I go out I represent Muslims and [must not] do anything [that would cause people to] blame Muslims," a young woman in Bradford said.[9] The Muslim migrants are themselves largely products of postcolonial countries where interaction with Europeans and European cultures has been lengthy. They are in no sense untouched "traditional" people encountering "the West." In moving to Europe, migrants from rural areas in many cases replicate processes common in their own countries when people move from countryside to city and settle among diverse populations coping with industrialization, electoral politics, modern architecture, and the assaults of transnational consumer culture on every side (Mandel, this volume). Many are people who have moved before (Shaw 1988). These processes are intensified in North America and Europe and given additional salience by the very fact of living in what is imagined as "the West," materialist, exploitative, licentious, and, at once, godless and Christian.

Werner Schiffauer, who has studied Turkish peasants in their home villages in Anatolia as well as in urban Turkey and Germany has coined the expression "the islamization of the self" to describe a central dimension of this "objectification." He describes a pattern of religious practice bound up with the rhythms of everyday life and shared by the whole society in

Anatolia; in contrast, among migrants, he finds withdrawal from the larger society to enter the religious community, which becomes, as he puts it, a counterweight, a place of respect (Schiffauer 1988: 134).

Similarly, Akbar Muhammad, using oral histories of African-American Muslims describing life up to the 1930s, has shown how mosques themselves were seen as a site of hijra and known as *mahjar* and given names like Masjid al Medina (to recall the Prophet's great hijra), in a way that did not have classical precedents. We are reminded of how the founding event of the Muslim community, the hijra, a charged spatial metaphor in itself, comes to stand for a properly conducted Muslim life. The mosques, like the Muslim home, were meant to stand apart from the mundane and alienating world (oral comments, May 13, 1991). So even practices exclusive to Muslims, even hidden from outside view, are changed by the very fact of their larger context.

For some Muslims, there is a particular sense of merit and satisfaction because of the difficulties of practice in a larger environment that is not Muslim. A Turk in Paris, for example, explained, "It is more important to live Islam in France than in Turkey: to know how to follow practices and customs in a society not yours is a greater achievement" (Kastoriano 1987: 841). Several New York Muslims interviewed during Ramadan made the same point. A Pakistani-American surgeon, for example, questioned the practice in Muslim countries of "artificially changing their schedules" during Ramadan (which requires daylight abstinence). "Absolutely, you get more benefit here than when you just make your A.M.'s your P.M.'s." And a Lebanese-American businessman agreed: "People get a joyous feeling because they have accomplished something in a place where they didn't have to" (*New York Times,* March 6, 1992).

A particular absence in a largely non-Muslim environment is the lack of Islamic sounds, the sound of the *azan* (call to prayer) and the sound of Qur'anic recitation, the latter especially marked in the nights of Ramadan. A Long Island Arabic teacher noted that he had a timer to turn on a recording of the azan in his home (*New York Times,* March 6, 1992).[10] Catalogues from Islamic shops and newspaper advertisements aimed at Muslims are full of such items to create the sounds of an Islamic space. An electronic "Azan Clock," for example, its digital display set in a replica of a domed mosque, can be set for the five daily prayers. Qur'anic tapes, produced in different styles and in different selections are widely available and certainly portable: as a poster at the Islamic Society of North America urged: "Use Driving Time to Listen to Holy Qur'an" (*New York Times,* September 3, 1990). Other devices ("qibla compasses") available in French and American shops allow one to orient oneself to Mecca throughout the world, a critical skill for prayer, as well as for sleep, toilets, and burial—see, for example, advertisements in the *Arrayah Newspaper* (Philadelphia) and *Al Nur: The Islamic Center Quarterly* (Washington, D.C.).

Special perfumes or essences worn by men to congregational prayer are also often available. I accompanied a young Zanzibar-born Canadian Muslim to a Cairo market to find perfumes to take home to American Muslims reluctant to use local products that might have an alcohol base. Again, there is the sense of satisfaction in overcoming obstacles to find ways to create the sounds, smells, and practices that define Islamic space. This very sense of achievement is a further distinction of contemporary practice in non-Muslim areas.

A second marked characteristic of Muslim practice in the diaspora, closely associated with "objectification" and "islamization of the self," is simply greater concern with Islamic practice. At the most basic level, increased wealth, even for those relatively poor in their new setting, allows ceremonial and ritual activities not possible for the poor in their place of origin. Indeed, normative practice and sponsorship of ritual events has often been associated with the well-born, so that, as Katy Gardner (1995) has shown for Sylhetis in Britain, migrant prosperity and observant religious style are linked in seeing migration as a source of blessing—and of enhanced social status.

A series of oral histories recorded in Bradford in the mid 1980s are suggestive of a transition to a higher level of religious practice in many individual lives. Thus a migrant from Mirpur, born in 1932, who arrived in Dewsbury to do factory work in 1961, described such change:

> Oh, we've been very fortunate . . . we're very grateful to Allah for keeping our children on the path of Islam. They haven't gone away from their culture or their religion, unlike myself, when I came over to England there was no mosque in England; there was no way of telling when . . . we have to fast . . . . We were quite isolated . . . so we just used to celebrate Eid whenever we could. (BHRU: CO123 8.9.87 Punjabi)

Migrants may thus distinguish themselves from their individual and collective pasts. A young Bradford-born woman, who spent her teenage years in Pakistan, recalled her own childhood education: "The teaching in Pakistan doesn't teach you to understand the words" (BHRU: CO83 29.10.86). Another criticized Pakistanis for having to *appear* religious (Mirza 1989: 26). For converts, of course, the very fact of a life of discipline and sanctioned behavior, typically seen as a dramatic break with one's past, often represents part of the great attraction of Islam.

Has practice also changed by the embrace of normative patterns—not only more practice but "correct" practice—at the cost of former local customary behavior? This has been the goal, indeed the expectation, of some

Muslim leaders, who have hoped that in a new setting, particularly when Muslims from different areas were joined together, individuals would examine their practices in the light of scriptural norms and focus on what was sanctioned and could be common to all.[11] Several of the essays below emphasize that kind of religious style, a style, of course, common among certain groups in Muslim places of origin as well. In the United States, the Islamic Society of North America, which is strongly linked to professionals and university populations, has particularly urged Muslims to overcome ethnic customs in favor of a shared normative practice. "The U.S. is the cutting edge," a Muslim graduate student at Harvard told me. "[Here] Muslims strip away centuries of innovation and succeed in getting to the essence."

The case of sectarian groups in the diaspora is particularly striking. In recent years, several such groups, long regarded as outside the mainstream have, in some respects, modified their interpretations and practices to conform more to those of the majority. The Isma'ilis, who have substantial communities in the diaspora, now conflate their relationship to the Aga Khan with patterns characteristic of a Sufi *tariqa* (rite, brotherhood), and cultivate cultural expressions shared by Muslims generally, among them architecture (in the project described in Holod 1983), and philanthropic work, including economic development. The Aga Khan himself has argued that the colonial period was one that encouraged groups to emphasize difference, whereas the contemporary situation allows for seeking commonalities. The Senegalese Mourides, Moustapha Diop has noted, have of late turned to emphasize shared Muslim symbols, encouraging the pilgrimage to Mecca rather than only that to Touba, site of their founder's tomb (cf. Ebin, this volume).

The Ahmadiyya, legally declared non-Muslim in Pakistan in 1974 and subsequently banned from Mecca, make a claim to a shared Muslim identity by the very architecture of the mosque designed by Gulzar Haidar, which he discusses below. Since 1984, the Ahmadiyya movement has made its headquarters in Britain (Lewis 1994: 98). The Ahmadi, like the Alevis in Berlin discussed by Ruth Mandel, illustrate greater opportunities for free expression than many old Muslim areas allow. The Alevis have flourished as they could not in Turkey, not only because of this freedom but because the very practices read as "libertine"—for example, in relation to women's behavior and dress—have been judged approvingly as "liberal" in Europe. Indeed, the British Muslim writer Shabir Akhtar has argued that "the freest Muslims live in the West and in Iran. Everywhere else, Islam is an outlawed political force" (Lewis 1994: 52).

The move to what is perceived as Islamically sanctioned, normative practice has, moreover, been encouraged by a range of other transnational movements not studied directly but alluded to in various essays, including

the Saudi Rabita al-'Alam al-Islami (World Muslim League). A wide variety
of media link Muslims as well. They may be geared to a particular country
even while communicating common themes: thus a call-in *fatwa* show in
France can advise on a problem at once French and Islamic: Are snails
halal? (Barbulesco 1987). The hajj is televised live in many Muslim countries and available later on video.

A final theme in the changed characteristics or emphases in religious
practice in the diaspora has been a push to a more dispersed leadership,
more popularly generated, for religious observances and community representation. Women appear to play a central role, whether formally in
mosque organization (Haddad and Lummis 1987: 131) or informally in
the context of devotional assemblies described below (Qureshi, this volume). In the United States and elsewhere, Muslims elect prayer leaders or
imams instead of receiving officials appointed by the state. Muslim prisoners in the United States have in some cases, as described by Dannin below,
struggled to sustain the practice of identifying their own leadership instead
of accepting state-appointed "chaplains," arguing that such practice reflects scriptural norms. Some mosque congregations in the United States
have no salaried imam at all, but rotate leadership among the members
themselves (Haddad and Lummis 1987: 61–62). Not only in the diaspora,
but everywhere, movements like the Tablighi Jama'at have made an emphasis on diffused, group-chosen leadership central to their operation, in
contrast to the exclusive leadership of the old elites. Thus changes in leadership roles, in some cases intensified by residence in the diaspora, are
part of changes taking place worldwide.

In looking at interaction among Muslims, the two final essays in Part 1,
on the Mourides and on Tablighi Jama'at, emphasize the way in which
shared behavior and devotional practice—shaped and given meaning in
all its different environments—create a world for adherents replicable everywhere. For Tablighis, the sentiment expressed by a Brooklyn shop-
keeper observing Ramadan—"the same food, the same moon . . . God is
everywhere"—reaches its extreme. It is themselves, and their fellow Muslims as embodiments of Muslim ritual and practice, that define any place
as Muslim space. Tablighis sit lightly on the earth. When a group of us
touring London mosques came to the Tabligh center (a former synagogue), a courteous young man explained that at this mosque "there was
nothing to see"; for that, we should go to the (Saudi-supported) London
Mosque in Regent's Park. Reverting to the juridical categories of classical
Islam, a young Toronto Muslim explained that where he was, was *daru'l-
islam.* Equally, the Mourides, with their icons, relationships, and cherished
qasidas, "carry Touba in their hearts," so that Marseilles or Manhattan are
ultimately indistinguishable. The Shi'a can reproduce Karbala, as described in Part 2 by Schubel, through devotion and ethical action

anywhere. In the very act of naming and orienting space through religious practice, we see a kind of empowering of Muslims and a clear form of resistance to the dominant categories of the larger culture.

CLAIMING A SPACE IN THE LARGER COMMUNITY: MOSQUES, PROCESSIONS, CONTESTATIONS

Even in the intimate spaces of domestic and ritual life, behavior and meaning are shaped by the context of the larger society. When, in turn, we focus on public expressions of Muslim life, such as the creation of mosques and organization of processions, we again encounter the enduring focus on worship and sanctioned practice coupled with "newness" both in meaning and in modes of institutional organization. What happens depends a great deal on the size and composition of the Muslim community. It also depends on the legal status of immigrant Muslims: whether they are treated as permanent settlers, as has been the case for most in Britain and North America, or are present in some different role, most extreme in the case of German "guest workers," where it has long been assumed that no permanent immigration takes place (Kastoriano 1987: 149–51).

Everywhere, moreover, religious life is shaped by the nature of the majority society, above all, by its assumptions about the relationship of state and religion. In each national context, Muslims may try or be encouraged to produce institutional and symbolic equivalences to non-Muslim forms; they may also strain at being thus constrained. Further, as Muslims make claims on public space, they encounter resistance to Islam, often defined by racism, that in turn shapes their behavior. Muslim institutional life in the diaspora, like Muslim ritual and practice, cannot be understood as mere continuity with an "Old World" past.

Converts, even if proportionately few, may play an important role in shaping Muslim institutional expressions. Kemal Ali, for example, described the anomaly of a New England mosque including Pakistanis, Middle Easterners, and African-Americans, implicitly ranked in that order in terms of social status and prestige. Yet it has been African-Americans like Ali, with his local knowledge of American society, who push for the kinds of mosque-based activities—basketball teams, for example—that conform to American expectations of the activities of religious congregations (oral comments, September 18, 1988). Khalid Duran (1990) has described the unusually active role taken by women converts in Germany in serving as political intermediaries to state institutions. In Britain, the rock star Yusuf Islam (Cat Stevens) has been at the forefront in seeking state support of denominational schools in order to benefit Muslims (Kureishi 1986: 156–59).

A widespread transformation in most communities has been the creation of "Islamic Centers" offering a variety of educational programs, bookshops, and sites for community gatherings, as well as places for prayer. They may be democratically organized. Or, equally novel, they may have a quasi-diplomatic status. The national flags flanking the Washington Islamic Center, for example, are a reminder of its foundation by diplomatic missions; the Islamic Center in London is served by an imam accredited to the Embassy of Saudi Arabia (Ruthven 1990: 54–55). The role of mosques in many cases has also been changed as they take on new functions. Imams may well serve in capacities beyond that of prayer leader, taking on pastoral, administrative, and ecumenical representational functions they would not do in areas of old Muslim settlement (Haddad and Lummis 1987: 59). In so doing, they replicate local non-Muslim religious organizations.

Beyond these local organizations, the British are particularly notable for their expectation that every religious community will evolve a single hierarchy and leadership: if there is an archbishop of Canterbury, there has, for example, to be a chief rabbi. One university center for the study of Christian-Muslim relations pairs the director-general of the London Islamic Centre with the archbishop as "patrons."[12] A Muslim activist and educator has called on the government to elevate a Muslim leader (presumably parallel to the Anglican bishops) to the House of Lords (Badawi 1981: 30). Nothing more astonishes continental European visitors to Britain than the official encouragement given to Muslim organizations.[13] Thus the Council of Mosques in Bradford was established in 1980 partly on the initiative of the city council, which wanted a single body representing mosques and other Muslim organizations to deal with (Ruthven 1990: 81). The Council of Mosques honed its political skills on issues related to the "Honeyford affair" (leading to the resignation of an allegedly racist headmaster), and it took a leading role in the book-burning and other actions of protest against *The Satanic Verses*.[14] A range of other issues, especially involving schools (costume, halal meat, objectionable classes, coeducation), have proven to be the sites at which "leaders" and "spokesmen" emerge. In this context, the efforts of Dr. Kalim Siddiqi (d. 1995), with Iranian support, to create a Muslim parliament within Britain took the current institutional logic to an extreme—whatever the disapproval of many Muslims and non-Muslims alike (*The Independent,* May 5, July 1, 1992).

The British expectation that religious institutions will play a role in public life and that religious education will be part of schooling stands in marked contrast to French secularism. Gilles Kepel has argued the merits of the French system, insisting that the state relate only to individuals and not to communities, and that all evidence of religious affiliation or teaching be kept from schools. The objection (both in France and Belgium) to Muslim girls' wearing scarves to school typifies this concern (Bloul, this volume). Despite their different positions on government secularism, Kepel lumps together the United States and Britain as Anglo-Saxon, arguing that both have given rise to politicized ethnic communities, breeding black ghettoes on the one hand and crises like the Rushdie affair on the other (*Le Monde,* November 30, 1989).

Almost inevitably, it is assumed that the content of Islam as a religion parallels that of non-Muslim religions, especially Christianity. While particularly encouraged as part of British "multiculturalism," the pattern is common. Heidi Larson (1990) in her conversations with schoolchildren in London was continuously educated in Islam in terms of equivalences: for example, 'Id becomes "our Christmas." Children are encouraged to visit religious centers of other faiths and to become familiar with other religions. Notwithstanding the concern of some parents, Muslim children in Britain learn to recount Sikh legends, act out the Hindu *Ramayana* epic, and play roles in the Nativity story (Durham 1992). Likewise, in elite schools in India, the same little boy who is a Shiva devotee in a production of the *Ramayana* may turn up as a shepherd in a Christmas nativity play.[15]

Some Muslims at least have protested what is implicit in all this: namely, that all religions are, fundamentally, the same and ultimately of equal value. This implication of "multiculturalism" has been explicitly denounced in Britain. Ali Kettani, who has served as a Saudi representative to guide diaspora communities, argues that Muslims in the diaspora must not accept "the belief that all religions are equally valid in the sight of the Creator . . . [this is] the first sign of religious assimilation" (Kettani 1980: 103).

Muslims have both entered into and strained against the institutional templates of their new societies. In Britain, of course, the Rushdie affair made evident different expectations of what was and what was not the role of government in relation to individuals' rights and in relation to the demands of specific groups. At root the crisis had as much to do with the colonial past as anything intrinsic to Islam. In British India, put simply, the government had little use for law at the cost of public order. Following communal disturbances in 1924 over the publication of a book called *Rangila Rasul* (The Merry Prophet), an article was added to the Penal Code allowing books likely to stir up religious sentiment to be banned. That law, like many others, was continued in the successor states and indeed used by Rajiv Gandhi to ban *The Satanic Verses* itself. Little wonder that British Muslims expected the government in Britain to act as it had in the colonies— but it never had and did not now (Ruthven 1990: 87, 102).

Taken up for political reasons locally and around the world, the actions of the British Muslims, which must be seen as a response on the part of those already assaulted by racism and insults to their culture, were to be the basis and pretext from right and left for even more insults. Muslim assumptions about the superiority of Islam, and the respect and bound-aries appropriate to its discussion, continue to sit uneasily in a context of secularism and cultural relativity.

In France, the strains against the allocated slot for religion have come with the desire to have religious practice in what is regarded as public space. The pressure for mosques within the *foyers* and factories was re-garded as regressive by labor movements whose triumph had been to keep Church authority at bay. The issue of scarves for Muslim schoolgirls simi-larly seemed to undermine the hard-won French principles of secular lib-erty in public space. The French have heard challenges such as, "You think you are in France, but the earth belongs only to Allah! It is our mission to 'Koranize' the region," however rare, with great concern (*The Times* [Lon-don], November 27, 1989).

As in the British case, the most cherished values of the culture seemed to be threatened: freedom of speech, secularism, the rights of women to equality (if the scarf was interpreted, as it was, as a symbol of restriction of women). Thus, on the scarf: "Ce fantastique retour en arrière: la légitima-tion, au nom de 'la tolérance' de l'inégalité entre les garçons et les filles" (Gaspard 1989).

In the end, both opponents of the veil, citing regression and women's rights, and the defenders, citing tolerance and pluralism, can be seen to converge in positing a fundamental Muslim difference. Beyond freedom of expression and women's rights, Muslims have been charged with flaunting yet more principles, those of architectural and landscape conser-vation, as described below by John Eade, and of animal rights, as noted in relation to animal sacrifice by Moustapha Diop. That at least some of these anxieties masked a "displaced discourse" of fear of difference and racism is indisputable. That very difference, constituted in part in the colonial relationship, had now come home. It had come home, moreover, at a time when the whole project of the nation-state as master of its own autonomous fate—whether economic or military—was clearly at stake. And in the case of Europeans, with the accomplishment of the European Com-munity, political autonomy and cultural identity seemed threatened as well.

Observers have watched with astonishment as Jean-Marie Le Pen's Na-tional Front in France has moved up to gain some 15 percent of the vote. Taking scant pleasure in the fact that "John Bull racists have made less headway over the past decade than their likes elsewhere in Europe," the *Economist* (December 7, 1991) expressed fear that hard economic times would be coupled with new kinds of nationalistic politics concomitant with the European union. Stanley Hoffman (1992) attributes recent protest votes in Germany, France, and Italy in large part to the issue of immigra-tion (noting, however, that in France that protest vote was equally divided between Le Pen and the ecologists). Issues of "clandestine immigration"

(Miller 1991) and the scientifically specious "threshold of tolerance" target all nonwhites as a problem (Silverman 1991). Attacks on Turks in Germany in the early 1990s were linked to expressions of defensive German nationalism.

Ironically, it has been precisely in such divisive issues as the Rushdie affair in Britain and the affair of the scarves in France that Muslims have shown themselves most clearly as participants in their states of residence. In Britain, as Werbner has perceptively observed, spokesmen for the banning deployed arguments of democracy, equal rights (for example, in application of the blasphemy law), and multiculturalism (Werbner, forthcoming). Similarly, as Bloul shows below, Maghrebi defenders of the right to wear scarves in public, just like opponents, invoked what they saw as normative French values. In part, then, the conflicts represented arguments of emphasis and interpretation in a shared democratic or republican discursive tradition, a point largely missed both by those fearful of the Muslim presence and by those who invoked cultural relativity and tolerance in the name of liberalism.

Yet crises have, in fact, also seen Muslims assert the difference between "Islam" and "the West," linking the plight of diaspora Muslims to that of Muslims in Palestine, Bosnia, Kashmir, and so forth. African-Americans stress their links to Muslim societies elsewhere, evident in home decoration (McCloud, this volume), the names of mosques such as Sankore recalling the great centers of learning of Timbuktu (Dannin, this volume), and educational and Sufi exchanges with Muslims in places like Senegal (Kemal Ali, oral comments). This stance of Muslim minorities has provoked fears of foreign funding and political conspiracy, but must be seen as only one strand in Muslim political orientations and imagination. Muslims who have taken on a politicized public identity may question the totalizing culture of the nation-state and assert that they are, in fact, distinct (Asad 1990). In this, they participate in the new solidarities that contribute to the changed context of the state today and to the creation of transnational networks of every kind. The "claims" on space are thus complex and not exhausted by ties to the homeland or participation, on whatever terms, in the new state, however important both may be.

The essays on communal religious expressions in mosques and processions must be seen against this context. Gulzar Haider's architectural career (chapter 1) moved from the creation of mosques meant to obscure a Muslim presence to mosques meant to proclaim it. This change mirrors major shifts in architectural styles quite apart from Islam and is as true in old Muslim areas as new. Meanwhile, as Susan Slyomovics documents in the case of a movie theater (chapter 11), some of the old "Orientalist" buildings can now be "reclaimed." Mosques now announce a Muslim presence.

The new mosque in Bradford is, for example, to be built on a hill and

Figure 3. Laying a mosque foundation, under the gaze of receding photogra-
phers, Fairfield Road, Bradford, England, 1986. Bradford Libraries and Information Services, Bradford Historical Research Unit, Oral Histories Project.

is meant to be observed; it is a symbol of vigor, surrounded by run-down
houses and an abandoned church. Figure 3 shows the groundbreaking
being immortalized by a photographer from the mosque, who is himself
being photographed by a reporter (presumably) from the local *Telegraph
and Argus,* while a British ethnographer photographs them both in the act
of taking photographs. What Muslims in Europe and North America do is
watched. "We expect [the mosque] to stand here long after we are gone.
People are observing us and in a sense we are representing Islam in
France," the Algerian imam of a Turkish–North African mosque in Lorraine explained to a reporter (*New York Times,* November 20, 1990).

The emphasis on architectural expressions in recent decades has been
criticized as an undue accommodation to non-Muslim ideas of "sacred
space" (Eade, this volume). Thus Hajji Taslim Ali, a participant in the
Tablighi Jama't (Metcalf, this volume), insists that the only importance of
a mosque is its function: "You can pray anywhere so long as it is neat and
clean. In the Western world we need a mosque because in the winter you
can't pray outside. This country is cold and draughty" (*The Independent,*
October 17, 1990). The noted architect Abdel Wahed el-Wakil argues,
however, that "sacred architecture" is in fact inherent in Islam (ibid.).
For many Muslims in the diaspora the importance of the mosque has,

moreover, come to rest in its symbolic role as a mark of their presence (Poston 1992: 94–95). Sacred or not, mosques increasingly represent Islam in the West to Muslims and non-Muslims alike.

Muslim processions, like mosques, address a non-Muslim audience. The meaning of Muhurram is different if the participants are concerned to demonstrate that "Islam is Peace" to non-Muslims and to show civic goodwill by transmuting self-flagellation into a blood drive (Schubel, this volume). Muslim processions, as Susan Slyomovics notes of the nonritual procession of Muslim World Day in New York, are also walking texts, emphasizing the sacred Word. Although the signboards may be directed at other Muslims, as Werbner notes, they may also address outsiders.

Self-presentation and contestation with the larger community, within the context of the nation-state, contribute to the formation of an ethnic identity defined as Muslim. At the same time, differences among Muslims may, in some contexts, also be salient. In the essays presented here, Islamic practice and behavior take place largely in milieux defined by language, ethnicity, and sect. Indo-Pakistanis meet in one another's homes to sing, recite, and pray;[16] African-Americans form neighborhoods and worship together in prisons; North African and West African workers in France tend to interact separately; mosques are often ethnically defined. A metaphor for such difference is the design of the mosque in Lorraine mentioned above, which explicitly joins North African and Turkish motifs (*New York Times,* November 29, 1990). This at once underlines the fact that there are two distinctive communities involved, but that, in this context, they unite as "Muslim."

IMAGINING MUSLIM SPACE

The imagined maps of diaspora Muslims, and the definition of centers and peripheries, like the identities they help focus, may also be multiple and may well vary in different times and contexts. Mecca, usually coupled with Medina, is, of course, for all Muslims a transcendent center (not to be confused with contemporary Saudi Arabia, which is to some Muslims anathema and not a center at all). But the West may also be seen as a center, as many of the essays included here suggest, by reason of the positive value placed on new homes in largely non-Muslim settings—value that is not merely worldly but is linked to deep religious aspirations.

Werbner, for example, shows Muslims deeply involved in life in two countries, Britain and Pakistan. The Manchester Sufis are tied to their current place of abode and employment as well as to the Pakistan mountain setting of their Sufi shrine, a site that is neither their birthplace nor a locus of family ties. Both, Werbner argues, are part of their larger "global sacred geography." While the Kohat shrine holds special charisma for them, Manchester has also become a site of spiritual power. Both places have been subsumed under the powerful metaphor of "tamed wilderness" through the efforts of a holy saint and performative ritual acts, especially *zikr.* Katy Gardner's recent work similarly shows how, to Sylheti peasants at home, Britain, a site of material gain linked with a shift to more rigorous Islamic practice, has now become "the sacred center" at the expense of once charismatic Sufi shrines (Gardner 1995). Comparisons in Europe's favor also come from newly observant Tunisians, who speak with disapproval of a secular state committed to such "modern" symbols as the Tunisian president eating on television during Ramadan in the interests of industrial productivity. Similarly, they come from Turks who have chosen to abandon Kemalist secularity.

Muslim intellectuals in the diaspora have articulated a heroic role for themselves and their communities. The late Fazlur Rahman, suspect for his modernism in Pakistan and long a professor in the United States, for example, explicitly expected Islamic renewal to come from Muslims in the West, and he himself set such a pattern in his own work. Khalid Duran (1990) has recently made the same point, mentioning by name such Islamists as Bassim Tibi, Smail Balic, and Muhammad Arkoun, a list to which one could add Seyyid Husain Nasr and others based in America and Europe. Zaki Badawi has expressed the same confidence in Islamic intellectual life in the West, convinced that the most profound formulations will come, not from the United States, where life is too easy for Muslims (cf. Haddad and Lummis: ch. 3); not in Britain, where he himself is based; but in France, where Muslims will be challenged by the hardness of life, the deep-held convictions of republican secularism, and the depth of racism (oral communication, 1991). Badawi himself, with the patronage of the Libyan Call Society, has established a college in London to train a new class of Islamic leadership, freed of national traditions, educated in European cultures, and trained in the technologies of new media (Badawi, n.d.).

In describing the choice to reside in non-Muslim territories, certain terms resonate, notably *hijra* and the always linked term of *jihad* (see Masud 1990). Various ideas about these terms coexist. Hijra may long have been understood as movement from a land where one could not lead an Islamic life, typically one of non-Muslim rule, to a land ruled by Muslims. Today, it can continue to mean physical movement, this time from a land of Muslim settlement, but of poverty, to a non-Muslim land of greater opportunity. It is this kind of migration that the late Isma'il al-Faruqi addressed, arguing that a hijra can only be justified if understood as a providential opportunity for Muslims to lead other people to Islam and ultimately to reform Islam among Muslims as well (al Faruqi 1985).

Hijra today is also construed as psychic and moral withdrawal, whether from support for governments only nominally Muslim (as in the well-known case of the Egyptian Islamist party, Takfir wa'l Hijra) or in one's personal life from practices deemed not Islamic. *Jihad* similarly takes on a range of meanings, derived from its root, "effort," in corporate and individual commitments of various kinds.

A theme articulated by an engaged observer of Muslims in Australia runs through the essays presented here: "While many, perhaps most, migrants, would see economic betterment, or other non-religious factors, for their decision to migrate, many eventually begin to see the maintenance and strengthening of their Muslim identity and commitment, some even see *daʿwa*, as [their] important or primary roles" (Ahmad Shboul, personal communication, 1989). This has been the argument of influential thinkers associated with Islamist movements such as the Jamaʿat-i Islami, notably in the writings of Khurram Murad, who was educated in the United States and has long been resident in Britain; his writings include *Islamic Movement in the West* (1981) and *Daʿwah among Non-Muslims in the West* (1986). Others, like Muzzamil Siddiqui, who has been an active religious leader in California, have insisted that any residence in "Dar ul Kufr," the "Place of Infidelity," should be temporary and for some limited objective like training or travel; but this seems to be a minor voice (Poston 1992: 81–90; 32). The challenge of creating communities in new settings, the creation of new Islamic institutions and networks, and the embrace and elaboration of practice and ritual have all been evident, not for all, but for many, of those Muslims who find themselves in the new political, economic, and cultural settings of the West.

In all this, we see Muslims negotiating relationships with other Muslims and non-Muslims in ways that forge communities of larger or smaller scale among those who share loyalty to sacred texts and symbols. This community means that even in situations of hardship like prisons and prisonlike foyers, Muslims are able to speak—in spatial metaphors—of "places of safety" (Diop, this volume) and "islands of knowledge" (Dannin, this volume) apart from the society as a whole that surrounds them.

To return to mosque architecture, in some of the best examples we can find an emblem of diaspora Islam as distinct both from the homeland and the surrounding culture. The builders of Manhattan's new mosque, reflecting in architecture what some have sought for Islam as a whole, have eschewed what might be seen as design characteristics of particular national architectural styles (fig. 4). Shaped by the specific functions needed of a mosque, and drawing on the classic Islamic aesthetic fascination with geometry, the mosque design overlaps with many characteristics of contemporary taste. But in its grassy setting, skewed some 29° from the Manhattan street grid to have the proper orientation, the mosque asserts its Islamic distinction. In the judgment of one architectural critic, "the mosque is an island, self-possessed, hewing to a rhythm different from

Figure 4. The Mosque of New York at Third Avenue and Ninety-sixth Street, designed by Skidmore, Owings & Merrill. Photograph Chester Higgins, Jr. / *New York Times*, April 15, 1991.

Manhattan's . . . its gently sloping, grassy site stand[ing] apart" (Dunlap 1992).

From Muslims in the West, we learn much about how Islam, like any historic tradition, exists in the process of redefinition and reappropriation in new contexts. In the situations of cultural displacement or marginality in which these populations find themselves, characteristic Islamic themes and processes of cultural negotiation are thrown into particularly high relief. In seeing this, moreover, we witness the vitality, variability, and creativity of populations who, in large part, live in settings characterized by racism, prejudice, and grim material realities. As we look at the specifically Islamic spatial expressions of these communities—the use of space, claims on space, the architecture of built forms, and conceptualizations of space—we encounter both patterns of everyday life and themes of the religious imagination, broadly construed.

Many observers have sought to interpret that identity through comparison to other groups marked by migration and/or religion. Dervla Murphy (1987), for example, looks to the historic experience of her fellow Irish in the north of England as the model for the South Asian Muslims in Britain today, for both groups were consigned to the drab settings of old industrial towns and both disparaged for cultural and religious difference. The Brad-ford Heritage Recording Unit, in a publication of historic photographs of immigrant groups to the city (1987), partly by juxtaposition of similar photographs (Ukrainian boarding house / Bengali boarding house) insists on a common pattern—now framed by the concept of "multiculturalism," where cultural equivalences of institutions, festivals, and so forth are meant to form a harmonious whole. In the French context, Rémy Leveau (1988) has found what seem to be compelling similarities to the experi-ence of Jews in the case of North African Muslims.

This hopeful, liberal, perspective (put at risk, Leveau suggests in his case, by contemporary French attitudes) has been questioned by some, not on the grounds of Muslim "difference," but on the basis of what actually happened in the past. Thus, Albert Bastanier, studying the Muslim popula-tion in Belgium, wonders if the assimilation of earlier immigrants entailed "mutilation," or if somehow an "underground" identity persisted: "Aware-ness of these matters required the experience of the immigration from Muslim countries" (Bastenier 1988: 134). In fact, however, the past is not an adequate guide to the present—let alone the future. The reason for that difference is not specific to Muslims.

Muslims represent a striking case of what might be called postmodern pluralism. Today's world is one of utterly transformed communications, so that groups can at times be enmeshed in more than one country—Hispan-ics in the United States—or be so engaged with an ethnic or interest group—activist Sikhs, Greens—that their closest ties are to others like themselves, transcending states. The postmodern dissolution of certainties also means that assimilation and integration may no longer be perceived, even by the majority, as unquestioned goods.

The Muslims studied here are immersed in deep affective and informa-tional networks of personal ties, organizations, and political concerns that define diverse and far-flung maps; at the same time, they are resident in nation-states whose own contours are ever more fluid. Their experiences of cultural displacement, their negotiations of hybridity and authenticity, are at the heart of contemporary life.[17] We do not know what patterns will finally emerge, but we are convinced of the importance of this moment, captured, as best we are able to do, in the words and images that follow.

NOTES

1. This introduction does not attempt to survey the literature on diaspora Mus-lims, which is by now very extensive, but rather to set out shared themes in the papers, some of the discussion of the conference, and relevant points from the editor's own (idiosyncratic) reading. Citations of individuals identified only by dates refer to comments made at preconference meetings listed in the acknowledg-

ments above; comments attributed to the individuals without citation were made orally at the conference that produced this volume. In addition to the works I cite, the larger literature includes recent edited volumes by Bernard Lewis and Dominique Schnapper; Felice Dasseto; Jochen Blaschke; and Jorgen Nielsen, as well as a bibliography by Steven Vertovec (1993). (With thanks for these references to Pnina Werbner.)

2. This is the conclusion of Bruno Etienne, quoted in Markham 1988. Given the extreme French anxiety about Muslim politics, however, one wonders if interviewees might be hesitant to acknowledge any religious activity at all.

3. I am grateful to Paul Titus for helping clarify the implications of using the term *space*. See his "Social Space, Cultural Space, and Ethnicity in Balochistan" (paper delivered at the Western Conference of the Association of Asian Studies, Claremont, Calif., October 21, 1994). This emphasis on what people do, not only what they say, follows an approach charted by such theorists as Pierre Bourdieu and Anthony Giddens.

4. See my discussion of the possibilities of vernacular architecture in this setting as a contribution to an *American* Islamic architecture (Metcalf 1989). Neighbors raised objections based on noise, traffic, neighborhood homogeneity, and architecture at public hearings on the proposed mosque (cf. John Eade's essay, chapter 12 below).

5. Clifford Geertz, oral comments at a conference to consider approaches to organizing an exhibit on Islamic cities/space (Smithsonian Institution, Washington, D.C., June 17–18, 1991).

6. These patterns may suggest the limitations of using the mosque as a focus for study of Muslim religious life (as is done in Haddad and Lummis 1987).

7. Meridian Productions produced a significant variation on this variety of films on rituals for the BBC with its "The Guests of God," first shown June 1991. This film on hajj does indeed focus on Europe, but the central figures are converts, not migrants, and the converts are based in Germany, not England.

8. Prepared by Dr. Khalid Duran, the films emphasize the behavior of privileged participants, nostalgic about, but distant from, customary observations. Thus, "Care was taken to avoid the more popular events, which can often be outrageous." A third film, on 'Id al-Adha, was in fact filmed in Germany because Turkish officials feared that outmoded "bloody customs" might be included and prohibited filming in Turkey itself.

9. BHRU interview #CO83, 1986. The interview itself suggests something of the alien world in which an immigrant is likely to live. With all the best will in the world, the interviewer's very questions suggest the stereotypes widely held about Islam: they include queries about the repression of women, how the interviewee feels about the need for religious change, and whether she believes the West is more materialist than the "East." She in fact does not buy into any of these themes: women are fine; Islam does not need to change (Muslims do), and everyone wants to live comfortably. The interviewer (or the typist), transcribing a description of the five pillars, turns the fast into "Rosa [Arabic: *roza*], the mother [month?] of Ramzan."

10. For a worldly failure who, like "all Moroccans dream[ed] of getting a passport and working in Europe" (p. 88), went there from 1964 to 1973, but ultimately

came back, the *azan* became a poignant symbol of Muslim space. "Sometimes I feel sad because I have no son and no house of my own. Then I hear the call to prayer and it washes my heart . . . .I was never happy working in France and Belgium because I missed hearing the call to prayer" (Munson 1984: 82).

11. Jacques Waardenburg (1988) ventures to predict a future "Islam without ethnicity" in large part as a result of the heterogeneity produced by migration, but many might doubt the likelihood of any single trajectory and expect variations depending on the contexts that emerge.

12. They are so listed on the letterhead of the Centre for the Study of Islam and Christian-Muslim Relations, Selly Oak Colleges, Birmingham.

13. This is the experience of Philip Lewis, the (Anglican) bishop of Bradford's advisor on community relations, who regularly meets ecumenically oriented visiting delegations (personal communication, July 1991).

14. On the Honeyford affair, see Murphy 1987, Kureishi 1986, and Ruthven 1990: 75–80. Yunas Samad (1991) explains the prominent role of Bradford in the Rushdie affair in large part as owed to the organization and experience of the Council of Mosques. A thinly disguised docudrama about the Honeyford affair was broadcast on British television on December 16, 1991.

15. For example, Benjamin Metcalf, then aged five, at the Playhouse School, New Delhi, 1981–82.

16. Werbner's description of the "interhousehold women-centered spirituality," focused on Qur'an reading and food sacrifice, among Muslims in Manchester complements Qureshi's study of Canadian domestic rituals below (Werbner 1988).

17. The Social Science Research Council has in recent years sought to stimulate a wide range of projects on transnational phenomena (Hershberg 1992).

WORKS CITED

"Architecture: Prosaic Approach to the Divine." 1990. *Independent,* October 17.

Asad, Talal. 1986. *The Idea of an Anthropology of Islam.* Center for Contemporary Arab Studies Occasional Papers Series. Washington, D.C.: Georgetown University Press.

———. 1990. "Multiculturalism and British Identity in the Wake of the Rushdie Affair. *Politics and Society* 18, 4: 455–80.

Badawi, Zaki. 1981. *Islam in Britain.* London: Ta Ha Publishers.

———. N.d. *The Muslim College: Provisional Prospectus.* London: Muslim College.

Barbulesco, Luc. "Les Radios arabes de la bande FM." *Esprit* 6 (June 1985): 176–85.

"Behind the Veil." 1989. *Times* (London), November 27.

Bastenier, Albert. 1988. "Islam in Belgium: Contradictions and Perspectives." In *The New Islamic Presence in Europe,* ed. Gerholm and Lithman, pp. 133–45.

Bradford Heritage Recording Unit. 1986–87. Oral Histories, Catalogue, and Transcripts, Bradford Public Library. Cited as BHRU.

"Britain: On the Seamier Side." *Economist,* December 7, 1991, pp. 31–32.

Diawara, Manthia. 1990. "Black British Cinema: Spectatorship and Identity Formation in *Territories.*" *Public Culture* 3, 1 (Fall): 33–48.

"La Droite refuse d'envisager un nouveau recours à l'immigration." 1991. *Le Monde,* July 31.

Dunlap, David W. 1992. "A New Mosque for Manhattan, for the Twenty-First Century." *New York Times,* April 26.

Duran, Khalid. 1990. "Muslims in the West: The Muslim Diaspora in Western Europe and the United States." Typescript.

Durham, Michael. 1992. "Children from All Faiths Tell the Christmas Story." *Independent,* December 14.

Eickelman, Dale F. 1989. "National Identity and Religious Discourse in Contemporary Oman." *International Journal of Islamic and Arabic Studies* 6, 1: 1–20.

Eickelman, Dale F., and James Piscatori. 1990. *Muslim Travellers: Pilgrimage, Migration, and the Religious Imagination.* Berkeley: University of California Press.

"Extremism in a Vacuum." 1992. *Independent,* July 1.

al Faruqui, Isma'il. 1985. *The Hijrah: The Necessity of Its Iqamat or Vergegenwärtigung.* Islamabad: National Hijrah Council.

Gardner, Katy. 1995. *Global Migrants, Local Lives: Travel and Transfomation in Rural Bangladesh.* Oxford: Oxford University Press, Clarendon Press.

Gaspard, Françoise. 1989. "Pensons aux musulmanes qui se battent!" *Le Nouvel Observateur,* October 26–November 1, pp. 79–80.

Gerholm, Tomas, and Yngve Georg Lithman, eds. 1988. *The New Islamic Presence in Europe.* New York: Mansell.

Grabar, Oleg. 1983. "Symbols and Signs in Islamic Architecture." In *Architecture and Community: Building in the Islamic World Today,* ed. Holod, pp. 25–32. Aga Khan Awards for Architecture. Millerton, N.Y.: Aperture.

Haddad, Yvonne Yazbeck, and Adair T. Lummis. 1987. *Islamic Values in the United States: A Cooperative Study.* New York: Oxford University Press.

Hershberg, Eric. 1992. "An Agenda for Transnational and Comparative Research." *Items* 27 (June/September 1992): 27–30.

Hoffmann, Stanley. 1992. "France Self-Destructs." *New York Review of Books,* May 28, pp. 25–30.

Holod, Renata, ed. 1983. *Architecture and Community: Building in the Islamic World Today.* Aga Khan Awards for Architecture. Millerton, N.Y.: Aperture.

Kastoriano, Riva. 1987. "Definition des frontières de l'identité: Turcs musulmans." *Revue française de science politique* 37, 6 (December): 833–54.

Kepel, Gilles. 1989. "L'Integration suppose que soit brisée la logique communautaire." *Le Monde,* November 30.

Kettani, M[uhammad] Ali. 1980. "The Problems of Muslim Minorities and Their Solutions." In *Muslim Communities in Non-Muslim States,* pp. 91–108. London: Islamic Council of Europe.

Kureishi, Hanif. 1986. "Bradford." *Granta* 20 (Winter): 149–70.

Larson, Heidi. 1990. "Culture at Play: Pakistani Children, British Childhood." Ph.D. Diss., Department of Anthropology, University of California, Berkeley.

Leveau, Remy. 1988. "The Islamic Presence in France." In *The New Islamic Presence in Europe,* ed. Gerholm and Lithman, pp. 107–22.

Lewis, Philip. 1994. *Islamic Britain: Religion, Politics and Identity among British Muslims.* London: I. B. Tauris.

Markham, James M. 1988. "If the Racism Tastes Sour, How Sweet Is Success." *New York Times,* November 16.

Masud, Muhammad Khalid. 1990. "The Obligation to Migrate: The Doctrine of the Hijra in Islamic Law." In *Muslim Travellers: Pilgrimage, Migration, and the Religious Imagination,* ed. Eickelman and Piscatori.

Metcalf, Barbara. 1989. "Chapel Hill Mosque Should Utilize Local Culture to Express Distinctiveness of Islam." *Chapel Hill Newspaper,* November 26.

Miller, Judith. 1991. "Strangers at the Gate: Europe's Immigration Crisis." *New York Times Magazine,* September 15, pp. 32–38, 49, 80–81, 86.

"Minaret Is Silent, but Has Much to Say to France." 1990. *New York Times,* November 29.

Mirza, Kausar. 1989. *The Silent Cry: Second-Generation Bradford Muslim Women Speak.* Muslims in Europe #43. Birmingham: Centre for the Study of Islam and Christian-Muslim Relations.

Munson, Henry, Jr., trans. and ed. 1984. *The House of Si Abd Allah: The Oral History of a Moroccan Family.* New Haven, Conn.: Yale University Press.

Murphy, Dervla. 1987. *Tales from Two Cities: Travels of Another Sort.* London: Penguin Books.

"Muslim Fast in U.S. Holds Difficulties." 1992. *New York Times,* March 6.

"Muslims Open 'Parliament' with Defiance." 1992. *Independent,* May 5.

Poston, Larry. 1992. *Islamic Daʿwa in the West: Muslim Missionary Activity and the Dynamics of Conversion to Islam.* New York: Oxford University Press.

Riding, Alan. 1991. "France Sees Integration as Answer to View of Immigrants as 'Taking Over.'" *New York Times,* March 24.

Robinson, Francis, ed. Forthcoming. *The Cambridge Illustrated History of the Islamic World.*

Rouse, Roger. 1991. "Mexican Migration and the Social Spaces of Modernity," *Diaspora* 1, 1 (Spring 1991): 8–23.

Ruthven, Malise. 1990. *A Satanic Affair: Salman Rushdie and the Rage of Islam.* London: Chatto & Windus.

Samad, Yunas. 1991. "Book Burning and Race Relations: Political Mobilization of Bradford Muslims." St Antony's College, Oxford. Typescript.

Schiffauer, Werner. 1988. "Migration and Religiousness." In *The New Islamic Presence in Europe,* ed. Gerholm and Lithman, pp. 146–58.

Shaw, Alison. 1988. *A Pakistani Community in Britain.* Oxford: Blackwell.

Said, Edward. 1978. *Orientalism.* New York: Pantheon Books.

Silverman, Maxim. 1991. "Citizenship and the Nation-State in France." *Ethnic and Racial Studies* 14, 3 (July): 333–49.

"6000 U.S. Muslims Meet; The Enemy: Stereotypes." 1990. *New York Times,* September 3.

Starrett, Gregory. 1992. "Our Children and Our Youth: Religious Education and Political Authority in Mubarak's Egypt." Ph.D. diss., Department of Anthropology, Stanford University

"TV Introduces West Germans to Islam." *Arabia,* November 1984, pp. 87, 91.

Vertovec, Steven. 1993. *Annotated Bibliography of Academic Publications Regarding Is-*

lam and Muslims in the United Kingdom, 1985–1992. Bibliographies in Ethnic Relations, 11. Coventry: Centre for Research in Ethnic Relations, University of Warwick.

Waardenburg, Jacques. 1988. "The Institutionalization of Islam in the Netherlands, 1961–86." In *The New Islamic Presence in Europe,* ed. Gerholm and Lithman, pp. 8–31.

Werbner, Pnina. 1988. "'Sealing' the Koran: Offering and Sacrifice among Pakistani Labour Migrants." *Cultural Dynamics* 1, 1: 77–97.

———. Forthcoming. "Diaspora and Millennium: Islamic Narrations, Identity Politics, and the Aesthetics of the Religious Imagination."

PART ONE

Making a Space for Everyday Ritual and Practice

ONE

Muslim Space and the Practice of Architecture

A Personal Odyssey

Gulzar Haider

In 1960, courtesy of Fulbright-Hays, I was sent from Lahore to the University of Pittsburgh for six weeks to be "oriented" to American cultural, political, and educational systems. I was assigned to a host family, the Waynes, who were active in the YMCA and numerous other voluntary organizations. The Waynes took it upon themselves to help this stranger see some fascinating sides of America. Socially active Christians, they were also devout Americans. They took me to different church services, and I naturally asked if there were mosques in Pittsburgh. Mr. Wayne offered to take me to one, a building he confessed to not knowing too much about.

As we turned onto a minor street on the University of Pittsburgh campus, he pointed to a vertical neon sign that said in no uncertain terms "Syria Mosque." Parking the car, we approached the building. I was fascinated, albeit with some premonition. I was riveted by the cursive Arabic calligraphy on the building: *la ghalib il-Allah,* "There is no victor but Allah," the well-known refrain of Granada's Alhambra (fig. 5). Horseshoe arches, horizontal bands of different colored bricks, decorative terra-cotta—all were devices to invoke a Moorish memory. Excitedly, I took a youthful step towards the lobby, when my host turned around and said, "This is not the kind of mosque in which you bend up and down facing Mecca. This is a meeting hall–theater built by Shriners, a nice bunch of people who build hospitals for crippled children and raise money through parades and circuses. They are the guys who dress up in satin baggies, embroidered vests, and fez caps." [1]

For a few seconds I felt as if the Waynes were playing a strange practical joke on me. And then I realized they were quite serious, composed, and a touch jubilant at their find. Two Americans and one Pakistani in search of a mosque had comically ended up in front of an architectural joke, a

Figure 5. The Shriners' theater known as the "Syria Mosque," Pittsburgh, Pa.
Photograph by Gulzar Haider.

tasteless impersonation. A big poster in the lobby promised a live performance of *Guys and Dolls* later that month, proceeds to go to the Syria Mosque campaign for a children's hospital.

We returned to a restaurant on the campus. From my seat, I could see the tall, spirelike building called the "Cathedral of Learning" through the glass, and a reflection of the "Syria Mosque" superimposed on it. With the passing years, I have realized that it was in that restaurant that the inherent ironies of the Muslim condition in the West, as expressed through architecture, got branded on my heart. *Cathedral,* a word from the sacred lexicon, had been appropriated by the university for its tallest and most celebrated building, aiming at the sky and daring it to open its gates and surrender its secrets. There were chapels for some denominations on the campus, but this "cathedral" was the seat of a new faith: the secular-humanistic pursuit of knowledge. And, by extension, the tall towers marking the heart of the American city were "cathedrals of Capitalism."

And there was the "Syria Mosque," emblem of a pirated tradition used by the pirates to identify their "secret" brotherhood. Though charity, service, and volunteerism legitimized the Shriners, they could not erase their insensitive and callous misuse of another religion's artistic vocabulary and symbolic grammar. This was the "oriental obsession" of the otherwise "puritanical" Europeans and Americans (Sweetman 1988). How was "Islamic architecture" represented in the West? Beyond the Shriners, there were movie theaters (fig. 6), casinos with names like "Gardens of Allah" and "Taj Mahal" (fig. 7), and—summing up the fantasies of the luxurious and exotic—the 1920s planned city of Opa-locka, Florida, whose vision sprang from a multimillionaire's fascination with the film *The Thief of Baghdad.* In Opa-locka, *everything* had a dome and minaret (Luxner 1989).

I brought to my encounter with this American landscape an architectural ambivalence of my own, articulated as the draw of "modernity" against "tradition" in every sphere. My father had already made the choice to leave our ancestral home in the countryside, a choice redolent with symbolism, since that home had adjoined the shrine of a legendary saint whose descendants we were. My father chose to migrate to Lahore, a city of schools and colleges, of progress and promise for his sons, and the seat of the British governor of Punjab. There the "indigenous" was old and terminally ill, and the "alien" was modern and exemplary. We lived in Mughalpura but aspired to move to Modeltown. There were the Shalimar Gardens but we preferred to see the white-dressed white gents and ladies playing tennis in the Lawrence Gardens. There was Shah-ʿAlam bazaar selling essence of sandalwood, but we felt special buying lime cordial from the Tolinton Market. Study of Urdu, Persian, and Arabic was a refuge of romantics or the last resort of the rejected; English was the essential requirement for those aspiring to serve the Raj. Kashmiri Bazaar led only to

Figure 6. Movie theater, Atlanta, Ga. Photograph by Gulzar Haider.

the then-decaying Wazir Khan Mosque. But the Mall, with its Government College, Mayo School of Arts, YMCA, Lloyds Bank, Imperial Bank, Regal Cinema, Charing Cross, Victoria Monument, and Aitcheson College was the road to the bright future. "Modern," "European," "British" and, later, "American"—in general, "foreign"—these words were the stuff that dreams were made of.

India got its freedom, and Pakistan came into being. Shakespeare Lane became Koocha-e-Saadi, one poet giving way to another, but the seeking heart did not change its bearings from Stratford to Shiraz. Thus, despite my heritage, I intellectually grew up, with much curiosity and some guilt, on the books and magazines of the British Council, United States Information Service, and Goethe Institute reading rooms. It was there that I met Christopher Wren and was mesmerized by the drawings in Banister Fletcher's *History of Architecture* (1896). It was there that a book showed me for the first time the grand strokes of Sir Edwin Lutyens's New Delhi. I was quite willing to trade Shah Jahan's old "genie" for the new genie of the Raj.

Figure 7. Trump casino: the Taj Mahal, Atlantic City, N.J. Photograph
by Gulzar Haider.

Perhaps the most precious gift I received was the architecture of Frank Lloyd Wright and, through him, the works of Louis Sullivan and the words of Walt Whitman. I can still recall the moment I "found" architecture. I had barely picked up a little book, *Towards a New Architecture,* by Le Corbusier (1927), when these words, "Eyes Which Do Not See," leapt at me:

> A great epoch has begun.
> There exists a new spirit.
> There exists a mass of work conceived in the new spirit; it is to be met with particularly in industrial production.
> Architecture is stifled by custom.
> The "styles" are a lie.
> Style is a unity of principle animating all the work of an epoch, the result of a state of mind which has its own special character.
> Our own epoch is determining, day by day, its own style.
> Our eyes, unhappily, are unable yet to discern it.

In the title "Eyes Which Do Not See" I sensed a resonance with the qur'anic parable of ignorance. And in the lines I sensed the clue to knowledge. Youth had found its manifesto! Already skeptical of "tradition," now repelled by the casual use of "Islamic architecture" I encountered abroad, I wanted to be part of what was new. I resolved to resist dream makers like the pious South Asian Muslim in Miami who had retrieved a discarded pressure tank, placed it on a flat-roofed tract house as a "dome," and topped off the whole thing with a crescent.

WIMBLEDON AND THE ISNA MOSQUE IN PLAINFIELD: INTERIOR REALITIES

When I reached the West, like the immigrants described in Regula Qureshi's essay (this volume), I welcomed the company of fellow Muslims at prayer in makeshift settings. It was the practice that mattered in my case, as no doubt in many others, a practice promised to my mother when I left home. En route to America, on my very first Friday in the West, I prayed in a small English house on a corner lot in Wimbledon. There was no *mihrab* niche, just a depression in a side wall, a cold fireplace with a checkerboard border of green and brown ceramic tiles. A small chandelier with missing pieces of crystal was suspended asymmetrically in a corner. A rickety office chair with a gaudy plush rug draped over its back acted as the *minbar* pulpit. The prayer lines were oblique to the walls of the rooms and the congregation overflowed into the narrow hall and other nooks and corners. Was there anything mosquelike about this building, except that people had sincerely spread their mats in a common orientation, willingly performed their *sajud* in unison, and listened to someone's sermon, accepting him as their imam?

Via the Syria Mosque, the Cathedral of Learning, and a few Fridays in transit I arrived at the old Georgian campus of the University of Illinois. About twenty of us prayed in the Faculty Club in the Illinois Union Building. We rearranged the furniture, spread rolls of green towel cloth at an estimated skewed angle, and listened to the sermon of a mathematician from Jordan, our "imam of the week." I was awed by his audacity in presenting Divine Unity as a sphere and in talking of Asma' al-Husna, Allah's Beautiful Names (see also n. 5 below), as an ordered state of points defining that sphere. As I recall this, I wonder whether he was—as I would later become—a lost son seeking authentication, in this case through his grandfather's philosophical geometry.

Soon I felt at home in a community of Muslim students. My turn to lead the prayers finally had to come. In my maiden sermon, I recited those verses of the Qur'an wherein God affirms Abraham and Ishmael's building of the Ka'ba as a House for Him.[2] Being away from the elders of my own culture, I felt safe in proposing my own exegesis: that the verse alluded to the sacred nature of architecture in support of the Divine commandments. And, by logical extension, I concluded that architecture could potentially be idolatrous when committed in defiance of the commandments. By 1963, a continental organization had been founded on our campus, the Muslim Student Association of USA and Canada. At its second annual convention, I again spoke, this time on nothing less than the architectural heritage of Muslims.

That year also, I was given permission to substitute for one of my studio projects the design of a mosque in North America. My understanding of Muslim architectural tradition was based on some memories of Lahore,[3] a childhood trip to Agra, and my recent visual encounters with six volumes of A. U. Pope and Phyllis Ackerman's *A Survey of Persian Art* (1938–39). But tradition was definitely not a burning issue for a student "going abroad for studies in America." Our dizzyingly optimistic, forward-looking American campus environment did not present the traditional versus the modern even as a legitimate question. Old was of interest only to historians. Old was the "problem."

Thus the shift of orientation of the Masjid-e-Shah against the great maidan of Isfahan was posed as one of the problems that needed a new solution. I confronted the problem by eliminating it. My prayer hall was circular in plan: a symbol of "unity," and free from the demands of orientation. I solved the problem of columns by using a single inverted dish-thin shell. I took the pool from the courtyard, made it much larger, and let my mosque float in it like a lotus. Finally, I proposed a bridge that was symbolically the path from the worldly—the profane parking lot—to the other-worldly, the prayer hall. Inventive energy has its own obsessive momentum, so I cut a laser slice of space right through the circular wall of the prayer hall to create a mihrab ending in the garden beyond. Perhaps the most daring gesture was to propose large-scale calligraphy on the top of the dome. The idea was to let the modern man in flight look down and recognize that this was a contemporary mosque in the West.

The project was graded excellent, and I was sincerely proud of my achievement. Three decades later, I am grateful to God that there was no government, nor any other patron around me, to help me commit this crime on a real site. There are grand projects of that decade across the Muslim world, designed when young architects who had studied in Sydney or London or New York returned to build their modernity-driven, metamorphosed mosques. These are places that distort the imagination of the one who prays. Modernity, in the design context, was too self-consumptive, self-driven, ever-changing, to be relevant to the timeless protocol of the human body on a humble prayer mat engaged in *qiyam* (standing), *ruku'* (bowing), *sajud* (prostration). . . . May God be Merciful to the one who recognizes his mistakes.

My next mosque design was in 1968–69, after I had earned my bachelor's degree in architecture from Illinois. This was a joint project with Mukhtar Khalil, another Muslim student. We entered the competition for the Grand National Mosque in Islamabad (now the well-known Faisal Mosque). The site and the beautiful surroundings, complex program, and grandiose scale encouraged us to provide an equally heroic design response. We conceived an Islamic "St. Mark's": a trapezoidal setting, with educational blocks on three sides, a horizontal plaza with geometric stone patterns, and an artificially twisted entrance to create an element of surprise. The mihrab area was a round sculpted form inspired by Ronchamp. And further to avoid any remote chance that someone might mistake our building for a "traditional" structure, we proposed a minaret tower four hundred feet high and fifty feet in diameter, visible from the peaks of the Murree Hills, covered with turquoise-glazed tiles, containing a library and a museum on the model of the Guggenheim Museum in New York. St. Mark's, Ronchamp, the Guggenheim, and a heavy dose of abstract calligraphy, all in one project! The sirens of modernity had cast their spell. It was my good fortune that the design got eaten by termites in a Post Office warehouse.

For about ten years I struggled with various Muslim communities in search of an opportunity to design a place of prayer. It was a period of trials and professional wanderings (Haider 1990). Nothing is more telling of the communal fragmentation of ideas and images than the kinds of mosques people carry in their minds. Recalling my encounters, I have sometimes felt like a volunteer nurse in a room full of Alzheimer's patients at various stages of their condition. My own mind being a page with far too many images stamped on it, I have always empathized with community luminaries heatedly debating what their mosque should look like—not infrequently illustrated by pages torn from a mosque calendar offered by a Muslim bank or an airline. Usually the majority side favors a modern style and the other aims for recognizable "conventional" imagery.

In 1977–78, while spending a sabbatical year in Saudi Arabia and traveling through Pakistan, Iran, and Turkey, I saw the destructive and alienating force of architecture in the name of progress. I started to experience a certain ecology of architecture, literature, belief, philosophy, commerce, culture, and craft still operating in the old bazaars behind the modern façades of the cities I visited. I began seeing architecture as a formative element in culture rather than a mute expression of it—an isolated bit of gallery artwork to be reviewed, honored, bought, sold, and collected.

In 1979, I was invited to design a national headquarters mosque in Plainfield, Indiana for the Islamic Society of North America (ISNA), which had evolved from the Muslim Student Association founded sixteen years earlier. It was the same MSA that had started at my university in Urbana, and the person who invited me was Mukhtar Khalil, my co-contestant in the Islamabad mosque competition of 1968. The invitation was an honor I received with many self-doubts. I recalled Abraham's House for God, and started my search for a place of prayer for those who, at home or in "occidental exile,"[4] turn their faces to that Blessed House in Mecca and recite:

Lo I have turned my face
Firmly and truly
Toward Him who willed
The heavens and the earth
And never shall I assign
Partners to Him.
          (Qur'an 6:79)

I was also very intrigued by the Divine attributes expressed in two of the names of God, "The Hidden" and "The Manifest." I wanted to find in them a special wisdom for the designer, who must create but not confront, offer but not attack, and yet withal express the profound in a language understandable and pleasing to the listener.[5]

To distinguish the exterior from interior, I chose to veil this mosque, evoking the need for meaningful and purposeful dissimulation. I thought of my building as an oyster whose brilliance and essence were internal, while the expressed form sought human ecological harmony, modesty, even anonymity. This was the period, after all, when I had gotten used to friends Americanizing my name to "Golz" and my wife's from Santosh to "Sandy."

In my design, I resisted Western exploitation of the visual symbols of Islamic "tradition" rather than the tradition itself. During the nineteenth century and the prewar twentieth, Muslim reality had been observed and

Figure 8. The Islamic Society of North America headquarters mosque, Plainfield, Ind. Photograph by Gulzar Haider.

projected through many distorting prisms. There were paintings, romantic fictions, exotic travelogues, and, later, circuses, movies, movie theaters, magic potions, exotic foods, and music—all capitalizing on immediate expectations of magic fortunes and paradisiacal sensuality. From Las Vegas and Atlantic City "pleasures for sale" to Barnum and Bailey's "Greatest Show on Earth" to Shriners' temples, all had exploited, with gluttonous appetite, the symbols associated with the Muslim past (Said 1978).

The project was built and has been used since 1982 (fig. 8). It has no expressed dome, although inside there are three domes creating an unmistakable space of Islamic prayer. Those who have been inside are struck by the "mosqueness" of it all. It remains an enigma, however, especially to those Muslims who are used to seeing mosques and not praying in them. Like the makeshift mosque in Wimbledon, what mattered in the Plainfield mosque was the practice—in this case intended to be fostered by the design—within.

THE BAI'TUL ISLAM MOSQUE, TORONTO, AND BACK TO WIMBLEDON: EXTERNALIZING ISLAM

The demand for what is seen as visual authenticity in the mosque, however, has intensified over the past decade. On the one hand, this is a natural sign of the maturation of the first wave of postwar immigrants, many of whom came for education and then settled for better economic and professional opportunities. On the other hand, this is also a sign that efforts at "melting into the pot" have given way to assertion of a Muslim identity as a better alternative. There are also global movements afoot that have given Muslims in the diaspora a sense of identity and linkage as part of the *umma,* or worldwide Muslim community. Some have now started to express "dome and minaret envy," in relation, for example, to the Plainfield mosque.

These years have also been a period of intense energy in architectural-academic discourse as modernism started to come under questioning and later open attack. The word *postmodernism* came to evoke everything from zealous commitment to ridicule. New terms such as *postfunctionalism, poststructuralism, deconstructivism, logocentricism,* and even *reconstructivism* made their appearance.

Even so, the postfunctionalist search for "meaning" and the return of "philosophical inquiry" through architecture has been timely for the emergent discourse on sacred architecture. For Muslims, there has been much discussion about the value of the Islamic heritage within a technologically homogenizing world. The symposia of the Aga Khan Trust for Culture, in particular, have brought the protagonists of tradition and those of modernity around the same table under the mostly civilizing gaze of some philosophers and itinerant sages. These symposia have taught me to treat my most cherished architectural conceptions with a humbling doubt.

For me, the academic inquisition against modernism has provided numerous opportunities. As the design canons of modernist minimality and pure composition have come under attack, there has been a new air of respectability for the study of ornament, craft, tradition, form, symbol, text, inscriptions, and, above all, the philosophical underpinnings of architectural intentions. There is now legitimacy for seeking to know culture though the direct experience of art—"tactile knowing," as we ended up calling it. It was the interpretive drawing of carpets, miniatures, and gardens, as well as the recitation of poetry, that opened up Islamic culture for many of my Canadian students.

In 1987, almost ten years after the ISNA mosque, I received a commission to design a large mosque in Toronto. By then, numerous North American Muslim communities had shown a desire for assertion through architecture, rather than anonymity through dissimulation. This desire was particularly keen in this case: the mosque was to be the national headquarters of the Ahmadiyya Movement in Islam, a community declared out of Islamic bounds by act of the Government of Pakistan in 1974, which now, quite simply, wanted all the architectural help it could get to express its Islamic presence in Canada (Haider 1990). I was advised to reject this commission, lest I risk my future and never get another job, or even risk my hereafter by "partnership in the crime of Ahmadiyyat." I am not an Ahmadi Muslim, and I am not qualified to make pronouncements on Islam or meter others' Islamicity. I *am* convinced, however, that I have designed a *mosque,* and that what are performed there are prayers in the finest tradition of Islam.

In designing the Toronto mosque, I used the prayer rug as a conceptual inspiration, as well as a source of formal and decorative discipline. Conceptually, the prayer rug, as it is spread out and *qibla-*directed, defines the elemental place of prayer. As the believer positions and orients his or her body on it and goes through various stages of *salat,* the Islamic ritual prayer, a place-space is defined, in the physical and temporal as well as experiential sense, that has all the essential attributes of a mosque. As the prayerful body interacts with the qibla-directed Cartesian planes established by the prayer rug, so the collectivity, the parallel rows of the community of believers, resonates with the architectural space of the mosque. All design decisions, especially the proportions of the space, the pattern and the placement of fenestration, the sequential placement of entrance and arrival, tile patterns and carpet layout are aimed at achieving this resonance. The prayer rug rises out of its horizontal plane and wraps itself around the space.

This mosque started with the study of prayer rugs; and its final act of design resulted in a prayer rug that has been sand-etched in the glass of the doors marking the entrance to the prayer hall. If the Plainfield mosque might seem like a corporate headquarters to the freeway observer driving by, the Toronto mosque boldly asserts an Islamic profile, reclaiming the conventional minaret and dome for their appropriate ends (fig. 9).

Twenty-five years after the first encounter, I had a chance to visit Wimbledon again. The house-mosque was now wrapped with a glazed finish; arched windows sat squeezed into what were at one time rectangular openings; the parapet had what seemed like an endless line of sharp crescents; and there were a number of token minaret domes, whose profile came less from any architectural tradition than from the illustrations of the "Arabian Nights." By now, they, too, had felt compelled to "Islamize" that sometime English house.

My innocent but bizarre encounter with the "Syria Mosque" has never left me. Like a plow in the field, it turns inside out what would otherwise have been quiet, sedate, but decaying chambers of my mind. I have never ceased raising questions about what a North American mosque might be and become. The mosque will have to attain its rightful and self-assured place in world society, so that later generations who choose to come to North America will not be faced by a theater garbed in Moorish dress.

Muslims living in the non-Islamic West face an unparalleled opportunity.

Figure 9. The Baiʿtul Islam mosque, Toronto. Photograph by Gulzar Haider.

Theirs is a promising exile: a freedom of thought, action, and inquiry un-known in the contemporary Muslim world. They are challenged by a milieu that takes pride in oppositional provocations. Those who can break free of the inertial ties of national and ethnic personas will be the ones who will forge an Islamicity hitherto unexperienced. They have the freedom to question the canons of traditional expression. Their very exile, understood as separation from the center, will make the expressions of Islam more profound, whether in literature, music, art, or architecture.

Muslim minorities in the non-Muslim world will ultimately realize that their history has put them in a position somehow reminiscent of the Proph-et's Meccan period. Their isolation will purify and strengthen their belief. It will refine their thought and make their tools precise, and at an appro-priate time, they will start to send "expressive" postcards home. Then there will begin another migration, not in space and time, but from blindness of a certain kind to a clearer vision, from spiritless materiality toward expres-sive spirituality.

NOTES

Editor's note: I prepared this essay from a draft paper by Gulzar Haider, "Prayer Rugs Lost and Found: In Search of Mosque Architecture" (1993), a slide presentation at the SSRC (May 13, 1989), and the published essays cited. I have organized and edited the material, provided linkage where necessary, and chosen the illustrations.—BDM

1. The Shriners are formally known as the Ancient Arabic Order of Nobles of the Mystic Shrine, "an auxiliary of the Masonic order . . . dedicated to good fellowship, health programs, charitable works, etc." (*Random House Dictionary,* 2d ed., s.v. "Shriner").

2. "Call to mind also when Abraham and Ishmael raised the foundations of the 'House' and (having done so) prayed: O Lord, accept this offering from us, it is Thou Who are All-Hearing, All-Knowing" (Qu'ran, 2:128).

3. Lahore is well known for such masterpieces of Islamic architecture as the Badshahi Mosque, Jahangir's Tomb, and Shalimar Gardens.

4. The phrase is borrowed with respect and apology from the great Muslim sage Shihab al-Din Yahya al-Suhrawardi, who spoke of *al-ghurbat al-gharbiyya* (translated by H. Corbin and S. H. Nasr as "occidental exile") as the state of the soul separated from its divine origin. See Nasr 1964: 64–68.

5. Al-Batin (Hidden), al-Zahir (Manifest), two of the "Ninety-nine" Asma' al Husna (Beautiful Names of God). Of much philosophical interest through Muslim history, the "Names" are sometimes proposed to be irreducible facets of the Divine Being that may reflect the seeker's self to himself and thus make possible gnosis, the cognizance of the destiny of the seeker's soul. The two names al-Batin and al-Zahir are of special interest to architects in pursuit of the silent eloquence of space and the quintessential presence of form. For an initiation into the relationship between esoteric philosophy of Islam and its architectural expression, I am indebted to Ardalan and Bakhtiar 1973.

WORKS CITED

Ardalan, Nader, and Laleh Bakhtiar. 1973. *The Sense of Unity: The Sufi Tradition in Persian Architecture.* Chicago: University of Chicago Press.

Fletcher, Banister. 1896. *A History of Architecture for the Student, Craftsman, and Amateur: Being a Comparative View from the Earliest Period.* 2d ed. London: B. T. Batsford.

Haider, Gulzar. 1990. "'Brother in Islam, Please Draw Us a Mosque.' Muslims in the West: A Personal Account." In *Expressions of Islam in Buildings,* pp. 155–66. Proceedings of an International Seminar sponsored by the Aga Khan Award for Architecture and the Indonesian Institute of Architecture, Jakarta, October 15–19, 1990. Aga Khan Award for Architecture, Geneva.

————. 1992. "The Bai'tul-Islam Mosque: Architectural Intentions." In *Ahmadi Muslims: A Brief Introduction,* pp. 10–12. Ontario: Ahmadiyya Movement in Islam.

Le Corbusier. 1927. *Towards a New Architecture.* Translated by Frederick Etchells. New York: Brewer & Warren.

Luxner, Larry. 1989. "Opa-locka Rising." *Aramco World Magazine,* September–October 1989, pp. 2–7.

Nasr, S. H. 1964. *Three Muslim Sages: Avicenna, Suhrawardi, Ibn 'Arabi.* Cambridge, Mass.: Harvard University Press.

Pope, Arthur Urban, and Phyllis Ackerman, eds. 1938–39. *A Survey of Persian Art.* London: Oxford University Press.

Said, Edward. 1978. *Orientalism.* New York: Pantheon Books.

Sweetman, John E. 1988. *The Oriental Obsession: Islamic Inspiration in British and American Art and Architecture, 1500–1920.* New York: Cambridge University Press.

TWO

Transcending Space

Recitation and Community among South Asian Muslims in Canada

Regula Burckhardt Qureshi

Islamic practice is central in creating meaning and community among many first-generation Muslim families in Canada. Characteristic of that practice are the four recitational assemblies described below, all focused on shared articulation of religious and cherished words: *milad,* hymns and homilies in praise of the Prophet; *zikr,* Sufi invocational phrases and hymns; *qur'ankhwani,* one or more complete recitations of the Qur'an; and *ayat-e-karima,* 125,000 reiterations of a qur'anic verse.[1] South Asian Muslims have become well established across the urban landscape of Canada, and they have created a strong community life on the foundation of shared events internal to the community.

Advantaged by their access to English and English institutions, as well as by their successful entry into higher education, professions, and services, South Asians stand out among immigrants from the Muslim world. Originating mainly in Pakistan, but also in India, Bangladesh, East Africa, and Sri Lanka, they are linked by a common language, Urdu, and by a cosmopolitan culture shared by urban Muslims all over the Indian subcontinent. Immigration to Canada has largely come from upper- and middle-class families, who have also set the tone of community life in the new country; only recently, liberalized Canadian sponsorship laws have enabled immigration from socially and educationally less privileged backgrounds. These later immigrants benefit from the growing community network and the Canadian government's multicultural outreach. As a result, with their social, educational, and health needs met by a comprehensive governmental support system, South Asian Muslims in Canada are overall reasonably prosperous and upwardly mobile, owning and replacing cars and homes, directing their children into preferred professional training, and sponsoring the immigration of relatives from the home country.

South Asian Muslims have, in the course of time, built mosques and become involved in the public representation of Islam through its buildings and organizations. In Edmonton, for example, to celebrate the 'Id holidays (and, for a few, to attend weekly prayers), they initially joined the Arab-Canadian congregation in the small al-Rashid Mosque,[2] contributed to its impressive new building, and eventually built the Markaz ul Islam as a mosque for the Pakistani community. But to focus on this public face leaves the observer on the outside and on the surface; it misses a strong community life that is deeply meaningful and quite private. This privacy is far from exclusive, since South Asian Muslims hold sharing and hospitality as primary values. People love to open their homes to share special life events and religious practices integral to their warmly social community life.[3]

Islam has been a major determinant of individual and group identity among these immigrants in Canada, mediated by their shared language and regional lifestyle. More important, it offers its ideational foundation and a rich set of practices to give salient articulation to the uncharted exigencies of life in Canada. This process of "making Muslim space" for the Muslim diaspora within the larger Western context must take as its starting point one that is community-internal, one that defines, not what outsiders see, but what insiders identify as creating "space" for Islam.

In his comprehensive search for visually perceptible symbols and signs in Islam, Oleg Grabar cautiously but inevitably concludes that "Islamic culture finds its means of self-representation in hearing and acting rather than in seeing," for "it is not forms which identify Islamic culture . . . but sounds, history, and a mode of life" (1983: 31, 29). Remarkable for coming from a specialist in the visual domain (Islamic architecture), this insight completely affirms my own experience as a specialist in sound; more important, it resounds from a chorus of Muslim voices speaking in both poetry and prose. Starting with the Prophet of Islam himself, these voices say in essence that Muslim space is where Muslims prevail (Abel 1965: 127). From the *hadis* of the Prophet Muhammad, which universalize the mosque as any place where Muslims pray,[4] to Sufi literature, where a tavern can become a cell (al-Hujwiri: 409), the theme of "multiplicity of purpose and flexibility of space" is a persuasive one in Islamic discourse. It also marks the history of Islamic "built space" itself (Jones 1978: 162).

Spatial cannot, therefore, be reduced to meaning visual and accessible to reification, as in a good deal of Western scholarship (Durkheim 1938; Moravia 1976). The new ethnography based on dialogue and process considers itself more appropriately represented by the modalities of the aural and oral (Fabian 1983; Ong 1970), which provide a better starting point for a dialectical communication giving access to the voices of those who are being studied.

Running counter to the widespread Western view of an Islam located in minarets, calligraphy, and carpets, what Muslims have taught me to associate with their religion are its commitment to universality, its resources of portability, its focus on a single sacred center, and its singularly verbal message. Islamic praxis transcends local space primarily by aural, not visual, communication. Consider the following vivid images of Canadian Muslim living: ritual prayers recited using towels as makeshift prayer rugs on any available floor area, subject only to identifying the direction of the Ka'ba; of reading the Qur'an during spare moments at the office desk; of holding a Sufi zikr seated informally across the space facing an unlit fireplace; of a funeral oration in the gymnasium that is part of the mosque complex; of breaking the fast during Ramadan in front of a TV or anywhere in the house; of a list of qur'anic invocations held by a magnet on the refrigerator door. What expresses Muslim identity—or experience, or faith—is *process,* at the core of which are words: the words of the qur'anic Message, words that explain and interpret the Message, words that praise God and his Messenger, words that express the believer's submission—"Islam." This emphasis resonates throughout the essays in this volume.

Key to proper utterance is the believer's intent. This is most clearly articulated in the classical Sufi writings on the assemblies for the performance of zikr and *sama'* (listening to mystical poetry). These texts postulate neutral space and time,[5] for what creates the actual ritual are its words, appropriately uttered and received. Muslims are linked by words, above all the divine Message of God in the Qur'an, and by the Ka'ba, toward which they all face during ritual prayer (*salat*). Such words are rendered visual and even decorative, but the purpose is to remind the Muslim to *utter* these words by reading or reciting them. Thus in a mosque all the outstanding spatial features are directly linked to both the Word and its actualization: from the minaret for reciting *adhan* and qur'anic calligraphy on the outside to the *mihrab* niche for the imam to lead the prayer and the *mimbar* from which he speaks the *khutba* (sermon). In the home, the Qur'an is always present; it is not displayed but placed in an elevated location as a mark of respect. What needs to be stressed is that for Muslims neither the Qur'an nor any visual Islamic display is a locus of contemplation; they are meant to initiate articulation and action.

As for the visual articulation of Muslim identity in today's South Asian Muslim home in Canada, what dominates is the qur'anic word (fig. 10). Artistically calligraphed qur'anic verses are displayed in many forms: prints in a Western-style rectangular picture frame, ornamental trays or plates of etched or embossed brass or copper, religious words on art objects collected from different parts of the Islamic world, including the South Asian homeland. Pakistan, especially, offers items that are both traditional, such as enamelled ceramic plates or tiles, and modern, such as calligraphic sculptures made of recently discovered marble. What all these calligraphic items have in common, regardless of differences in material, style, or connotation, is their primary function: to convey a religious verbal message. The messages may be the names of God or the names of the Prophet, or the *kalma,* "La Ilaha-il Allah, Muhammad al-Rasul Allah" ("There is no god but God, and Muhammad is his Prophet"). They are often a part of the Qur'an, for example, the sura al-Rahman (sura 55), on divine beneficence, and include the words that open the Qur'an and preface each sura: "In the Name of God most Gracious, most Merciful" ("Bismillah al-rahman al-rahim"); they are recited when a Muslim begins any task, from beginning a meal to starting on a journey. Also favored are the four *qul,*[6] especially the sura al-Ikhlas ("Qul hu wallahu ahad . . . ");[7] these are short suras beneficial for any place and occasion. A special passage selected to give safety to home and family is the "Ayat al-Kursi."[8] Complementing these verbal messages are occasional pictorial representations of the Ka'ba, which can take the place of a painting to adorn the living room.[9]

Aesthetically less relevant, but all the more clearly action-oriented in function are words that convey information to facilitate religious observances, mainly in the form of an Islamic calendar that marks the lunar months and days, religious holidays, and times for starting and ending the fast during the month of Ramadan and perhaps for the five daily prayers. In addition, families with children may display words for Muslim living, for their children to absorb, perhaps qur'anic verses on a calendar supplied by the local mosque or simply a list of religiously appropriate responses to different life situations in Arabic—for instance, "Masha'allah" ("by the grace of God") or "Insha'allah" ("God willing"). Individual homes, of course, differ widely in the kind, extent, and style of visual-spatial expression of Islamic words.

Engaging in the articulation of Islamic word and performing the relevant actions form the basis of individual Muslim identity; sharing that engagement links Muslims into a community. The primary ritual of a Muslim is salat, the prescribed ritual prayer offered five times each day, for which South Asian usage employs the Persian term *namaz.* Even though a Western observer's visual attention may be directed to the ritual gestures of prostration, it needs to be stressed that the primary action of namaz is verbal: one "says" or "recites" the prayer (in Urdu: *namaz parhna*).[10] Another form of individual recitation is *qir'at,* the reading of chosen passages from the Qur'an, either following namaz or at any other suitable time. Normally silent, such recitation or reading may also be chanted; this sets apart the sound of the words by making them beautiful (*khushilhan*), while the act of recitation is set apart by a respectful and modest posture and physical attitude. Most important, religious recitation means actually saying the words, even when reading silently, not just visually perusing them, as in the

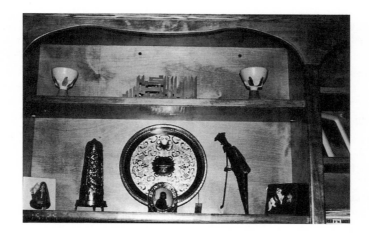

Figure 10. The verbal-visual presence of Islam in a Canadian home. Photographs by Regula Burckhardt Qureshi.

Western sense of *reading*. Indeed, the fact that Urdu speakers apply the term *reading* to both silent reading and voiced recitation or chant denotes less a limitation in vocabulary than a fundamentally different conception of the act of reading itself (Tomlinson 1993).

In addition to namaz, reading or reciting religious words is also carried out as a structural, collective activity in the four kinds of assemblies described here. They fall into two different formats. Milad and zikr follow a traditional performative format of South Asia in which one or several persons recite to the assembled audience. Led by reciters, they require competence and result in a structured performance sequence. The Shi'a *majlis* (Schubel, this volume) follows the same pattern (Qureshi 1981). Qur'an-khwani and ayat-e-karima, on the other hand, are participatory gatherings of silent recitation, which is shared by all. All four assemblies share basic features of setting and overall procedure.

First of all, the prime locus for holding these assemblies remains the home, community associations and public buildings notwithstanding, for the processes of community formation emanate essentially from individual families, as do the rituals or religious "performance events" that link people of the same group. The distinct subcultures of men and women contribute to and are shaped by these occasions. Visually apparent in separate seating arrangements and formal social space generally, what this "segregation" means—rather than what it displays—is interaction and mutual reinforcement among members of the same gender within and across families. Supported by their single-gender network, both men and women mobilize support for initiatives such as the holding of religious assemblies appropriate to their family's personal circumstances.

Over the years in Canada, spatially separated socializing has visibly increased. On the surface, this trend would seem to run counter to increasing adaptation to the Western host society. In fact, it represents an "internal adaptation" to more extensive familylike socializing among people not related by family ties. Given this reality, spatial separation is a response, for example, to the concerns of elderly parents, especially grandmothers, who are unaccustomed to mixed socializing. It also reflects concern for creating an appropriate social environment for growing daughters by reinforcing the traditional pattern of restricted interaction between the sexes (Qureshi 1991). This trend has been further reinforced by the conservative impact of transnational Islamic movements.

In reality, however, networks of connectedness among women and among men have always been strong. This point bears emphasizing, precisely because the spatial element of female seclusion tends to claim much attention at the expense of recognizing the autonomous role of women in South Asian Muslim homes. Home-based affairs are always in the hands of women, who also, of course, produce the repasts provided for social or religious "functions" outside the home.

The key change in religious assemblies from the pattern of the home-land is that they now take place largely in this context of domestic hospital-ity and socializing (Qureshi 1972; 1980: v; 1981). The separation of men and women is facilitated by modern house plans that include both a draw-ing room and a family room, with men typically in the formal drawing room, leaving women to the family room or other less formal parts of the house. A similar use of space has been described for the typically modest homes of South Asian Muslims in Britain (Shaw 1988) and for African-American Muslims (McCloud, this volume).

MILAD

Milad is the devotional assembly in the most traditional sense, celebrating the Prophet's birth on the twelfth day of the month Rabi ul-Awwal. Prac-ticed by Muslims all over South Asia, the milad has an established format. A small reciting group presents a sequence of chanted[11] hymns in praise of the Prophet (*na't*), alternating with spoken homilies (*riwayat, bayan*) and interspersed with Arabic praise litanies (*durud*). Like all religious events, a milad begins with God, often in the form of a hymn of praise to God (*hamd*); sometimes it is preceded by qur'anic recitation. A saluta-tional hymn to the Prophet (*salam*) followed by an intercessory prayer to God (*du'a*) and a recitation of al-Fatiha (sura 1), the sura dedicated to prayer for the dead, conclude the event (fig. 11).

Milads are held during the entire month of Rabi ul-Awwal and also on auspicious occasions such as a move into a new house, professional success, and family events such as the arrival of a daughter-in-law from Pakistan or the birth of a healthy grandchild. Milads are predominantly a women's tradition, and even in South Asia, they take place mainly in homes, with women reciting.[12] In Canada, the smaller Muslim community of the 1960s and 1970s saw milads that included both women and men and their then mostly small children.

One of many such events from the late 1970s stands out in my memory, a milad held in conjunction with a bismillah celebration, a ceremony that initiates a child's education, traditionally at the age of four years and four months. The milad was organized to precede the brief ceremony as an expression of praise and thanks, and to invoke blessings. The ceremony itself bespeaks the centrality of reading and reciting the qur'anic word: a religious teacher or family elder guides the child's hand to write the first letters of the Arabic Urdu alphabet and recites with her the opening words of the Qur'an: "Bismillah al-rahman al-rahim" ("In the name of God, the all-compassionate, the all-merciful").

As friends gradually arrived, they were invited to settle down in the liv-ing- and dining-room area, which was cleared of furniture and covered with white sheets, back support being offered by pillows and bolsters, as

durūd (Litany in praise of the Prophet)

naᶜt (Hymn to the Prophet)

salām (Salutational Hymn to the Prophet)

du'a (Intercessory Prayer)

Figure 11. Hymns recited at Milad-e-Akbar: Durud (litany in praise of the Prophet); Na't ("Allah Allah Allahu"); Salam ("Ya Nabi Salam Alaika"); and Du'a.

Figure 12. Recitation of the great-grandmother. Photograph by Yasmeen Nizam.

well as by the walls. A special carpet was placed against one wall for the reciters. An attractive cloth packet containing the book *Milad-e-Akbar* (Akbar Warsi n.d.), a compilation of hymns and prose sermons from which recitations would be chosen, was placed on a decorative raised pillow. The guests sat down along the other walls, eventually forming a loose circle around the entire area. Men and women naturally chose to sit in different areas of the L-shaped space, joining friends among their gender group and talking informally. The hostess had previously asked a friend who was a competent reciter for the recitation, and the latter then asked two other invited friends to join her. The milad was relatively short, with only two sets of hymns and riwayat, followed by the salam and then the du'a.

Then the bismillah ceremony followed, all conducted by the women, with the men participating as listeners. Everyone's attention was on the beautifully dressed little girl and her words of recitation. The joyous event concluded with a sumptuous dinner.

Today, preference has shifted to all-female milads, supported by the trend noted above toward separating social space by gender. Excluding men also allows the hostess to include participants from twice as many households, which is socially desirable given the expanding personal circles brought about by the larger numbers of immigrants. These events are now multigenerational. Overall, the recitation may lack the performative creativity of the seasoned semiprofessionals of the Indian subcontinent. But, as in a recent "housewarming" milad where the grandmother of the young hostess presided over four generations (fig. 12), milads often do achieve an intensely religious mood in a setting of relaxed intimacy.

ZIKR

Zikr ("recollection") is the Sufi practice of remembering God by repeating His name. The most commonly recited zikr phrases are linked to the articulation of the kalma: "Allahu" (God is); "La ilaha il-Allah" (There is no God but God); and "il-Allah" (The only God). Their constant repetition is intended to create a spiritual-emotional experience of nearness to God. The zikr assembly is convened by a spiritual leader, who is responsible for intoning and coordinating the repeated reiteration of these powerful invocations, as well as for providing spiritual guidance for the experience.

Zikr assemblies are relatively uncommon in Canada because of the scarcity of Sufis among South Asian Muslim immigrants, and among middle- and upper-class Muslims in South Asia generally. Many Muslims do not really approve of the practice. At a zikr gathering held in the 1980s, non-Sufis were invited as personal friends, or as an outreach gesture on behalf of Sufism and of the host's Sufi lineage. After a fine dinner, the guests were seated in the family room, oriented around the host, who informally introduced the significance and purpose of the zikr. He then initiated the zikr recitation with the universal opening phrase of the kalma, speaking the words rhythmically and accompanying them with the traditional gesture of bowing the head and placing the right hand on the heart, whose pulse is understood as the Sufi's inner zikr. The participants joined in with either voiced or silent zikr (*zikr-e-jali* or *zikr-e-khafi*).

Here the performer-audience opposition is less total than in the milad because of active audience participation. Ideally, a Sufi assembly would also offer the listeners the spiritually involving experience of *sama'*, listening to mystical hymns (*qawwali*), but that is rarely possible because of the lack of trained performers. For this reason, the few Sufis who have held such assemblies in Canada reach for the resource of zikr, which requires only a modicum of recitational skill. Another recent trend is the playing of qawwali recordings to evoke the experience of sama'.

QUR'ANKHWANI

Qur'ankhwani and ayat-e-karima are distinctly nonperformative and therefore differ from the other two assemblies fundamentally in their organizational structure. In these participatory assemblies, people gather to share in the task of completing a major task of recitation: the complete text of the Qur'an in qur'ankhwani, and 125,000 utterances of a specified qur'anic verse in ayat-e-karima.[13] Each individual recites soundlessly, so that neither spatial nor temporal management is required, although there is informal coordination between reciters. Women and men gather in separate rooms with sheet-covered floors, seated along walls or furniture for back support, their heads covered "as a mark of respect." Participants focus on the task of reciting, their lips often moving silently as they speak each word to themselves.

Qur'ankhwani entails the recitation of the whole Qur'an.[14] This is done traditionally during Ramadan and on the occasion of a death, as well as on the *soyem* and *chehlum* (commemorations on the third and fortieth days after death), and the anniversary of a death (*barsi*). In recent years, qur'an-khwani has also been organized on auspicious occasions, and more generally to invoke a blessing (for instance, on a new home). The aim is to complete the reading of at least one and preferably several Qur'ans, for these represent accumulated blessings dedicated to the person or cause for whom the qur'ankhwani is being held.

One senior widow holds a qur'ankhwani, followed by a meal, each year on the weekend following the death anniversary of her husband, who died ten years ago. In order not to fall short of at least one complete reading of the Qur'an, her two sons and daughters-in-law begin to read one or two hours before the event starts, and if many people arrive early, a second or even a third Qur'an might be completed. If the reading still falls short of the goal, the recitation is completed later by members of the household.

The host has made the Qur'an available in the form of thirty separately bound sections, the *siparas*, which form the traditional units of qur'ankh-wani recitation and are familiar to everyone. On this occasion, a friend brought a second set, so that instead of sharing, the men's room and the women's room each had its own. Each guest picked up one siparah, per-haps selecting a particular siparah containing a favored sura. Completed siparahs were placed separately to avoid duplication. Someone already present quietly provided newcomers with directions as needed. Anyone not *ba-wuzu* (ritually clean) [15] did not recite but sat quietly. Those who read quickly soon added their siparas to the pile of completed ones, and each picked up another. When none were left in the women's room, unread siparas were brought in from the men's room, since they, being fewer in number, had not been able to read as much. Each person who had com-pleted his or her last sipara sat quietly or, in the case of women, went to the kitchen to help and socialize. On completion of the Qur'an, the host's daughter placed a tray with a dish of halva on the sheet-covered floor of the living room where the women had been sitting, and everyone recited the sura al-Fatiha, followed by the du'a to bring peace to the dead person and to bless the food that was later placed on the table along with the halva.

Now everyone rose, removed their head coverings, and proceeded to enjoy the company of friends and a delicious meal. Participants in a qur'ankhwani work hard for the host to gain religious merit or blessings; this generates a special sense of reciprocity between host and guest, arising from a genuine sense of religious commitment.

AYAT-E-KARIMA

Ayat-e-karima denotes the famous qur'anic verse in which the Prophet Jonah, in the belly of the whale, cries out to God admitting his wrong, and God then saves him, saying, "and thus do we deliver those who have faith" (21:88).[16] The words of the ayat thus recall and invoke God's mercy, hence the name *karima* ("merciful"): "La Ilaha Illah anta subhaneka inni kunto min az-zalemin" (There is no god but Thou; glory to Thee; I was indeed wrong.) When God's help is needed for something important, this verse is chosen to be recited a total of 125,000 times. The task is undertaken collectively in this least structured of all assemblies, for the recitation consists of a single phrase known to all, so that there is no need for either leadership or printed text.

In 1986, a Pakistani-Canadian invited her friends to an ayat-e-karima when her husband was recovering from a serious illness. Given the immensity of the task, a late morning time on a Sunday was chosen, and many friends were invited. A large number came to support this effort; most brought along their *tasbih*s (rosaries) of one hundred beads to facilitate counting, or they picked up one of the tasbihs provided by the host. To add up individual counts, fifty sheets with twenty-five circles each had been drawn up and placed among both men and women, so that circle by circle could be marked off for each tasbih completed, in contrast to the old system of counting with almonds. Participants took care of their own counting, until all the circles were marked off. The recitation completed, a du'a was recited for the desired purpose. Then people rose to recite their namaz and to socialize; as usual, the event concluded with a sumptuous dinner, after which people quickly dispersed.

In this recitational event, no one stood out in any way; attending it was simply to reinforce the bond of mutual support that can always be activated among members of the community. In its own way, each of the four assemblies adds profoundly and significantly to this support, invoking shared ways of reaching God and shared means of coping with present-day life situations.

FROM HOME TO MOSQUE

This shared religious life appears essentially private, personal, and deeply conservative. The prime constant in this experience has been the home domain, although not in the sense of a specific home, since families readily move, and not in the sense of a specific urban area, since there are no signs of a South Asian Muslim quarter emerging. At the same time, the Muslim sense of community and, even more so, the sense of religious identity, has increasingly been extending beyond the home. The two main mosques in Edmonton, the one originally Arab and the second South Asian, reflect a gradually evolving sense of community, serving less as "sacred space"[17] than simply as loci for religious observance. The mosque is also the place where South Asian Muslims are today negotiating a communal identity that has both religious and sociocultural facets. This is evidenced in the way they selectively attend both mosques on different occasions. For instance, for 'Id prayers many Pakistanis go to the original al-Rashid Mosque, with the aim of joining in one single Muslim congregation on 'Id day, as they do in their homeland.

Notable is the participation of women in mosque worship, a practice pioneered by Arab Muslims and now practiced by South Asians, although in their homelands, mosques are attended only by men. Another Western innovation is the use of the mosque basement for community "functions"—and, of course, for children's religion classes. The significance of participation becomes obvious if one compares such centers of Muslim worship as the Shi'a *imambara* (or *imambargah*) or, even more so, the Isma'ili *jama'tkhana,* where women, and thereby children, participate in complementary roles as fully as men, so that for these Muslims their centers have become truly a community space.[18]

Increasing mosque activity no doubt reflects a recent and slowly growing trend toward solidifying and projecting a collective Muslim identity in the public domain, while also negotiating ethnocultural and linguistic differences vis-à-vis the universalizing thrust of transnational Islamic movements. Muslim Canadians themselves, however, often debate and deplore the fact that they are not "well organized" as a community.

Where South Asian Sunnis have constituted themselves into public community groups, it has been as narrower linguistic, regional, and national associations, such as the largely Punjabi-speaking Pakistani Association of Alberta. On the other hand, Urdu speakers, who hail from urban areas across the Indian subcontinent, lack a national focus in addition to a specifically Islamic one.[19] Individuals and families also express themselves through association with earlier and differently defined communities of Muslims—the Muslim Student Association; its parent organization, the Islamic Society of North America; a Muslim youth or women's group; a Sufi group; a mosque association. Over their history in Canada, self-identification for Muslims has ranged within a universe extending from the single family to the *umma* of all Muslims; Muslim self-expression can therefore draw from anywhere in this rich reference base.

A gradual shift toward the mosque as a center of identity has been taking place during the past ten years. With the establishment of the South Asian mosque, or "Pakistani *masjid*" (as the Markaz ul Islam is commonly called), a deep involvement in the building, funding, and running of the mosque has created a sense of solidarity among men, on the one hand, and women, on the other, of many families. Contributing to this solidarity has been the desire of families to strengthen the religious identity of their growing children by encouraging joint activities. Recitational assemblies, especially qur'ankhwani assemblies held after a death, are beginning to take place in the mosque. Out of respect for its sacred content, qur'anic recitation is done in the mosque's area for worship, on the main floor for men and the balcony for women. Both men and women arrive individually and choose a sitting place on the floor, using the walls for back support; one or two chairs are provided for the infirm. The event proceeds exactly as in the home. Those who finish their reading sit quietly, silent or talking softly; some individually assume prayer position to say optional *rak'at* preceding the regular namaz that will follow the completion of the qur'ankhwani. After prayer, everyone repairs to the basement, where an appropriate re-past has been laid out by the hostess and her women friends.

Ayat-e-karima, too, is sometimes held in the mosque, so as to involve a much larger number of reciters. As in the home, women of the host's fam-ily organize the event, but here with the help of friends who share the tasks of preparing the food and of telephoning a large number of people to recite, using a list that circulates for this purpose. What stands out is that women continue to manage these events even in the mosque.

Unlike qur'ankhwani and ayat-e-karima, the milad is held in the meet-ing area in the basement of the mosque, given the nonliturgical status of its texts. In this space, men and women are, beyond the cloakroom area, separated by movable screens acquired earlier to create separate classroom spaces for an Islamic school. In contrast to the home situation, the pro-ceedings are under male leadership, including *riwayat* and individually re-cited *na't*. Na't are also recited by a group of children, mainly girls, but not by women.

The milad is concluded by a repast; but occasionally now another, more public, way is chosen to conclude a large milad by offering everyone a share of *tabarruk* (blessed food). Thus there are signs of a more "public" or communitarian hue in these mosque events. On the other hand, they are hosted by—or often in the case of a death, on behalf of—a particular family, just like the same events held in the home of such a family. The issue of female participation in mosque basement activities is an evolving one, influenced on one side by the lack of precedent for women taking any active role on mosque premises vis-à-vis men, other than providing refreshments, and on the other by the recognition of women's actual con-tribution toward the genesis and maintenance of this mosque.

Zikr does not have the community appeal to warrant being held in the mosque.

At this point, the frequency and importance of mosque events is minor as compared to home-based assemblies; it remains to be seen whether the desire to articulate a public Muslim identity will in the future supersede other, nonreligious facets of community identity, which up to now have continued to motivate South Asian Muslim bonding and self-expression.

FROM PERFORMANCE TO PARTICIPATION

Placing the four assemblies in the historical perspective of three decades clearly indicates a movement toward the increased prevalence of the participatory, soundless, leaderless gathering of Arabic recitation. The growing preference for qur'ankhwani, not only in North America but also in Pakistan, probably reflects the impact of influential transnational Islamic movements. The general shift toward participatory, silent recitation appears moreover to be a function of two aspects of contemporary South Asian Muslim life in North America. One is a lack of performance resources, given the absence of traditional service professions, whether hereditary musical specialists, such as *qawwals* who perform mystical hymns for Sufi assemblies, or musically adept artisans and tradesmen. Second, the participatory assembly reflects the Canadian reality of a voluntary association among individuals who share a bond of religion and community activated only by mutual goodwill, leaving behind the ties of dominance and dependence that characterized social relationships in the homeland. The qur'ankhwani accurately represents this reality where everyone's voice is speaking, but no one dominates. This contrasts clearly with the milad model, which projects dominance, submission, and temporal-spatial coordination within the group.

This trend represents a confluence of several trajectories, all of which are relevant to the larger issue of self-representation by South Asian Muslims in North America. First, identity is asserted vis-à-vis the West and in the face of its perceived "threat to valued social relationships" (Metcalf 1989) through an acting out of those relationships, reinforcing them by means of the shared verbal articulation of religious identity. Second, space is functional. Structural spatial expression of Muslim identity resides in the mosque, the processual spatial expression of Muslim identity is the *qibla,* and the social expression of family and gender relationships is the home. Finally, linking all three in dynamic action are the Word and its articulation, embodied in both the ritual of prayer and of the recitational assembly. Ritual prayer serves to universalize; recitational assemblies, to actualize the particular community of South Asian Muslims in Canada.

Seen in a wider context, the life of the four recitational assemblies forms a salient part of the unique and dynamic process of this Muslim community's creating itself in the West. Its primary action has been to focus self-expression inward in order to articulate community identity to its own members, largely disregarding the presence of a larger society of outsiders. But as their sense of community has strengthened, the focus of self-expression is expanding toward self-representation vis-à-vis the larger society. Recitation, too, is affected by this shift, but it remains to be seen how South Asian Muslims transform the living Islamic Word as they move from adapting Western space to Muslim uses toward the creation of a Muslim space displayed to non-Muslims in the West.

NOTES

1. This paper is drawn essentially from the life involvement of one who is both an outsider and insider among Muslims in Canada, a socially entrenched participant and translator across the margins. Its focus is on Muslims who have become, over the years, more like family members than friends, and what I write must reflect their sense of self-representation. My collaborators' wish to stay outside this text accounts for the absence of the personal voices so attractive to read (see also Qureshi 1991). Special thanks go to Saleem Qureshi, Siddiqua Qureshi, Amera Raza, Atiya Siddiqi, Yasmeen Nizam, Zehra Hameed, Aqil Athar, Anisa and Nazir Khatib, and Najma Hossain. I am particularly grateful to Atiya Siddiqi, Anisa Khatib, Ansa Athar, and Yasmeen Nizam for sharing photographs of their homes. This chapter is dedicated to all of you!

2. Built in 1938 by a small group of Arab immigrants, Edmonton's al-Rashid Mosque is the oldest in Canada. The newly built al-Rashid Mosque was opened in 1982. Today, the original small building has been moved to the historical site of Fort Edmonton. The Markaz ul Islam was opened in 1986.

3. For a discussion of basic concepts in South Asian Canadian community formation, see Qureshi 1983.

4. "The whole world is a *masjid* [mosque] for you, so wherever the hour of prayer overtakes thee, thou shalt perform the *salat* and that is *masjid*" (*Sahih Muslim* 1977, vol. 1, ch. 194, no. 1057, p. 264; see also Samb 1991: 645).

5. The classical formulation is by Ghazali (Macdonald 1901–2; see also During 1988).

6. Qur'an, suras 109, 112, 113, 114.

7. Ibid., sura 112.

8. Ibid., sura 2:255.

9. In Shi'a homes, names include members of the Prophet's family ('Ali, Fatima, Hasan, Husain), and pictures of their tombs at Karbala (Husain) and Najaf ('Ali).

10. If disabled, a Muslim can recite a namaz without the gestures, just as dry cleaning can be substituted in ablutions (*wuzu*) if water is unavailable. Flexibility vis-à-vis ritual observance is characteristic of Islam and clearly serves to facilitate individual observance.

11. Despite the highly musical presentation, the term *singing* is inappropriate, since Islamic tradition does not approve of music in association with religious expression.

12. An informal alias for milad is *auraton ki qawwali* (women's qawwali)—that is, a women's equivalent of the (male) Sufi devotional assembly convened for listening to the performance of mystical hymns (Qureshi 1995).

13. Also chosen sometimes for repeated recitation are the words of the first qul, for which the appropriate number is 11,000 times. The practice of undertaking a fixed number of repeated repetitions is collectively termed *wazifa*.

14. The term *khatam-e-qur'an* (completion of the Qur'an) is also used for qur'ankwhani (see, e.g., Werbner 1990).

15. For example, during menstruation.

16. All qur'anic translations are taken from Yusuf Ali 1986.

17. In my experience, the term *sacred* does not resonate positively with Muslims.

18. My long association with both the Shi'a and Isma'ili communities leads me to think that their prior experience as endogamous minority groups (especially in East Africa) may have endowed them with an institutional religious life that furthered their adaptation and self-definition in Canada. The swift establishment of thriving imambaras and jama'tkhanas after the two groups emigrated from East Africa contrasts strikingly with the very gradual establishment of South Asian mosque activities. Also striking is the fact that before the substantial immigration of Khoja Shi'as from East Africa, South Asian Shi'a religious life in Canada was not more publicly organized than that of South Asian Sunnis, possibly because of low numbers. See Schubel, this volume.

19. In Alberta this is exemplified by the now-dormant Urdu Muslim Cultural Association. The more recently established Bazm-e-Sukhan is explicitly secular and includes anyone interested in Urdu culture.

WORKS CITED

Abel, A. 1965. "Dar-ul Islam." In *The Encyclopedia of Islam,* ed. B. Lewis, C. H. Pellet, and J. Schacht, 2: 127–28. Leiden: Brill.

Akbar Warsi, Khwaja Muhammad. N.d. *Milad-e-Akbar.* Delhi: Ratan.

Durkheim, Emile. 1938. *L'Evolution pédogogique en France des origines à la Renaissance.* Paris: Felix Alcan.

During, Jean. 1988. *Musique et extase: L'Audition mystique dans la tradition soufie.* Paris: Albin Michel.

Fabian, Johannes. 1983. *Time and the Other: How Anthropology Makes Its Object.* New York: Columbia University Press.

Grabar, Oleg. 1983. "Symbols and Signs in Islamic Architecture." In *Architecture and Community: Building in the Islamic World Today,* ed. Renata Holod, pp. 25–32. Aga Khan Awards for Architecture. Millerton, N.Y.: Aperture.

al-Hujwiri. 1911. *Kashf al-Mahjub.* Translated by R. A. Nicholson. Gibb Memorial Series, no. 17. London: Luzac. Reprint, London, 1959.

Jones, Dalu. 1978. "The Elements of Decoration: Surface, Pattern, and Light." In *Architecture of the Islamic World: Its History and Social Meaning,* pp. 144–75. London: Thames & Hudson.

Macdonald, Duncan Black. 1901–2. "Emotional Religion in Islam as Affected by Music and Singing, Being a Translation of a Book of the Ihya Ulum ad-Din of al-Ghazzali." *Journal of the Royal Asiatic Society*, 1–28, 195–252, 705–48.

Metcalf, Barbara D. 1989. "Making Space for Islam: Spatial Expression of Muslims in the West." Proposal for SSRC Conference, Boston, November 1–4.

Moravia, Sergio. 1976. "Les Ideologues et l'age des lumières." *Studies on Voltaire and the Eighteenth Century* 154: 1465–86.

Ong, Walter J. 1958. *Ramus: Method and the Decay of Dialogue*. Cambridge, Mass.: Harvard University Press.

Samb, A. 1991. "Masdjid." In *The Encyclopedia of Islam*, ed. C. E. Bosworth, E. van Douzel, B. Lewis, W. P. Heinrichs, and C. H. Pellet, 6: 644–707. Leiden: Brill.

Qureshi, Regula Burckhardt. 1972. "Indo-Muslim Religious Music: An Overview." *Asian Music*, 15–22.

———. 1980a. "India, Subcontinent of: IV Chanted Poetry, V Popular Religious Music, Muslim." In *The New Grove Dictionary of Music and Musicians*, 9: 143–47. London: Macmillan.

———. 1980b. "Pakistan." *The New Grove Dictionary of Music and Musicians*, 14: 104–12. London: Macmillan.

———. 1981. "Islamic Music in an Indian Environment: The Shi'a Majlis." *Ethnomusicology* 25, 1 (January): 41–71.

———. 1991. "Marriage Strategies among Muslims from South East Asia." In *Muslim Families in North America*, ed. E. Waugh, S. Abu-Laban, and R. B. Qureshi, pp. 185–212. Edmonton: University of Alberta Press.

———. 1995. *Sufi Music of India and Pakistan: Sound, Context, and Meaning in Qawwali*. 1986. Reprint. Chicago: University of Chicago Press.

Qureshi, Regula Burckhardt, and Saleem M. M. Qureshi. 1983. "Pakistani Canadians: The Making of a Muslim Community." In *The Muslim Community in North America*, ed. E. Waugh, B. Abu-Laban, and R. B. Qureshi, pp. 127–48. Edmonton: University of Alberta Press.

Sahih Muslim. 1977. In *Al-Jami'-us-Sahih by Imam Muslim*, trans. Abdul Hamid Siddiqi. 4 vols. New Delhi: Kitab Bhavan.

Shaw, Alison. 1988. *A Pakistani Community in Britain*. London: Blackwell.

Tomlinson, Gary. 1993. *Music in Renaissance Magic: Toward a Historiography of Others*. Chicago: University of Chicago Press.

Werbner, Pnina. 1988. "'Sealing' the Koran: Offering and Sacrifice among Pakistani Labour Migrants." *Cultural Dynamics* 1, 1: 77–97.

Yusuf Ali, Abdullah, trans. 1986. *The Holy Quran: Full Arabic Text, Roman Transliteration and Translation*. Lahore: Sheikh Muhammad Ashraf.

THREE

"This Is a Muslim Home"

Signs of Difference in the African-American Row House

Aminah Beverly McCloud

Muslims over history have varied widely in their cultural lives. They have, however, generally shared certain practices dependent on space. Muslims' submission of their will to God ideally reappropriates space and reorganizes temporality. *Salat* (formal prayer) requires space both physically and mentally. Fasting makes demands of mental and spiritual space, while altering temporality. The Hajj demands its space and time. In salat, for example, boundaries are formed when the prayer space is isolated. The calling of the *adhan* and the *iqamah* signal movement from one reality to another as the Muslim and Muslimah stand before ALLAH. In salat, the individual merges with the worldwide (and local) *umma* in a time for God that is distinct and unbounded. Both the practical needs of ritual and the profound juncture of the coterminous nature of the time and space of salat with the time and space of the world have a fundamental influence on space.

This essay first briefly describes the main Muslim communities and their congregational spaces in Philadelphia and then turns to a discussion of the city's African-American Muslim homes. Muslims make these homes, built on standard models, into a distinctive "Muslim space" through signage, decoration, and practice.

THE PHILADELPHIA COMMUNITIES AND
CONGREGATIONAL SPACE

Philadelphia has been a microcosm of Muslim activity at least since the 1940s. Most Islamic groups in the United States either have members living there or some ties with residents. By the middle of the 1970s, numerous Muslim communities were evident in Philadelphia, among them the

Moorish Science Temple of America (1913), the Ahmadiyah movement (1921), three Nation of Islam communities (1930), the American Muslim Mission (1980), the Darul Islam (ca. 1971), and several communities associated with the Muslim Student Association.

"Our divine national movement stands for the specific grand principles of Love, Truth, Peace, Freedom, and Justice," the Moorish Science Temple's statement of belief begins. "It is the great GOD ALLAH alone, that guides the destiny of the divine and national movement" (Ali 1927). The community expect "the end of tyranny and wickedness" against African-Americans and seek to connect with their Muslim heritage in general and with the descendants of Moroccans in particular. They identify the qur'anic *kufars* (disbelievers, or the ungrateful) as the European-Americans, who face imminent destruction as a result of their apparent disbelief and unaccountability while engaging in evil conduct. They understand the nature of reality as spiritual and human existence as co-eternal with the existence of time. They believe that the Christianity taught by European-Americans was designed to enslave Africans, and they regard heaven and hell as conditions of the mind created by individual deeds and misdeeds.

Moorish Science members usually meet in a designated house in a room painted beige or eggshell, with neatly ordered rows of chairs on an uncarpeted floor polished to perfection. In one house I visited, all the chairs faced a small stage with a podium, behind which were seven chairs signaling some persons of importance. On the wall behind the stage were nicely framed portraits and documents: Noble Drew Ali's mother dressed in white, with a long white veil; Noble Drew Ali by himself, looking regal; a charter for the community; and a set of bylaws. All the other walls were bare, and the only other fixture was a red flag with a green five-pointed star in its center. The sect offers members a space of neatness, cleanliness, and order.

The Ahmadiyyians, who originated in the Indian subcontinent in the late nineteenth century, assert that God is active in this world, determining and designing the course of events. They hold that there should be a living relationship with God, from whom revelatory experience is still possible. Because of this belief, other Muslims have accused them of denying the finality of Prophethood (cf. Haider, this volume). Ahmadis do, however, believe in the Oneness of God, observe the prescribed prayers, fast during the month of Ramadan, pay *zakat,* and perform the pilgrimage to Mecca. They also uphold the Al-Hadith (Friedmann 1989). They are active missionaries, and their journals, *The Review of Religions* and *The Moslem Sunrise,* have been widely used.

In Philadelphia, this community meets in a large house, where there is strict adherence to the code of gender separation, with women having a separate entrance and a separate prayer room. The walls are bare, with the exception of an occasional piece of Arabic calligraphy. Distinct prayer areas are carpeted. Chairs are provided for eating and classes. The Indian subcontinent influences furnishings and other decorations.

The American Muslim Mission, which has largely replaced the Nation of Islam founded by Elijah Muhammad in the 1930s, is also active. The mission dates from an address delivered in Atlanta in the late 1970s by Elijah Muhammad's son, Warithudeen Muhammad, who disbanded the central authority of the Chicago *masjid,* encouraging decentralization of the community. He "revived true Islam," instituting salat at the proper times and encouraging the five pillars. Imams were to be trained in Arabic, *tafsir,* masjid administration, and marriage counseling. The AMM continues to emphasize concerns of African-Americans such as self-development, self-accountability, racism, and poverty.

American Muslim Mission communities refurbished their places of congregation to be "orthodox"; they were no longer called "temples" but "masjids" or "mosques." Pictures of Elijah Muhammad, Clara Muhammad, and W. D. Fard were removed, along with the characteristic elegant chandeliers, heavy velvet drapes, chairs, and wall lighting. Search areas were turned into cloakrooms to serve as foyers leading into the masjid. Women, who had always been present side by side with men, were now separated from men inside the prayer area (the *masala*).

The Darul Islam, finally, used a rehabed house, which in the 1970s was open neither to the general community of Muslims nor to the surrounding community. The members sought seclusion and protection after reports of police mistreatment of their mentors in New York. Guards at the bare entranceway sat behind a counter to scrutinize visitors as to their intent. The community held its prayers upstairs, out of range of observation, with women in a separate room, linked by loudspeakers. Believers lived close to the masjid and schooled their children there. The mosque was open twenty-four hours a day.

As these examples illustrate, although the concept of umma is very important to African-American Muslims, it is provincially conceived. Their buildings reflect their many divisions and their perception of American hostility to the Muslim world. For all their sectarian differences, however, African-American Muslims share a great deal, including their use of the home.

"THIS IS A MUSLIM HOME"

African-American Muslims in large cities have continually attempted to replicate the earliest Muslim communities by locating themselves in physical communities in close proximity to the masjid. Some jointly purchase small apartment buildings when available. In a few cases, entire communities have moved to rural areas to be able to live together.

Muslims often mark their homes as a space of difference and separation by a sign on the door. This is especially important for those living outside a Muslim enclave. The sign creates a boundary that signals both a warning and a welcome. To non-Muslims, the sign serves as a polite warning that the visitor is about to enter a different space and time. For other Muslims, it is a sign denoting a refuge. The phrase, "THIS IS A MUSLIM HOME / PLEASE REMOVE YOUR SHOES" is on the door of hundreds of African-American Muslim homes and apartments in Philadelphia and probably in other major cities as well.

Muslims say that these signs, selling for only fifty cents, appeared in the late 1960s on the tables of Muslim vendors. Non-Muslim workmen, repairmen, salespersons, and social workers may be annoyed by the sign and resist removing their shoes. Neighbors simply grow used to it.

For the owners of the space, the sign symbolizes the success of having created a boundary that defines an area of control. The sign dictates an attitude: in this house, it says, the hostile environment of racism, religious intolerance, and discrimination are locked out; prayer space and hospitality are guaranteed.

African-American Muslims self-consciously and deliberately organize the use of domestic space in the light of teachings found in the Qur'an and Al-Hadith, as well as through the example of immigrant Muslim homes and homes in the Muslim world. These Islamic norms thus inform the basic daily needs characteristic of domestic space—shelter, food storage and use, ritual activities, and social interaction. For African-American Muslims, the home becomes a space for learning and practicing Muslim behavior and for being separate from the larger society.

One of the classical divisions known in Islam, between Darul Islam (the House of Islam) and Darul Harb (the House of War), translates in American usage as the domestic space and the outside community. Domestic space is consciously separated from the space of the House of War, which is viewed as a space of religious intolerance and racism. The use of domestic space creates, moreover, a sense of shared spirituality with Muslims elsewhere in the Muslim world, while fostering a sense of well-being in an environment perceived as hostile.

Juan Campo has recently argued that "the religious meanings of domestic space is an important part of the study of sacred space" that has long been neglected (Campo 1991: 8). In examining the Islamic aspects of Egyptian homes, Campo links a terminology and discourse related to domestic space to a discourse related to God's house (the Ka'ba), sacred history, rules of behavior, and the Hereafter. Campo suggests that the social etiquette and some of the ritual observances defined for the Ka'ba have served as the prototype for all human dwellings. The Qur'an reminds Muslims that the people before them who committed serious errors perished, along with their dwellings (cf. Haider, this volume). Thus, everyday social

Figure 13. Philadelphia row house. Note Islamic signs in window and door.
Photograph by Aminah Beverly McCloud.

life is linked to "ideas about God, right and wrong, purity, and blessings."
Many rules relate to women (Campo 1991: 27). As for Paradise, "In each
of these descriptions, the quality of life in Paradise is an idealized rendering of the best aspects of domestic life in this world" (Campo 1991: 25).
Thus the Qur'an's exhortations about the space and time of the Hereafter
implicitly remind believers of the importance of the home. The Al-Hadith
explicitly makes people's houses and behavior in them regular objects of
discourse. Campo argues that because of the moral restrictions on wom-
en's movement and seclusion, a great deal of a house's sacrality depends
on the reputation of its female occupants.

These issues shape the lives of African-American Muslims living in Philadelphia row houses. There are row homes throughout the city, usually
three-bedroom, two-story structures, often with no yard, some with small
porches (fig. 13). The interior design is largely uniform. There are few
houses with central hallways in the areas where Muslims predominately
live. Rooms interconnect, with or without doors, with a small staircase leading upstairs to the small bedrooms and a centrally located bathroom. African-American Muslims have lived in these houses for several decades.

Stories of the Prophet Muhammad's life yield a central paradigm for
living within the house. The house should be austere and near the masjid.

Prophet Muhammad lived in a one-room dwelling, furnished with the bare necessities for living, with access to prayer space.

Al-Hadith regulate the accumulation of wealth and delineate the responsibilities attached to its use; African-American Muslims furnish their homes within these constraints.

Within their homes, Muslims live a distinctive life. Even their concepts of time differ from those of non-Muslims. The Muslim community is seen as a dot on a continuum that began with creation and does not end but shifts focus in the afterlife. Ritual practices define Muslim schedules, beginning with the pre-dawn prayer while most non-Muslim neighbors are sleeping. Fasting during the month of Ramadan has led school officials and neighbors to alert social workers to the possibility of child abuse or neglect, causing some Muslim households to become even more insular.

Life in the house is characterized by cleanliness and minimal consumption. There is only one requirement for Muslim space—a place for prayer. The Muslim not only retreats internally for experiencing *taqwa* (piety) for salat, but also requires a physical place to face the Ka'ba and to perform the prayer undisturbed. This space should above all be free from pollution. Muslims have developed some creative strategies for overcoming the physical structure of their homes. They enter this space by removing their shoes, leaving them in baskets, shoe racks, bookcases, crates, or just a designated space near the front door, since most houses do not have foyers. Women, who typically carry an extra pair of socks to wear inside, are escorted to one portion of the house, while the men are escorted to another. The members of the household also divide themselves along gender lines at this time.

The house is usually decorated with Islamic texts and calligraphy, framed as well as unframed, and bronze plates engraved with various Qur'anic suras, much like the Canadian homes described by Qureshi above (fig. 10). Qur'anic recitations are the only music generally played in the public rooms of the home. In most living rooms, families have the latest copies of various Muslim newspapers, journals and pamphlets but not issues of *Time, Ebony, Essence,* or *Woman's Day.* Bookcases hold the Qur'an on the top shelf by itself, at least one set of Al-Hadith, and several sets of commentary by Maulana Ali and Yusuf Ali just below them. Other texts, generally originating in Pakistan or Egypt, are also religious. These books are purchased from merchants, the masjid, and conventions. The bookcase may hold prayer rugs and veils, and may itself configure the room toward Mecca. The *qiblah,* or direction toward the Ka'ba in Mecca, may also be indicated by a wall plaque or by some other piece of furnishing, such as the carved screen in figure 14.

Muslim space is replete with Arabic calligraphy, "oriental" rugs, brassware, latticed screens and so on. Since African-American Muslims are not

Figure 14. Living room with calligraphy, Qur'an, and objects from African and Asian Muslim countries. Photograph by Aminah Beverly McCloud.

tied to any particular country, they have drawn on the entire Muslim world for interior design. African-American Muslim adoption of a wide variety of Muslim cultural interior designs has generated probably the only "melting pot" of Muslim culture since the earliest centuries of Islamic history. In some homes, the furnishings for seating remind the visitor of a Moroccan restaurant: fat pillows made from synthetic oriental rugs, tables no more than a foot tall, couches with no legs, or mattresses used as couches. Other homes have traditional American furnishings. Living-room furniture is kept to a minimum in order to be able to turn the living-room space into prayer space without difficulty. Dining rooms are often sparsely furnished so that, along with the living room, they too can become a prayer area. In Philadelphia row homes, the dining room is usually situated between the kitchen and the living room; a *maida* (tablecloth) can be spread on the dining-room floor for meals and a few pillows, usually stacked in a corner, put out for seating.

Window shades, curtains, and drapes are always closed to exclude the view of neighbors in adjoining row houses. When visitors are not present, women are free to unveil and wear any appropriate clothing. When there are visitors, if there is even one adult male in the house, all the women will remain in the kitchen. They only leave to serve food or to pray.

The kitchens may accommodate a small dinette set, which doubles as a space for food preparation, an ongoing event. Halal meat (meat raised and then ritually slaughtered according to Islamic law) is purchased at great expense, either shipped in (by United Parcel Service or U.S. mail) or, in some communities, slaughtered by designated men in contractual arrangements with local farmers. Families then buy portions of the slaughtered meat. Breads are often homemade or are purchased from immigrant Muslim bakers or grocery stores. Dietary restrictions are strictly adhered to in all communities, and a great amount of time is thus spent in grocery shopping. Storage of foods is a critical skill. Vegetables are usually bought fresh and cooked daily. Foods regarded as Muslim food include falafel, couscous, humus, curry, lentils, pita bread, and basmati rice. Muslims prefer to cook elaborate dishes with spices, learned from immigrants, and avoid fast foods. Women highly esteem culinary skills.

Muslims do not linger in the bathroom (*hamam*) where jinn (creations of fire and thought in general to be evil) are thought to be present. Bathroom doors are kept closed for this reason. Those entering a bathroom wear special shoes or slippers. The bathroom is a space both of pollution and purification. The believer enters with the left foot, acknowledges the dangers of the space with a *du'a,* performs the necessary acts, and leaves on the right foot, reentering prayer space. Some people place pictures or other decorative items in bathrooms that could not be placed in spaces for prayer. There may also be signs with instructions on ablution. In some homes, a curtain or screen is positioned around the toilet to separate it from other facilities in the bathroom, while in others a closed toilet lid suffices.

Full participation in the Muslim community requires certain responses in the domestic space. Homes must reflect Islamic injunctions on prayer space and diet. They must also reflect Muslim prohibitions of certain kinds of art, social entertainment, and mixing of men and women. Muslims recognize some shared values in American life, such as charity, but in general they find non-Muslim values, especially in relation to sex, overwhelming. They seek an ideal Muslim atmosphere inside the home that is wholly separate.

Unlike most of the Muslim world, which welcomes television and radio, African-American Muslims try to shut out Western values and open the door to Muslim values. Fear of compromise of Islamic values prompts many parents to prefer either Islamic education or home schooling, so that in several communities, children have had only brief contact with the larger community.

Dress is also distinctive. Women may wear long-sleeved blouses under short-sleeved dresses or pants under dresses that are above the ankles. Men occasionally wear long shirts reaching the thigh under suit jackets with traditional Muslim headwear. Young girls wear scarves as an early deterrent to assimilation into "Christian" society (cf. Slyomovics, fig. 40, this volume). To enjoy public entertainments, Muslims may rent an entire roller rink for the evening so that girls or boys can skate, or hold an outdoor picnic in some remote part of a park.

African-American Muslims have taken small portions of various Muslim cultures and woven their own tapestry. Living rooms may contain Berber-patterned rugs, rattan furniture, Victorian lamps, Indian brass vases, and Arabic calligraphy on walls, all together an enthusiastic mixture of worlds. Arabic has mixed with black English. The expression "Masha'allah," which is generally understood to mean "It is what Allah decreed" in happiness over some event or occurrence, is used by most African-American Muslims only as a lament.

African-American Muslims have clearly found that their American nationality is but one small aspect of their identity as prescribed by Islam. They are part of the larger Muslim world and interact with immigrant Muslims, while at times clashing with them and even encountering racism. African-American Muslims are likely in the near future to seek a greater blending of African Islam with African-American Islam and thus to engender an even more distinct African-American Islam. Then, as now, the home will be central to its expression and will be seen—whether explicitly signposted or not—as a separate and explicitly Muslim space.

WORKS CITED

Ali, Noble Drew. 1927. *The Holy Koran of the Moorish Science Temple.*

Campo, Juan E. 1991. *The Other Sides of Paradise: Explorations into the Religious Meanings of Domestic Space in Islam.* Columbia, S.C.: University of South Carolina Press.

Friedmann, Yohanan. 1989. *Prophecy Continuous: Aspects of Ahmadi Religious Thought and Its Medieval Background.* Berkeley: University of California Press.

FOUR

"Refuge" and "Prison"

Islam, Ethnicity, and the Adaptation of Space in Workers' Housing in France

Moustapha Diop
Laurence Michalak

In the intense public debate about migration issues in France, there has been a general tendency to treat the religious affiliation of labor migrants from predominantly Muslim countries as their most salient feature. Migrants in France are, indeed, almost all Muslim—Arab North Africans, West Africans, and Turks. Yet we should not assume that religious affiliation necessarily plays a preeminent role in the position of labor migrants vis-à-vis the host country. For example, almost all Latin American migrants to the United States in recent years have been Christian, but religion plays no role in American discourse on migration. In France, however, where most migrants are of a different religion than their hosts, "Muslim" has become a synonym for "other"—or, some would argue, code for "non-white." If migrants increasingly speak as "Muslim," finding such an identity natural and effective in the new contexts where they live, we must see that in part as a label thrust upon them.

Muslims in France do not act to any significant degree—or at least not yet—as a corporate group, with a consciousness of unity, a sentiment of solidarity, and a consensus for collective action. Islam appears to be increasingly an aspect of "ethnicization," which may or may not transcend national and other social divisions. The importance of domestic settings for constructing such social identities is evident throughout this volume. One of those settings is the densely populated, highly charged, semipublic space of the *foyers* created in France for migrant workers, whose space has sometimes, in important ways, been made Islamic.

THE FOYERS IN FRANCE

The foyer is a ubiquitous aspect of the French urban and architectural landscape wherever there are high concentrations of foreign workers. The term *foyer*, or "home," with its domestic connotations, is ironic, in that the foyers rarely house families and typically forbid couples and children. The migrants in the foyer are frequently married, but they have left their families in their countries of origin. The foyer is a social universe of non-French males, an island of workers, usually unskilled or low-skilled, away from their homelands and isolated from their families. In fact, foreign workers have had high rates of unemployment in recent years, so that the foyer has become a kind of reservoir of cheap foreign labor.

The function of the foyer is to provide sleeping accommodations and common facilities for its inhabitants. Several workers may share a room or a group of small individual bedrooms, grouped around a shared kitchen/dining facility and a bathroom.

A single building or group of buildings with multiple clusters like this forms the foyer. The foyer may also have common rooms, such as a room for Muslims to perform their daily prayers, like the makeshift room shown in figure 15. The foyer tends to be isolated—located away from the urban center, contiguous to places such as cemeteries and garbage dumps, typically found at urban peripheries. To compare the foyers to concentration camps or minimum security prisons or urban reservations would be too harsh. To compare them with youth hostels and student residences seems too mild.

The first modern foyers for migrant workers in France date from the early 1950s, but their rapid spread began when the French government passed a law (Article 116 of Law No. 56–780 of August 4, 1956), creating SONACOTRAL, the Societé nationale de construction de logements pour les travailleurs algériens (National Company for the Construction of Housing for Algerian Workers), to finance, construct, and manage housing for "Muslim French from Algeria come to work in metropolitan [France], and for their families." SONACOTRAL was clearly expected to help keep closer control over Algerian workers in France, but *algérien* was dropped from the name in 1963, and the organization is now called SONACOTRA. By the early 1980s, other organizations—such as the ADEF (for management of construction-workers' foyers), AFTAM (which included students and had a mainly sub-Saharan clientèle), and AFRP (for North Africans in the Paris region)—together accounted for another 128 foyers with 35,338 beds (Ginesy-Galano 1984: 28–48). By the end of 1988, SONACOTRA controlled 69,000 rooms and 1,800 apartments in 330 establishments, with a staff of 1,100 (Gagneux 1989). SONACOTRA today justly describes itself as "France's Number One Host"—it is the largest entity in France in the field of hotels and housing. Figure 16 shows a small room in a SONACOTRA foyer. The next largest foyer organization is an umbrella group of organizations called UNAFO, the Union nationale des Associations gestionnaires des foyers des travailleurs migrants (National Union of

Figure 15. A makeshift room for prayer in a foyer in the Var region of southeastern France. Note the rugs and the hanging with the Kaʿba image to indicate the direction of prayer. Photograph by Laurence Michalak.

Associations Managing Foyers for Migrant Workers), which includes most of the smaller foyer chains, totaling nearly 50 associations with about 260 foyers, 52,000 beds, and 2,200 staff, housing a mobile population (Brun-Melin 1989).

WEST AFRICANS IN THE FOYERS

The modern history of black African immigration to France began after World War I, when former African soldiers (known as *tirailleurs sénégalais,*

Figure 16. A Tunisian worker in a room in a SONACOTRA foyer. Photograph by Laurence Michalak.

or Senegalese infantrymen) were allowed to work on merchant ships as kitchen hands, coal trimmers, and stokers. In 1945, West Africans were employed as seamen in the context of government concerns about shortages of labor. After World War II, however, French seamen urged that French be hired ahead of foreigners—notwithstanding that many West Africans were French citizens. Between 1954 and 1959, the immigration of seamen, along with many unskilled and low-skilled workers, continued.

After 1960, African immigration to France increased with colonial independence. A multilateral agreement between France and the African states allowed members of the Franco-African Commonwealth to move without restriction to France or to the other African states that had formerly been components of the French empire (namely, Mali, Mauritania, and Senegal). African migration to France during the 1960s was usually temporary, lasting about four years. But after 1974—the official date suspending immigration into France—black Africans began to settle in for good.

There are officially 172,689 Africans in France from eighteen nations, making up 4.5 percent of the foreign population, according to the 1982 national census. The largest African group are from Senegal (33,242 people), followed by migrants from Mali (24,340), Cameroun (14,220), Ivory Coast (11,680), and Mauritania (5,060). West Africans work in industry (38 percent), in services (32 percent), in building and civil engineering (8 percent), in domestic services, and in the textile and confectionary industries.

In the 1950s and early 1960s, West Africans were housed in slums, including old factories adapted for housing, in cities such as Marseilles, Rouen, Le Havre, Paris, and Montreuil. In Paris, they were mainly concentrated in the eleventh, twelfth, eighteenth, nineteenth, and twentieth *arrondissements*. In 1962–64, under a 1901 law, associations were created for the purpose of lodging black Africans: Accueil et promotion (Welcome and Support); ASSOTRAF, the Association d'aide sociale aux travailleurs africains en France (Association for Social Aid to African Workers in France); and SOUNIATA, the Association pour le soutien, la dignité et l'unité dans l'accueil aux travailleurs africains (Association for Support, Dignity, and Unity in the Welcome of African Workers). These associations were directly or indirectly created by the government and were run by French political figures who claimed that they were "friends of Africa," some of them with links to former French colonies. Thus, in the late 1960s and the 1970s, while SONACOTRA took care of the Maghrebis and European migrants such as Portuguese and Yugoslavs, these other associations looked after the West Africans. SONACOTRA began giving rooms to black Africans in the mid 1970s, when it was ordered to do so by the prefecture of Paris. In the Ile-de-France, a quarter of UNAFO's 126 foyers serve mixed populations, while only 11 of SONACOTRA foyers do.

West African foyers usually house people either from the same region or of the same ethnic origin, or at most perhaps two or three different ethnic groups or nationalities. All or nearly all of the people in these foyers are Muslims. Two main groups are usually to be found in the foyers—the Soninke, or Sarakolle, and the Tukuleur (from the Senegal River Valley, shared by the three countries of Mali, Mauritania, and Senegal). In Paris, the foyers are mostly Malian, while in Les Mureaux and Mantes-La-Jolie (Yvelines), the Senegalese are the majority. There are other ethnic minorities in the foyers as well, such as the Bambara (Mali and Senegal), the Manding (Senegal and Mali), and the Manjak (who are Catholic and come from Senegal and Guinea-Bissau).

The social life of the residents replicates significant features of life in their homelands. All the ethnic groups—except for the Manjak—have strong hierarchical organizations, and despite the overcrowding, divisions between nobles and commoners are respected through invisible barriers. Every man has his place. The head of the community, or the village, is always a man of high birth. Among the Soninke, the head is helped in his task by a council of nobles, who see to the administration of the community or village. The council looks after the morality of the group, monthly dues for food, and the lodging of newcomers or people in need (because of illness or unemployment). It also provides help for the village of origin with mosques, schools, sanitary arrangements, and so on.

Just below, or sometimes at the same level as, the notables stands the *marabout*. He is very important in the group, serving simultaneously as secretary, confidant, teacher, leader, and talisman-maker, and is usually well trained in qur'anic and Islamic studies. The marabout is also expected to moderate the tendency of the *griot*—a kind of troubadour and historian— to rekindle ancient quarrels between noble families. The griot is Janus-faced. According to the circumstances, he can act on the "pagan" side of the nobles, rekindling memories of the glorious past of the Soninke people, or he can put on Islamic dress and go hand in hand with the marabout. At the bottom of the social pyramid are the lower categories of traditional craftsmen (cobblers, smiths) and the "slaves"—the descendants of former prisoners of war.

There is a complicity between the noble, the marabout, and the griot— a web of collusion so well spun that the lower-status groups assent to their conditions without making too much fuss, even when and if they are more educated and more knowledgeable about French society than their "masters." In the Soninke communities, the cooking must always be done by the "slaves." In return, the "masters" must be lavish toward them, especially during traditional feasts such as those at initiations. On these occasions, the dividing up of space in the meeting rooms reveals the underlying principles of exclusion and inclusion. Women sit apart from men, and Islamic rather than traditional practices are invoked. There is a subtle spatial segregation between nobles and commoners. As for the lower social categories, they are busy helping the nobles and their guests. The boundaries are subtle. Everyone knows where and next to whom to sit.

Residents of the foyers are outspoken and articulate in describing the negative aspects of their lodgings. They perceive their lodgings as "prisons" or "concentration camps," and individual rooms as "tombs." Still, despite these criticisms, most West African residents also acknowledge positive aspects of the foyer: "The foyer is my second village"; "It is a place where things go well"; "It is very secure, a welcoming place compared to the aggressiveness of the town"; "In the foyer, people come and go without problems."

Were the foyers created in order to further the segregation of migrant workers? Whatever the answer, one must acknowledge that foreign residents have transformed the space of the foyers, using it to their liking. In place of the official rules of the foyer, they have substituted unofficial rules of their own.

In the 1970s, the foyers, whether Maghrebi or West African, were strictly supervised by directors who were, for the most part, French army veterans who had served in Indochina, Algeria, or West Africa. Administrative rules were drastic. Visits from people outside the foyer were severely controlled, largely limited to male relatives, at fixed hours and in the television room only. After 8:00 P.M., the director could enter and inspect any room. The director would play off one nationality against another, first of all by separating nationalities into specific floors, and secondly, by emphasizing the cultural or religious differences between nationalities or ethnic groups. This period of military-style rule came to an end after the widespread 1975 strike about living conditions in the foyers. From that time on, the African foyers were open to free visitations and susceptible to "stowaways"—illegal residents from outside.

Nowadays in an individual room there may be the "official" bed, plus two or three folding beds, like the rooms of Mourides or Turks (see Ebin, Mandel, this volume). During weekends, the rooms are filled with visitors in traditional dress, sitting wherever a place can be found, chanting in loud voices, and drinking tea—which is perceived as an Islamic beverage. Meals of meat, or fish, and rice are also served, whereas during the period of military directors, it was forbidden to eat in the rooms. In some rooms of Muslim residents, one can see, among other decorations, a Hegira calendar, pictures of Mecca, ornate qur'anic calligraphy, and perhaps photographs on a table of a spiritual leader or a new mosque in an African village of origin. In the rooms of marabouts or educated Muslims, there are Islamic and Arabic books and a prayer rug in a corner. Thus sanctified, the place can become a site for prayer or religious education, so that space is defined by practice, not convention, much as it is described in several chapters of this book.

In the quest for identity, black Africans have endeavored to appropriate different collective areas of the foyers, including the corridors, the communal dining rooms, and the courtyards. The foyer has become multifunctional—a place of business and a place of worship. In nearly every African foyer, there are traditional activities such as craftsmen's workshops, markets, and restaurants. The latter are run by women, Malians for the most part, who are helped by "slaves," and sometimes by unemployed young commoners. The food usually consists of rice, meat stews, and sometimes chicken and chips (called a "European meal"). The price varies between eight and ten francs. The midday meal draws customers from outside, both migrants and French workers, into the foyers.

In most of the foyers, the common rooms and the corridors also serve as marketplaces. The market is usually conducted by men of high rank from the community, and their rooms become warehouses. The market provides different types of products—cigarettes, soap, chewing gum, sweets, African toothpicks, kola nuts. At weekends, the market increases in size, and, in some foyers, it is "sanctified" by such products as religious tapes, prayer rugs, Islamic calendars, religious books for different reading levels, prayer beads, incense, "Indian" perfumes, and even "halal" meat. The markets that specialize in these products are situated in foyers in which the "mosques" and village association meetings draw from five to eight hundred people on weekends.

In summertime, the courtyards of the foyers are taken over by men selling both raw and roasted ears of corn. An ambience conducive to informal socializing is created. The smell of roasted corn fills the air, and people stay up late. These marketplaces become places for meeting, discussion, and the construction and the consolidation of different kinds of identity.

In the 1970s, the landlords began to tolerate workshops in the foyers, so that black Africans could make a living related to their "tradition and culture." Tailors, cobblers, and smiths carry on their professions in tiny shops—perhaps fifteen square meters for five or six craftsmen. Some of these people work only on weekends; others work every day and even at night—especially tailors at the approach of Islamic festivals.

During the Islamic holiday of the 'Id (French: Ayd), people of lower status, especially cobblers, become butchers. The slaughtering of sheep in black African foyers began in 1971, after a social commission associated with the sixth national plan advocated support for cultural activities in the foyers. With the money that was allocated for this purpose, black Africans working through the foyers bought sheep for sacrifice at the Islamic new year and during the 'Ids, and invited lodgers, policemen, and mayors' delegations for these occasions.

In the France of the 1990s, however, ritual slaughtering has become a big issue, giving non-Muslims presumed moral ground to challenge the Muslim presence. This recalls "moral" causes discussed elsewhere in this volume in relation to Muslims: architectural conservation (Eade), "noise pollution" (Eade), and women's rights (Bloul). Petitions have been drawn up by humane societies, the National Front, and the French butchers' lobby to protest this practice. In January 1990, the famous movie star Brigitte Bardot vigorously attacked religious animal slaughter, both Jewish and Muslim, in an interview on French national television. She repeated these attacks in August in *Présent* (August 1, 1990), a newspaper sympathetic to the National Front, France's extreme right-wing party. But this time she objected, not only to the Muslim method of animal slaughter, but also to the French government policy, which "tolerates such ritual sacrifices and allows the spread of Islam in France. It's a shame." In the meantime, the Conseil de réflexion sur l'Islam en France, composed of Muslims of different nationalities and created in 1990 by the ministries of Interior and Culture, is trying to find ways to resolve this issue.

The foyer is also a place of worship. The first prayer room to be instituted in a black African residence appeared in 1967, located on the ground floor of the foyer "La Commanderie" in the nineteenth arrondissement of Paris. The next year a marabout living in the same building transformed his own sixth-floor room into a prayer room. He argued that a "mosque" should not be something given by non-Muslims; Muslims should themselves open their own prayer room. The marabout, who has now returned to Africa, thus drew a distinction between legitimate and illegitimate prayer places.

Only in 1977 did a second foyer introduce a prayer room. Despite this slow beginning, now almost all foyers have prayer rooms, which are subsidized by all residents of the foyer, whether Muslim or not. UNAFO, the principal organization of black African foyers, has, for example, 126 foyers in the Ile-de-France, of which 119 have prayer rooms.

The prayer rooms may be located on any floor—basement, ground floor, or various upper floors. The sizes vary, averaging around thirty to forty square meters. The prayer room is usually well furnished with multicolored carpets and contrasts with the rest of the building in its tidiness. A box for donations is always hung inside the room, next to the exit.

On weekdays, the prayer room may not be more than 20 to 30 percent filled. But on Fridays and during the 'Ids, it is completely full and people—both residents and outsiders—overflow into the courtyard. On such occasions, the nearby pavements become part of the prayer place, bewildering French neighbors, who talk about being "invaded," a telling metaphor. Two other dates offer opportunities for gatherings. The first is the Night of Destiny, the 26th to the 27th of the lunar month of Ramadan, when people assemble all night for prayer and recitation of the Qur'an, and food is brought in by the families of the residents and by outsiders. The second opportunity is Mawlud—the Prophet's birthday.

In some foyers, the prayer rooms are used as classrooms, albeit without tables or chairs. Qur'an and Arabic classes are conducted for children, with the lowest-level group next to the teacher and more advanced groups and individuals scattered about in different corners of the room. For the adults, lectures and talks follow the weekend afternoon prayer (*salat al asr*).

The "mosque" in the foyer contributes to the formation of Muslim identity. Even nonpracticing Muslims seem proud of its existence. The territory of the "mosque" is perceived, in principle, as a base that belongs to all Muslims, and, as such, it is a symbolic place of safety.

NORTH AFRICAN ARABS IN THE FOYERS

The collective life in the foyer of labor migrants faced with poverty and isolated from country and family would seem to offer the potential of comradeship, even of political action. The very fact of residence in a foyer has been important on occasion, as when foyer residents organized rent strikes in the 1970s. As the strikes led to improvements in conditions in the foyers, especially the relaxation of visiting rules noted above, tenants' organizations appeared to lose their raison d'être. Nor have the Tunisian, Algerian, and Moroccan *amicales,* or "friendship organizations," been very effective. All tend to be small groups dedicated to performing useful services, such as repatriating dead bodies. North Africans certainly tend to identify with their countries of origin, but this is not manifested through adherence to voluntary organizations such as the amicales, and their national sentiments are more cultural than political.

Islamic practices, often centered on the foyer, are typically part of those cultural sentiments. A 1985 survey conducted by Michalak in the Marseilles area included questions such as:

Of being Muslim, Arab, and [Moroccan/Algerian/Tunisian], which is
   most important for you?
How do you spend Ramadan in France?
Do you fast when you work?
Do you believe in God? Pray? Give alms?
Have you made or do you plan to make the hajj?
Do you drink alcohol? Eat non-halal meat?
Are you a good Muslim?
Have you changed your practice in France?
Is there a place to pray where you work?
Have you given money for a mosque?
Are you a member of an Islamic organization?
What is your opinion about Islamic political groups?

To the question of primary identity, all but one of those interviewed replied that their main identity was as Muslims. "There is no God but God," one worker said; "that comes before anything else." Some denied having any identity besides being Muslim; "My only nationality is God," said one. National identity usually came next, then regional identity. Everyone interviewed affirmed belief in God and in Muhammad as His Prophet.

All those interviewed, both formally and informally, claimed to fast during Ramadan, even those who did heavy manual labor on farms. As one person described it:

> During Ramadan it's hard and tiring, especially when Ramadan comes in the summer with long days and heat. I come home and fix dinner, eat at 9:00 or 10:00 P.M.—I fast longer than sunset because I have to cook. Then I go to the mosque [prayer room in the foyer] until 1:00 A.M. for the prayer—yes, for about 2½ hours. Then I come back to my room and sleep and get up at 2:00 A.M., eat, and go to work. I hardly sleep during Ramadan.

Another said:

> I work better when I fast, especially after the second or third day. I fast, I pray in the evening, I read the Qur'an, and I work. My children fast too.

Far fewer people pray than fast. About half of those interviewed performed the daily prayers—usually cumulatively, rather than at the five prescribed intervals, in order to avoid interrupting their work. Nobody interviewed had a workplace with a prayer room.

The foyers are sometimes focal points because of their prayer rooms. A typical prayer room in a foyer has minimal furnishings, such as a rack for shoes; rugs, which are rolled up and placed on shelves when they are not in use; a set of five cardboard clocks with movable hands posted on the wall to indicate the five times of prayer; and a small carpet with the image of the Ka'ba mounted on the wall to indicate the direction of prayer (fig. 17 below). Some prayer rooms in the foyers used to be canteens, which, among other things, served alcoholic beverages, but were converted to prayer rooms at the request of the residents. This is an example of the adaptation of French space by Muslims.

On Fridays, an imam usually leads the prayer in the foyer prayer room and gives the Friday sermon. One respondent described the imam in his foyer as follows:

> Our imam is sixty-three years old and is Algerian. On Fridays he gives a *khutba*—about Muslim life, the life of the Prophet, the words of God, what things are halal and haram. The imam was a worker, and we pay him with donations. People who earn good wages and don't have large family responsibilities give 50 or 100 francs a month each. One of the foyer residents replaces the imam for the Friday sermon when he is on vacation. On weekdays, anyone among those present, usually someone older, can lead the prayer.

The prayer rooms at the foyers are usually open to anyone, from within or outside the foyer, and outsiders do come in to pray, especially on Fridays and especially in places with no mosque. Of course, many pray privately. One agricultural worker said that he worked every day except Sunday and prayed in the fields. So attendance at the Friday prayer is not a reflection of the numbers of Muslims who actually pray.

One of the foyer residents told me that he sometimes prayed at his work-place in a relatively unfrequented room where broken equipment was stored:

> One day about two years ago—I've been working there for eight years now—I put down my cardboard in the tower in front of the door and was praying. Then my foreman came in. He was with a big boss of the company visiting from Paris, and the director of the refinery and a bunch of engineers—a whole crowd. I said to myself, he's going to say I'm stealing time from my job, and fire me. Well, I continued my prayer, and they visited the room as if I wasn't there, and left. Later I saw the superintendent and asked him about it, but he didn't know what I was talking about. He said yes, he had taken the group on a tour, but he hadn't seen me. I asked one of the other people who was in the group, and he hadn't seen me either.

The factory supervisors may have been avoiding potential controversy. The worker, however, believed that because he was engaged in prayer, he was rendered invisible and under divine protection from any harm.

The North Africans generally agree that it would be a good idea for there to be a real mosque to pray in—not just a room set aside for prayer in a secular building. As one worker said:

> I read in the newspaper the other day that there are 450 mosques in France and 33 in Bouches-du-Rhône. We Muslims should take care of building the mosques, and the consulates and the North African governments can help us. You have to get an authorization from the city hall to build one. I've given money for mosques. [Here] we need to get a bigger place to pray, to be on our own. There's a really good, big mosque in Marseilles, near the old city gate.

No worker in the sample had yet been on the pilgrimage to Mecca, although they all said they would like to go some day.

North African workers often try to time their vacations so that they can participate in *zardas,* the annual festivals at rural North African shrines. One worker said:

> The zarda of Sidi Tahar, who was a son of Sidi Abdelkader, is always in the late summer, after the harvest, starting on a Wednesday afternoon and lasting until Thursday morning, with a *hathra* (ecstatic dance) and a *draouch* (divination), but which week the zarda will be is always set at the last minute. Nobody ever has to tell me when it will be. I just wake up in the morning and I know. I go to work and tell the boss, I have to go, and he says, go. I've never been refused.

Another worker expressed an objection to zardas, reflecting the opinion of reformers and some transnational Islamic movements:

> The zarda is an error, a false Islam. You can't ask a marabout like Sidi Belka-
> cem for help. He wasn't a prophet. Muhammad was the last prophet. You
> can't ask Muhammad for help either. You have to ask God.

It is possible that the status of being a member of a Muslim minority in
France tends to make some workers more Muslim than if they had stayed
at home. That is, people become ascriptively Muslim when they are born
into Islamic settings, where minimal religious practice—for example, fasting—is expected. In a non-Muslim setting, practice of Islam may become
more self-conscious and linked to expressing a group identity.

In a situation of being part of a Muslim minority and encountering
hardship and adversity, some migrants may become more observant Muslims, or join Islamic groups that can organize with greater freedom abroad
than at home. The phenomenon of being treated as a Muslim by non-
Muslims also reinforces Islamic identity. None of the workers I interviewed,
however, expressed enthusiasm for Islamic political movements, for which
they often use the pejorative term *khawangiyya* (from the *ikhwan*, the Muslim Brotherhood). One worker associated Islamic political movements with
sabotage. Another, evincing absorption of French values (cf. Bloul, this
volume), remarked, "Politics and religion should not mix; you can talk
about politics in the amicale, but not in the [prayer room]." Several spoke
of increased practice:

> I prayed from when I was about seven because my father made me, and in
> school, and then for a while after I finished school, until I was eighteen.
> When I came to France that changed. I found another system of life. From
> 1971 to 1978, I worked in a factory in the Alps where they made jam and
> tomato paste and other preserves. In 1978, they wanted me to work in the
> kitchen and make preserves from pork. I explained that I couldn't. They said
> they would fire me if I didn't, but I wouldn't set foot in that kitchen. Then I
> came here, where I had friends. I found work after only two days. Ever since
> then, I pray every day.

One might argue that many people have become more observant in Islamic countries too, especially in these times when Islamic practice is being
intensified. In this instance and in many other instances, however, the return to Islamic practice was brought on by an experience of discrimination
abroad, which makes migration an important element in individual religious experience.

There is a political advantage to emphasizing Muslim identity in France.
In separating church and state, France guarantees religious freedom. Since
Catholics and Jews have the right to build churches and synagogues, for
example, Muslims logically have the right to build mosques. There has
been discussion in France of creating a commission for Islamic representation. Thus workers might adopt an Islamic stance, not only out of convic-

tion, but also as a strategy for dealing with the French authorities under certain circumstances.

ETHNICITY IN THE FOYER: INTERACTION BETWEEN WEST AFRICANS AND ARABS

In mixed settings, generally speaking, Maghrebis and black Africans do not emphasize their ethnic or national identities. Still, the foyer bears in itself the seeds of potential conflict. An illustration of this is a survey carried out in fifteen foyers in the Lyons region in 1978, since which time things have changed very little. The survey noted that quarrels frequently occurred over the use of kitchens. Muslims complained that European residents cooked pork on nearby stoves, which tainted their meals. Disputes between Muslims and Christians, between Turks and Maghrebis, and between Algerians and Moroccans arose for any number of reasons.

A serious example of strained relations between black Africans and Maghrebis took place in 1975 in a foyer in Villejuif (a suburban town near Paris), when a small incident developed into a major riot. A Maghrebi poured water down on some black Africans who were speaking loudly under his window. This escalated into a violent interethnic conflict, which lasted for three days, despite the intervention of the French Special Police (the CRS). There were six deaths in all—three on each side.

A basic source of contention is the difference in community life and the use of space in the foyers. The Maghrebis, in part because they have been in France longer, have become more individualistic. The black Africans have not only come more recently, but, as villagers, resist passage from wider spaces to the tiny and orderly spaces of the foyer. As a result, black Africans are seen as encroaching upon the territory of others.

Black Africans seek to increase their numbers. When a room becomes vacant, they press for it to be rented to someone from their community. In some of the foyers in Seine-Saint-Denis, this policy has worked so well that the Maghrebis have left one by one. Maghrebis tend to cook and eat individually, while for the black Africans a meal is a major social occasion for the exchange of news, jokes, and laughter. The black Africans thus gradually appropriate the whole collective space as their exclusive domain.

Faced with this situation, the Maghrebis may simply leave for private lodgings in towns; others stay, but withdraw into their rooms, which they furnish with television sets, telephones, and drinks (as in Val-de-Marne, for example). The majority of North Africans try to lodge with other North Africans through lobbying the residents' committees.

Some, however, confront the black Africans on religious grounds. They equate true Islam with Arabs only, and stigmatize the religious practices of black Africans. As Arabs, they look down upon black Africans as people who belong to Sufi *turuq* and are ignorant of the Arabic language, and therefore of the Qur'an. They try to assume the lead in the collective prayer in the prayer room and to exclude black Africans from directing prayers.

Foyer managers tried to use this division to break the strikes of the 1970s. Many foyer managers brought numerous black Africans into the SONACOTRA foyers, hoping to divert discontent into intercommunity conflicts. In fact, the two groups combined against SONACOTRA. Both French trade unions and the Algerian amicale tardily tried in vain to take over the strikes. The government's actions, including deportations, only hardened the resolve of the strikers. In the end, the strikes not only led to some improvement in living conditions, they gave the workers the opportunity to establish their own residents' committees, control the use of the foyers, and play a role in forging new identities.

One aftermath of the 1970s strikes has been the assertion of an Islamic identity. At that time, calls for the creation of more prayer rooms became more insistent. Requests for facilities for Islamic practice are clearly older than the Khomeini era. The "foyer mosques" are a mark of Islamic identity for all Muslims, be they regular or irregular in their attendance at prayers. From the late 1970s to the early 1980s, Maghrebis were reluctant to pray under a black African imam. Yet even then, the significant distinction began to be that between regular and irregular mosque attenders.

To claim to be a Muslim by birth was no longer sufficient. There appeared a coalition of observant Muslims, both black and Arab—who organized their lives apart from the others, offering an alternative to the traditional organization described above. They offered one another mutual support, especially in relation to the pilgrimage. On occasions such as Ramadan, and especially the Night of Destiny, they regularly assembled in the "mosque" for qur'anic recitation and prayer.

The brothers in the faith began campaigns to purify the "pagan" parts of the foyers. Beer was no longer to be served in the foyers, and prostitutes were forbidden entry to them. "Cleanliness is next to godliness" became the rule. The regular attenders began their *dawa* ("mission") among the infrequent attenders, who were invited to attend religious lectures. Celebrations of Islamic festivals became more elaborate. There were frequent discussions of the importance of true *jihad* during Ramadan. Clocks were displayed to show times of prayer (fig. 17).

Those who kept on living as usual—especially younger Maghrebis and black Africans—were marginalized as black sheep. Differences also emerged among the regular mosque attenders, again a cleavage not following lines of nationality. The believers in turuq opposed the people of the *hadith*. The Soninke belong for the most part to the Jama'at Tabligh (see Metcalf, this volume). The Soninke stigmatize the Tukuleur (who are faith-

Figure 17. Clocks set to show prayer times as part of an
effort within the foyer to encourage Islamic practice.
Photograph by Laurence Michalak.

ful to the Tijaniyya *tariqa*) and tend to associate instead with the Tabligh
Maghrebis. In some foyers in Les Mureaux (Yvelines), the prayer rooms are
divided in two after the main prayer of the day. On one side the turuq
believers gather in a circle, performing their *wird* (special recitation of a
tariqa). On the other side, the Tabligh assemble under the direction of
their amir to introduce newcomers to the finer points of the true religion.
The rivalry between religious groups gets more acute during Ramadan and
on the eve of the hajj. Every group tries to draw in more people to attend
lectures. This rivalry divides Maghrebis and black Africans among themselves.

CONCLUSION

The foyers, which were built to provide sleeping quarters for transitory men, have been transformed into multifunctional institutions for long-term and permanent residents. The different functions of foyer space accord with different aspects of migrants' identities. Thus the foyer residents engage in social interaction as Soninke or Tatouin in one context, Tunisian or Malian in another, sometimes as consumers, sometimes as Muslims.

In examining the foyers, we have called attention to the significant ways in which black West Africans and North African Arabs act to appropriate and transform foyer space. However, these foyer residents operate within contexts of considerable constraint. They cannot truly "appropriate" space in the foyer setting, and they can "transform" it to only a very limited extent. The foyer buildings are not "theirs" in any sense of ownership. Architecturally, the foyers are buildings conceived by non-Muslims for ends that have nothing to do with community, religious or otherwise. On the contrary, the foyer both isolates individuals (as in the small suites of the SONACOTRA model) or concentrates them in stifling density (as in the case of the West African foyers in the Ile de France and in some of the non-SONACOTRA foyers). To the extent that foreign workers succeed in adapting this foreign space, they work against the grain, making superficial modifications, within local and national political climates that are at best neutral and at worst explicitly hostile. Islamic practices such as prayer, 'Id, and wird have been one way in which workers have defined themselves as best they could and made this space their own. The capacity of the workers to create meaningful relations and ritual is the more dramatic in such harsh settings.

WORKS CITED

This essay is based on the research of Moustapha Diop on the predominantly black West African foyers of the Ile-de-France and of Laurence Michalak on the predominantly Arab North African foyers of the Bouches-du-Rhône.

Barou, J. 1978. "Les Causes de sous-location dans les foyers SONACOTRA de la région lyonnaise." Report. Paris: SONACOTRA.
Brun-Melin, Annick. 1989. *Les Foyers vus par les professionels.* Brochure. Paris: Union nationale des Associations gestionnaires des foyers de travailleurs migrants (UNAFO). June.
Diop, Moustapha. 1988. "Stéréotypes et stratégies dans la communauté musulmane de France." In *Les Musulmans dans la société française*, ed. R. Leveau and G. Kepel, pp. 77–87. Paris: Presses nationales des sciences politiques, Fondation nationale de science politique.

————. 1989. "Immigration et religion: Les Musulmans negro-africains en France." *Migrations-Société* 1: 45–57.

d'Orso, Louis (president). 1980. *L'Association des Foyers de Provence et de Corse à 30 ans: 1950–1980*. Brochure. Paris: AFPC.

Gagneux, Michel (president). N.d. [ca. 1989]. *SONACOTRA: L'Habitat en mouvement*. Brochure. Paris: SONACOTRA.

Ginesy-Galano, Mireille. 1984. *Les Immigrés hors la cité: Le Système d'encadrement dans les foyers (1973–1982)*. Paris: L'Harmattan / CIEM.

Labbez, Joelle. 1989. *Les Soviets des foyers*. Paris: Editions Albatros.

Leveau, Rémy, and Gilles Kepel. 1985. *Culture islamique et attitudes politiques dans la population musulmane en France: Enquête éffectuée pendant le mois de Ramadan (mai–juin) 1985*. Paris: Fondation nationale des sciences politiques.

FIVE

Making Room versus Creating Space

The Construction of Spatial Categories
by Itinerant Mouride Traders

Victoria Ebin

Studies on how people use space generally focus on groups identified with a particular setting. The Mourides, however, are itinerant traders who are nearly full-time travelers, constantly on the move in search of new goods and clients. These traders, who belong to a Sufi brotherhood based in Senegal, have neither the time nor the resources to transform their living quarters in any radical way.

This essay explores how, despite their transient lives, the Mourides use and appropriate space in ways that are specifically their own. If no one hears a tree fall in the forest, does it make a noise? If no Mourides are in the room, is the room, in any definable way, Mouride?

The Mouride brotherhood is a Sufi *tariqa* organized around a founding saint, Cheikh Amadu Bamba (ca. 1857–1927), a holy man who attracted a large following in the confused period following the French conquest of Senegal. Originally a rural brotherhood, the Mourides assumed a powerful role in national government by the late 1920s through their role in peanut farming. With the drop in peanut prices, drought, and the decreasing fertility of the soil, large numbers of Mourides have migrated to the cities over the past two decades. They have now become a trading diaspora, with trade networks stretching from Dakar to western Europe and on to Jidda and Hong Kong. In their long *boubous,* with red-and-blue-striped plastic bags, they are familiar figures in the wholesale districts of major capital cities in Europe and North America, and have been sighted in Istanbul (*Le Soleil,* August 22, 1992).

Despite their rural backgrounds and often barely functional French, they leave their homes in rural Senegal to make long intercontinental trips.[1] While they may occasionally pause for a few months, they are virtu-

Figure 18. A Mouride wearing the characteristic hat with pom-pom, Dakar. Photograph by Victoria Ebin.

ally nonstop travelers, with a beat that covers a good portion of the globe. As one Mouride put it, "Our homeland [in western Senegal] is built on sand, and, like the sand, we are blown everywhere. . . . Nowadays you can go to the ends of the earth and see a Mouride wearing a wool cap with a pom-pom selling something to someone" (fig. 18).

MOURIDE HISTORY

By the end of the nineteenth century, Senegal was almost completely Islamized. Islamic movements had been present in the region since the eleventh century, but at the end of the eighteenth century, the religion became more implanted when warriors from the north attempted to create Islamic states in Wolof kingdoms whose rulers were animist or only semi-Islamized (Cruise O'Brien 1971: 13). Battles between militant Muslims and animist chiefs continued for many years and virtually destroyed the social organization of Wolof society. By the mid nineteenth century, the region was divided by internal strife.

The Qadiriyya and Tijaniyya, Islamic brotherhoods that have their origins in North Africa and the Middle East, appeared in Senegal during the time of upheaval and division in the late eighteenth and nineteenth centuries (Cruise O'Brien 1971: 27). Based on the veneration of Islamic saints, who were regarded as carriers of *baraka,* or grace, they were a powerful unifying force and became centers of resistance against the animist aristocrats and the French colonizers, offering a haven to those who wanted to flee the French administration or the local chiefs (Cruise O'Brien 1971: 26).

The Mouride brotherhood alone had its origins in Senegal. Its appearance is associated with a series of crises—the disintegration of social and political structures after years of internal warfare, the French conquest, and the introduction of cash-crop agriculture (Copans 1972: 19–33, cited in Diop 1984: 46). Cheikh Amadu Bamba was from a learned Muslim family that had links with both the Tijaniyya and Qadiriyya. Initially, he drew followers from many levels of society, mostly artisans, traders, and slaves, who more than other members of the community had something to gain from the Mouride doctrine of hard work as the way to salvation. He also won over local rulers, for whom Mouridism represented a nonmilitary form of resistance to colonial rule (Diop 1984: 45).

The French initially viewed Amadu Bamba as a threat to their fragile authority, repeatedly sending him into exile, first to Gabon, then to southern Mauritania, and then to a remote region of Senegal. During his many years of solitude, he wrote voluminously and created a substantial body of religious writing, now housed in Touba, the Mouride center. He addressed the *murid,* or seeker after God, and the term gave the movement its name, Muridiyya. Exile confirmed Amadu Bamba's status as a saint. Upon each return, he was greeted by increasing numbers of admirers and followers.[2]

Toward 1912, Mouride relations with the French improved, and Mourides became actively involved with French agricultural projects. Mouride leaders organized their followers into efficient work groups, which cleared and cultivated land for peanut production (with sometimes disastrous results for the Fulani pastoralists).

More than any of the other brotherhoods, the Mourides became an economic community, united by an ethic of hard work and an internal organization that eventually made them the country's top peanut producers. The Mourides had certain qualities that fostered this role. First, Mouride doctrine emphasized work, discipline, and prayer, and valued physical labor. Indeed, Cheikh Ibra Fall, Amadu Bamba's foremost disciple, or *taalibe,* preached that fervent dedication to work replaced the obligations to pray and fast. Second, the leaders of the brotherhood displayed unusual organizational abilities in creating a highly disciplined work force among their taalibes. Finally, the cheikhs were highly skilled in mediating between the peasants and the French authorities (Fatton 1987: 98–99). As producers of one-quarter of the country's total crop, Mourides acquired political power in the administration that has continued until today (Cruise O'Brien 1971: 2).

One feature of the cheikhs' organizational genius was the work group, which Donal Cruise O'Brien has described as "probably the single institution which has most contributed to the brotherhood's success" (Cruise O'Brien 1971: 163). These groups also provided some education for the taalibes. Only after ten years of labor did taalibes receive their own land to farm, and even then they continued to work one day a week, generally Wednesday, for the cheikh. Today, when more Mourides are working in Dakar's markets than in the fields, a delegation goes from store to store collecting money for the cheikhs every Wednesday.

Under Mamadou Mustapha, Amadu Bamba's son, who succeeded him as khalifa-general, the Mourides became increasingly bureaucratized. Amadu Bamba's saintly qualities and "charismatic authority" gave way to hierarchy as kinsmen and associates, and their descendants in turn, assumed positions of authority (Robinson 1987: 2). The current and fifth khalifa-general is Serigne Salyiou, another of Amadu Bamba's sons.

With the transition to urban life and the migration of many Mourides abroad, the brotherhood has maintained its close ties by emphasizing the relationship between the cheikh and the taalibe. For a migrant, who may spend many years outside Senegal, the Mouride *da'ira* (Arabic pl. *dawa'ir,* circle, association) is crucial in maintaining contact with his cheikh and with Touba.

Each da'ira is founded to honor a particular cheikh, whose taalibes meet regularly in hotel rooms and apartments across western Europe and North America. They meet regularly to sing the *qasa'ids,* poems written in Arabic by Cheikh Amadu Bamba, and to share a meal (Cruise O'Brien 1971: 251).

Each da'ira elects officeholders, who keep in close touch with the cheikhs in Senegal. They collect money at each meeting to send back to the cheikh or, more typically, to the khalifa-general in memory of Serigne Touba (Cheikh Amadu Bamba). Important cheikhs, the khalifas of various lineages, have many da'iras scattered throughout other African countries, in Europe, and in America, which they generally visit once a year.

One of the most important da'iras in France, for example, is that of Serigne Mbacke Sokhna Lo, a great-grandson of Cheikh Amadu Bamba and son of Cheikh Mbacke, a major figure in the brotherhood. His appointed representative, who is in Lyons, is responsible for organizing the local da'ira and also makes regular visits to the cheikh's other da'iras in Europe.

Da'iras are also organized by occupation and by neighborhood. Sandaga market in Dakar has several da'iras that meet regularly on the roof of the market while tailors, gold workers, and factory workers in some towns have created their own da'iras.

Da'iras were initially for Mourides who had left the countryside for towns in Senegal, but today, with the large numbers of Mourides whose involvement in trade leads them to travel nonstop, they have acquired a new importance as a meeting place for Mourides on the road.

THE MOURIDE ECONOMY TODAY

Mourides are now involved in trade at all levels, from selling on the streets to organizing a flourishing international electronics trade. The majority of Mourides, however, are street peddlers, *bana-bana* or *modou-modou* (a nickname for Mamadou in the Baol region of Senegal, whose people are believed to be particularly astute and hard-working, and where many of the street peddlers come from).

The Mouride street peddlers have been characterized as "inward-looking and conservative" in contrast to the Mouride students and ex-students now living in Europe and North America.[3] The students are active proselytizers and have made many converts among other migrant groups in France, while the peddlers prefer to live among themselves, limiting their contact with the outside world to work.

The bana-bana's style is essentially the same wherever he goes. He deals in whatever he can sell, but for economic and practical reasons—quick turnover and small size—most specialize in Asian-made watches, "fantasy" jewelry, and novelty items such as fluorescent shoelaces and American cosmetics.

Being Mouride shapes a large part of their lives, whether they are urban migrants to Dakar or have settled abroad. A group of street peddlers from a village in the Baol region of Senegal live together in a room in Dakar— the same room that street-peddling migrants from their village have rented since the 1970s. Once a week they visit the local wholesalers, who are also

Mouride, and pool their resources to buy large quantities of merchandise. Each peddler then takes a portion of the goods and sets out to sell it on his special "beat." Bana-bana living in New York follow essentially the same routine. Every week, a household of migrants from Darou-Mousty in Senegal who now live in the Bronx set off for Chinatown to buy wholesale goods to resell.

Some bana-bana trade only seasonally. Mustapha and Moussa, for example, go to Marseilles every summer. They buy goods from their primary Mouride wholesaler and then set out for the small villages between Aix, Avignon, and Marseilles. Fellow Mourides have staked out the curve of Mediterranean beaches as their territory. At the end of the summer, most return to Senegal but some make their winter base in Lyons or Paris.

The circuit of one itinerant trader, Amadu Dieng, exemplifies Mouride entrepreneurial skills and adaptability. He set out from Senegal for Marseilles with two thousand "Ouagadougou" bracelets. In Marseilles, he stayed in a residential hotel with a cousin, whom he left some bracelets to sell, and also bought some Italian jewelry from a Mouride wholesaler. On to Paris, where he bought leather clothes made by Mouride tailors and items in the Turkish garment district to resell in New York. He sold everything in New York and bought up beauty products and music cassettes. Then on to Cameroon, where he sold the cassettes and sent the beauty products back to Senegal with a cousin. He then headed north to Libya to find work for a few months to make money to return to New York.

Other Mourides in Europe—students, tailors, or those with white-collar jobs—also rely on trade to supplement their incomes ("pour arrondir la fin du mois"). They too may become highly mobile at certain times of year as they take up trade, traveling across Europe or North America and relying on the brotherhood's scattered communities for lodging and essential connections in the wholesale districts.

Mouride tailors who specialize in leather, for example, often become bana-bana in the summer, which is the off-season in the leather trade. One Mouride leather tailor in Paris works six months of the year in a Turkish-owned workshop and spends the rest of the year selling on the streets in Milan and Marseilles. Students too are integrated into the trade community by kinsmen and friends, who supply them with goods and teach them the strategies necessary to street peddling.

Unlike Amadu Dieng, who had obtained a multiple-entry visa for the United States, most bana-bana, once in New York, remain for some time, since they are not certain they can return. Mor Ndiaye, for example, sold sunglasses and umbrellas on a corner near Times Square for four years, returned to Senegal for a vacation, and was unable to get a visa to return. He now sells shoes from a kiosk in Dakar's central market and plans how to get back to America.

Mouride businessmen who started their careers as bana-bana still travel extensively, buying and selling on a vaster scale. They buy television sets, VCRs, radios, cassettes, and compact-disc players in Jidda, Hong Kong, and New York, which they resell in Senegal. They also buy up smaller items such as African-American beauty products and television sets in New York. At least one Mouride trader who started out as a street peddler owes his fortune (several stores in Dakar and a factory making "hair extenders") to the sale of such accessories—he was the first to sell Ultra-sheen products in Senegal.

MIGRATION AS A THEME IN MOURIDE HISTORY

Mourides have been migrants since the early days of the brotherhood. In the past, cheikhs migrated with their taalibes to "pioneer lands" in the hinterlands in search of new farmland (Cruise O'Brien 1971: 60). Since their farming practices deplete the soil, Mourides were always in need of land, and even today Mourides continue to migrate within Senegal in search of new land.

The lives of New York street peddlers are also shaped by long years of travel. While other people from inhospitable regions migrate to establish themselves elsewhere, Mouride traders have continued, at least until now, to maintain their primary attachment to Senegal. A common saying is, "We are like the birds who think of home when flying high above the earth."

Mourides find an explanation and some consolation for their transient lives in the brotherhood's history. They say that travel leads to knowledge, *xam-xam,* which is essential to a young man's education.[4] Travel and life in another country, and perhaps a foreign wife, add to one's understanding of the world. The number of countries one has "done" ("faire la France [l'Italie, le Maroc, etc.]") and the languages one speaks are frequent subjects of conversation at Mouride gatherings.

Travel has become an almost sacred activity for Mourides, and its special status can be seen in the large round house in Diourbel where Cheikh Amadu Bamba was confined by the French, where his suitcases have been preserved along with his books (fig. 19). By also becoming travelers, Mourides emphasize their ties with their founding saint.

Travel entails hardship, and one Mouride trader, a migrant for thirteen years, explained that Amadu Bamba wanted his followers to leave home to test their faith. Another underlined the theme: "We know misery so well that we have come to love it, so much that now we conjugate it as a verb, 'Moi, je misère à New York; toi, tu misères à Paris.' "

Figure 19. Cheikh Amadu Bamba's suitcases, Diourbel, Senegal. Photograph by Victoria Ebin.

THE MOURIDES' SPIRITUAL AND SPATIAL CENTER

Despite their highly mobile way of life and their many years abroad, Mourides' point of orientation is Touba, the site of the mosque where Amadu Bamba is buried.[5] Touba ("finest or sweetest") is the name given by Amadu Bamba to the village where he had a prophetic revelation and where the Mourides' central mosque was later built. Its construction, authorized by the French in 1931, was undertaken by the first khalifa-general. The cost, not including the labor, has been estimated at equivalent to £1 million sterling, and it took thirty years build.[6]

The Touba mosque is said to be the largest in sub-Saharan Africa, with the central minaret almost three hundred feet high, four lesser minarets, fourteen domes, and two ablution baths (Nguyen Van-Chi-Bonnardel 1978: 869). Since its completion, the brotherhood has not built another major mosque. It has only one in Dakar, while other brotherhoods have built mosques throughout the city. In explanation, Mourides cite Amadu Bamba, who said that a true Mouride can pray anywhere as long as he is holy and "clean."

The mosque at Touba is a point of reference for Mourides everywhere.

Friday prayers led by the khalifa-general draw Mourides from all over Senegal. The annual celebration, the Magal, which marks the anniversary of Amadu Bamba's return from exile, brings hundreds of thousands of visitors to Touba. Mourides living abroad make a special effort to return to Senegal for the celebration, because they can then meet up with the greatest numbers of their comrades and kin.

Touba is a repository of Mouride history. The library there contains Amadu Bamba's writings, proclaimed by the faithful to weigh seven tons. Guides point out the well where Mame Diarra Boussou, Amadu Bamba's mother, went to draw water. The tallest minaret is named Lampe Fall, after Cheikh Ibra Fall, the most illustrious of Amadu Bamba's taalibes. Key events in Mouride history, Amadu Bamba's visions, and crucial moments from the Mouride past are identified with fixed points at Touba.

Touba is so closely identified with Amadu Bamba that he is called "Serigne Touba." Moreover, this conjunction of sacred place and person now includes his descendants, and people announce the visit of a cheikh by saying, "Touba is coming to town."

For Mouride travelers, Touba is the central point to which they always return, yet this center is infinitely reproducible. Throughout their travels, Mourides say Touba is always with them. They carry this sacred place in their hearts. As a young Mouride cheikh said, "Touba is a state of mind."

A favorite theme in Senegalese art, often depicted in paintings on glass, shows French sailors taking Amadu Bamba away on a boat. Since they refuse to let him pray in the boat, he has placed his prayer rug on the water and is kneeling on the waves, surrounded, in one illustration, by a circle of leaping fish. According to Mouride accounts, when he returned to the boat, the sailors found it was covered with sand from Touba. Mourides abroad continue, in their own way and less dramatically, to recreate Touba in their many settings.

TOUBA IN MARSEILLES

Marseilles is a crossroads for Mouride traders coming from the north (Lyons, Paris, and Brussels) and those heading south for the French and Italian coasts. Many Mouride wholesalers are based here, and "runners" carrying goods from southern Europe, Africa, and as far away as Hong Kong pass through this port city.

The Senegalese live mainly between the Gare Saint-Charles and the port. The tiny twisting streets—rue du Tapis Vert, rue Bagnoir, rue Thubaneau—that spangle the *quartier* are lined with narrow, shabby hotels and apartment buildings, wholesale stores and warehouses. The people who work and live here are generally not French. Most are from the other side of the Mediterranean—Algeria, Morocco, and West Africa.

This old quarter of the town has been more or less abandoned by the French and taken over by immigrants. Nonresidents who come here are generally looking for drugs or prostitutes, and fights are common. Nights are lively with sirens and flashing lights as police control the neighborhood. They occasionally throw tear gas bombs at groups that have become too large and stop people to demand their identity papers.

Marseilles may be notorious in France because of its level of organized crime, but neighborhoods where Mourides live in other places tend to be similar. Given their need for low rents and proximity to wholesale stores and the train station, it is not surprising that Mourides tend to live in neighborhoods where it is better not to go out after dark. With the heavy police presence and dangerous streets, the Senegalese remain psychologically and geographically enclosed in their quarter. They have little reason to venture out of their neighborhood except on business.

Even a shared Muslim identity does not broaden their social relations. Outnumbered by North Africans, whom they refer to as "Arabs," and with whom relations are rarely amiable, Mourides stick to themselves. Nor is Mouridism a vehicle out of their narrow lives as it has been for Mouride students, who have made converts among other groups (Diop 1985).

Relations with French neighbors are generally not much better. The French complain, as they do about other immigrant groups, of noise, cooking smells, and irregular hours. In return, the Mouride traders have their own views of the French. "What they're good for is butter and cheese," said one peddler.

Another joined in to describe a recent experience in Bordeaux, where a woman had allowed her dog to walk across his wares, saying, "Well, at least he's from Bordeaux." In such settings, Senegalese living abroad tend to stick together, creating a place of warmth against an outside world that is so pointedly unfriendly.

INSIDE MOURIDE SPACE

For Mouride traders on the road, home is a series of hotel rooms and apartments. In Marseilles, they live in residential hotels that resemble boarding houses, where they typically have developed good relations with the owners. The air of camaraderie, a welcome change from the streets, resembles that of a college dormitory.

Despite Mouride claims that they are never far from Touba, their rooms do not outwardly bear much resemblance to anything in their capital. They do, however, look like every other Mouride immigrant's apartment. Furniture is minimal, with one or two beds supplemented with mattresses brought out at night. Sleeping two to a bed, and with mattresses covering the floor, the population of the rooms is far above whatever the hotel initially intended. People generally sit on beds rather than chairs. A corner may be designated for cooking, or at least for making tea.

Emblems of Touba are the principal form of decoration. On the walls are posters of Mouride cheikhs, most often a copy of the only photograph of Cheikh Amadu Bamba—a slight figure in white with the end of his turban covering the lower half of his face. Sometimes, there are posters of other important cheikhs. One of the most popular is Cheikh Ibra Fall superimposed on the minaret that bears his name. Other items, equally transportable, are cassettes of the qasidas.

Amet's room in Marseilles is typical of traders' rooms everywhere. Because he is a major wholesaler, his room is especially crowded with people and merchandise. He receives visits all day long from bana-bana, who come to buy merchandise from him, to do business, to socialize, and to see the visiting cheikhs who stay with him. Wholesalers and "runners" from Italy, Switzerland, Hong Kong, and New York also meet there.

Amet holds court on his bed, seated on a satin bedspread, handing around samples of the latest arrivals—handfuls of jewelry from Italy or tangled heaps of shoelaces recently arrived from Spain. People come for sociability as well as for business. Several Senegalese come regularly for lunch and are joined by others who gather to drink the three glasses of tea customary during the long afternoons.

Crowded living conditions among migrants may seem due to lack of means, but values attached to sociability and the community also account for the large numbers who may occupy a space. Questioned about his noisy neighbors, a Mouride convalescing in a crowded ward of Bellevue hospital in New York replied, "Il y a ceux qui aiment la paix et ceux qui aiment les gens. La paix c'est la mort" ("There are those who love peace and those who love people. Peace is death").

The Senegalese, moreover, may count more than one place as home. Their more diffuse notion of family generates a greater choice of places to go to feel "at home." Migrants abroad may sleep, eat, drink tea, and spend time in different households.

INVISIBLE ARCHITECTURE: CHOREOGRAPHY, TIME, AND SPACE

Whenever possible, Mourides living in hotels designate rooms for specific purposes. Mbaye's room in Marseilles is the kitchen where neighbors take turns preparing meals. Amet's is a favorite place for drinking tea. The largest room is for the weekly da'ira meeting. In New York's Parkview Hotel, women have transformed their rooms into restaurants, where they sell *ceebu jen* (Wolof: rice with fish) to street peddlers and hotel residents.

But in these crowded living conditions, sometimes all activities must take place in the same room—praying, eating, watching TV, and doing business. Time, however, can be manipulated in the use of space. The simplest way to expand space, to make a single room serve a number of purposes—meeting room, kitchen, bedroom—is to separate these activities in time. These temporal divisions can be just as effective as spatial ones in separating activities. Occupying a room for a series of different purposes over time (diachronically) is equivalent to occupying several rooms.

Sometimes, however, these activities must all take place in the same room at the same time with no separations in space or time. People are praying, eating, and watching TV in the same room all at once. While these activities are adjacent and simultaneous, a difference in the quality of time separates them. A man unfolding a prayer rug is in a different time-space dimension than the one who is preparing for work. The man facing Mecca and reciting his prayers is linked to all the other times he has prayed and to all others who are praying.

Ritual/religious activities have their own metronome, and more than one metronome may be ticking simultaneously, creating different rhythms, in one space. When space is limited, people who cannot physically separate themselves enter into another measure of time as a way to maintain separations among categories.

The way people move within the space they occupy—their specific choreography—also orders the use of space. For example, upon entering a house, a Mouride shakes hands with everyone, sometimes with the distinctive Mouride handshake, bringing the other's hand reverently to his forehead, while the other person makes the same gesture. (With a cheikh the gesture is not reciprocal—he only allows his hand to be raised to the taalibe's forehead.)

This choreography becomes most evident on ritual occasions, when Mourides make a sharper distinction between states and beings considered sacred or polluting. For example, when a da'ira begins, separations between men and women become more important, and they separate to form two discrete groups. Women form their own group, perhaps in an adjoining room, while men come together to form a circle excluding women and non-Mourides. A cheikh's place is in the middle of the men's circle. The cheikh is physically set apart from the crowd in other ways, sometimes elevated above the others on a bed or in an armchair, while they sit on the floor (fig. 20).

Figure 20. A visiting cheikh in Paris gives his blessing to *taalibes*. Photograph by Victoria Ebin.

The choreography, how people move within space, follows the same pattern as the da'ira. The men gather in a circle and begin to sing *zikrs*, or chants in Arabic, new arrivals advance, approach the group, shake hands, and join the circle. Eventually, their individual shapes merge into one. Shoulders touching, they sway from side to side in unison as they sing.

This new choreography—men coming together in a circle, singing the praises of Cheikh Amadu Bamba—marks a change in mood. People say that singing the qasa'ids brings them closer to Cheikh Amadu Bamba. These sessions are a release from the usual limitations of everyday life (Trimingham 1971: 200). Da'ira meetings are intense emotional experiences that create close bonds and link people into a collective identity (Martin 1976: 2). "Now that we have sung the zikrs and eaten together, we are like that," one young street peddler said after a da'ira, holding up his fist, "tight and strong." Using a newly learned English phrase, he said, "All for one and one for all."

These traders live without a permanent space of their own and travel with few possessions. They do not have a mosque or a sacred place. They sanctify space by their own actions, by making the "inside outside."

A NEW CHOREOGRAPHY: TOUBA COMES TO TOWN

The arrival of a cheikh from Senegal, the personification of Touba, marks a starting point in a new set of movements. This sacred individual introduces a more formal order into the community, like the jolt of an electric shock to regulate an erratic pulse.

The cheikh's arrival activates notions of hierarchy, which seem somewhat less evident among migrants than in Senegal, where distinctions such as those based on occupational castes seem to carry greater weight. Far from their families, and without the backdrop of support they provide, the migrants seem more egalitarian. Mouride immigrant life breaks down some of the formality of Senegalese society.

The cheikh's arrival means that more attention is paid to these distinctions. The observance of these separations creates a different use of space. Separations between men and women and separations based on notions of hierarchy suddenly become more important. *Griots* (professional praise singers) come forward to sing the praises of the cheikh. Women of the community cover their heads and cook.

Once a year, Serigne Modou Boussou Dieng, a son of Serigne Fallilou, the second khalifa-general of the Mourides, and therefore a major figure in the brotherhood, visits his followers in Europe and America. The cheikh and his entourage travel the Mouride circuit somewhat the way a traveling troupe takes to the road. Every year they follow the same itinerary around Europe—Paris, Lyons, Rome, Barcelona, Madrid—to visit their taalibes.

Like other important cheikhs, Serigne Modou travels with an entourage of family members, always the same during the three years I have seen them in Paris and New York—a younger brother who acts as translator, a young wife who is his preferred traveling companion, a daughter, and her husband, who is also a cheikh. At each stop, they set up house in a lavish hotel, where Mourides come to visit, and, despite their frequent moves, the use of space remains the same.

While in Paris, the cheikh stays in a large apartment in a luxury hotel near the Eiffel Tower. At least three of the hotel staff have become his taalibes during the years he has been staying at the hotel. At lunch time, a fleet of friendly French cleaning women stop by the cheikh's kitchen for a Senegalese lunch.

The apartment has three bedrooms, a living room, a kitchen, and two bathrooms. Visitors leave their shoes at the entrance, where a large rug is set out and used for prayers. The cheikh's brothers share the room closest to the apartment's entrance, while the cheikh's wife and daughter receive guests in the adjacent room. Women visitors, who move within a limited space in the apartment, generally wait in this room for the cheikh to receive them. Men, however, move from room to room, sometimes stopping to visit the women. But the only time women enter the men's room is to distribute food.

The hallway leads into a large living room, where taalibes wait for the cheikh to make an appearance before his assembled visitors, who frequently number from fifty to eighty after work and on weekends. Most visitors, however, are waiting for a private audience with the cheikh, whose small room, entered through the living room, is in the innermost, most protected location in the apartment.

While the apartment's design is purely European, the use of space is similar to that in a cheikh's house in Touba. According to this plan, the cheikh's or ruler's house consists of an enclosure built around a series of concentric circles or squares, with the cheikh in the most interior, protected space.

In his *Esquisses sénégalaises,* Abbé Boilat describes how the plan of a midnineteenth-century house protected the Wolof king. "At the entrance is a large courtyard with armed soldiers at the door. One must pass through several such courtyards to arrive at the prince's's room; in each courtyard one traverses a house which serves as a sort of guard. The house of the sovereign is always at the end of the enclosure" (Boilat 1984 [1853]: 292).

The abbé's description of his visit to the queen of Walo in northern Senegal in 1850 shows how royal protocol organized the use of space. "We were obliged to wait an hour in the first court; a half-hour in the second; another half-hour in the third; finally, at 4:00 we were received by the prince, the husband of the queen. . . . It was only at 6:00 that the queen was visible; . . . we entered a large courtyard where Her Majesty was seated, smoking her pipe of honor, surrounded by more than 500 women" (Boilat 1984: 293).

Visitors to Serigne Modou in his Paris hotel must pass through similar protocol, which is often equally lengthy. The outer door of the hotel suite in Paris, as well as the entrances to each room, are station points for guards. In the small foyer at the main door, the cheikh's younger brother is always present, greeting taalibes, sometimes giving blessings, and also receiving offerings. The new arrivals, especially if they are close to the cheikh's family, may visit the young cheikhs in their room while waiting to see Serigne Modou Boussou Dieng.

All visitors must pass by an individual known as the *bëkk néeg,* or "confidant of the king," who controls access to the cheikh (Fal et al. 1990: 44). According to a Wolof proverb, a marabout needs more than one set of ears: the bëkk néeg is his second set. One bëkk néeg is stationed at the entrance to the living room and another is in front of the cheikh's private room.

In both the Paris hotel and the nineteenth-century king's house, the bëkk néeg choreographs the passage of visitors. He protects the space around the cheikh by guiding visitors to where they must wait and informs them when the cheikh is ready.

As in the nineteenth-century palace, the bëkk néeg choreographs the passage of visitors in the Paris hotel suite. He protects the inviolable space around the cheikh by directing the flow of people. In the past, the design of the king's house, with its series of concentric courtyards and guards, maintained a distance between him and visitors. Today's cheikh in a hotel suite is protected by a choreography that fulfills the same function.

CONCLUSION

The Mouride brotherhood is an example of a highly centralized body, organized around a hierarchy of saints, with the khalifa-general at its peak and Touba at its conceptual center. It is now also a highly mobile society (taalibes and cheikhs in a state of continuous motion) that places high value on solidarity and collective identity.

Itinerant Mourides reproduce aspects of this structure wherever they are. Touba multiplies and is recreated by a sort of spontaneous generation, which occurs when conditions are right—that is, when Mourides invoke its presence. These replications of Touba can be ephemeral, such as the ambience created at a da'ira or during the visit of a cheikh, or semipermanent, as they are in a hotel room where Mourides live. In creating their space, Mouride traders do not construct buildings or alter the arrangements of their space, but an invisible architecture structures their use of space just as clearly as walls and courtyards.

Three features seem essential to creating Mouride space. First, they bring Touba and everything it connotes—the mosque, Cheikh Amadu Bamba, the home of the saints—into their present space. The frequent visits of their cheikhs—when "Touba comes to town"—reinforce Touba's presence. The invariable objects in their living places—posters, tapes of the qasa'ids, the highly spiced "Touba" coffee—refer to the sacred town like a series of mnemonic notes.

Mourides carry Touba in their hearts. At the da'ira meetings, their chants and songs make the "inside outside." They claim that singing the poems of Amadu Bamba transforms the space where da'iras are held, creating sacred space and unity.

Second, the presence of other Mourides is essential. In creating space that is specifically their own, the group, or, as they say, "being numerous," is crucial. Mourides claim that everything is better when it is shared—eating, praying, and singing. Singing the zikrs and the qasidas brings Mourides together, physically and spiritually, binding them into a collectivity, the very foundation of their invisible house.

Finally, Mouride choreography, observing separations between sacred and polluting categories, is necessary. Divisions between these categories are maintained through specific strategies in the use of space and time.

Mourides claim and appropriate space as their own by recreating Touba, observing their specific choreography and simply being in a space—a

Mouride surrounded by other Mourides. *Minimal* is the only word to describe their living conditions, and the transformation of space into specifically Mouride territory depends on its occupation by Mourides.

Singing the zikrs, the foremost example of how Mourides transform space, can be done anywhere, in a train station, a hotel lobby, an airport. By this activity, they mark space and make it theirs. They do not need to possess space to make it their own. The paradox is that despite their patent lack of it, they constantly create space through their presence.

NOTES

1. This study focuses on Mouride men, because at the time of my fieldwork in New York and Marseilles in 1986–88, few women were involved in trade. Recently, however, the number of Mouride women traders has grown.

2. In 1895, Amadu Bamba had 500 followers; in 1912, a French official estimated their number at 68,350; by 1952, the figure had risen to 300,000, and by 1959 to 400,000 (Monteil 1966: 370).

3. Cruise O'Brien 1988: 137. For a discussion of the divisions among Mourides in Paris, see Diop 1985. For a comparison with Mourides in New York, see Ebin 1990.

4. *Xam-xam* is defined as knowledge, understanding, science (Fal et al. 1990: 250).

5. The importance of Touba for Mourides is highlighted by comparison with the behavior of migrants from northern Senegal in Paris, who form associations to carry out collective projects in their home villages; they build dispensaries and make village gardens. Mourides, on the other hand, make their collective donations to Touba.

6. Cruise O'Brien 1971: 47, 41–137. While other roots for "Touba" are possible, such as *tauba* (repentance) or *tuba* (a tree in Paradise), Mouride informants invariably define it as "sweetest" (Cruise O'Brien 1971: 47).

WORKS CITED

Behrman, Lucy. 1985. "Muslim Brotherhoods and Politics in Senegal in 1985." *Journal of Modern African Studies* 4: 715–21.

Boilat, Abbé David. 1984 [1853]. *Esquisses sénégalaises.* Paris: Karthala.

Cohen, A. 1971. "Cultural Strategies in the Organization of Trading Diasporas." In *The Development of Indigenous Trade and Markets in West Africa: Studies Presented and Discussed at the Tenth International African Seminar at Fourah Bay College, Freetown, December 1969,* ed. Claude Meillassoux. London: International Africa Institute.

Cruise O'Brien, Donal B. 1971. *The Mourides of Senegal: The Political and Economic Organization of an Islamic Brotherhood.* Oxford: Clarendon Press.

———. 1989. "Charisma Comes to Town: Mouride Urbanization, 1945–1989." In *Charisma and Brotherhood in African Islam,* ed. Donal Cruise O'Brien and Christian Coulon, pp. 135–55. Oxford: Clarendon Press.

Diop, A. M. 1985. "Les Associations murid en France." *Esprit* 6: 197–206.

Ebin, Victoria. 1990. "Commerçants et missionaires: Une Confrérie musulmane sénégalaise a New York." *Hommes et migrations* 1132: 25–31.

———. 1992. "A la recherche de nouveaux 'poissons': Strategies commerciales mourides par temps de crise." *Politique africaine* 45: 86–98.

Fal, Arame, Rosine Santos, and Jean Leonce Doneux. 1990. *Dictionnaire Wolof-Français*. Paris: Karthala.

Fatton, Robert. 1987. *The Making of a Liberal Democracy: Senegal's Passive Revolution, 1975–1985*. Boulder, Colo.: Lynn Rienner.

Martin, Bradley. 1976. *Muslim Brotherhoods in Nineteenth-Century Africa*. Cambridge: Cambridge University Press.

Monteil, Vincent. 1966. *Esquisses sénégalaises*. Initiation et études africaines, 11. Dakar: IFAN.

Nguyen Van-Chi-Bonnardel, Regine. 1978. *La Vie de relations au Sénégal: La Circulation des biens*. Dakar: IFAN.

Renaudeau, Michel, and Michelle Strobel. 1984. *Peinture sous verre du Sénégal*. Paris: Nathan; Dakar: Nouvelles editions africaines.

Samb, Papa Boubacar. 1992. "Du grand bazar à Taksim: Un petit coin du Sénégal." *Le Soleil* (Dakar), August 22–23.

Trimingham, J. Spencer. 1971. *The Sufi Orders in Islam*. Oxford: Clarendon Press.

SIX

New Medinas

The Tablighi Jamaʿat in America and Europe

Barbara D. Metcalf

THE TABLIGHI JAMAʿAT

The Tablighi Jamaʿat is a quietist movement of spiritual renewal that originated some seventy years ago in British India. The movement has spread widely in areas of Indo-Pakistani migration, among Muslims of North African origin in Belgium (Dassetto 1988) and France (Kepel 1987), and thence to North Africa (Tozy and Etienne 1986), as well as to many countries of Africa and to Malaysia.[1] A succinct summary by a British Muslim reviewing "Islam in Britain" might serve as an introduction to the movement, as well as an illustration of how Tablighis are often viewed:

> The founder of the Tablighi Jamaat in India was Maulana Muhammad Ilyas (1885–1944). A student of Deoband [a reformist theological institute founded in 1867], he became disillusioned with [conventional education] and wanted to project Islam in an extroverted manner. His main thrust was to do missionary work. . . .The Tablighis . . . travel in groups on *gasht* (tour) to bring other Muslims round to their way of thinking. They have been quite successful in this but [N.B.] like the Deobandis they are non-political.
>
> The center of the Tablighi Jamaat in Britain is Dewsbury [in West Yorkshire]. They are spread all over Britain through the mosques and are well organized. They are polite, courteous and well behaved, and can easily be spotted in the streets. They wear a cap, a beard, a long shirt which goes below the knees, and a pyjama or trousers which is shortened to be above the ankles. They might also wear a jacket and sneakers. They keep very much to themselves. (Raza 1991: 14–15)

The rationale behind the program described by Raza, as conceived by Maulana Muhammad Ilyas, was imitation of the practice of the early community of the Prophet, not only by following his *sunna* in general terms, but specifically by conducting "campaigns" to spread Islam. For Ilyas, the critical qur'anic teaching was that Muslims were "the best community" only insofar as they "enjoined the good and forbade evil" (Qur'an, sura Al Imran, 3:110). Although military forays were impossible, active preaching was equally a "struggle in the way of God," a *jihad*. Muslims were to go out on patrols (*gasht*) and excursions or forays (*khuruj*); and they were to be led by an *amir,* a ruler or chief, who need not necessarily be a teacher or spiritual guide. Every time they left home "in the way of God," they undertook a *hijra,* recalling the move to Medina.² The most distinctive dimension of Muhammad Ilyas's teaching was that the duty to preach was incumbent on all Muslims, not only on the learned or spiritual elite. Outsiders labeled them the "community" (*jama' at*) of "informing" or "notifying" (*tabligh*), in reference to this earnest preaching.

Since there are no formal criteria for membership, it is impossible to measure the spread or depth of Tabligh activity with any precision. Even participation in missions is a limited measure of the movement's influence: thus a recent doctoral dissertation on a Muslim community in Bombay attributes a radical change in religious style over recent decades to Tabligh preaching despite the fact that very few participate in the weekly gatherings, let alone the missionary tours (Fazalbhoy 1990). Tabligh includes many levels of participation, from those who have virtually no other activity, to people engaged in household or paid employment who yet manage to meet the movement's standards for participation in gatherings and travel, to those who join an occasional mission, to those who may occasionally or regularly pray where Tablighis congregate and listen to their discussions. The annual gatherings, drawing participants worldwide, are one measure of the movement's growth. In the subcontinent, the numbers attending the meetings in Raiwind (Pakistan) each November and Tungi (Bangladesh) each January are widely estimated to be over one million; similar numbers participated in meetings in India, but because of fears of anti-Muslim violence, such mass meetings have in recent years been suspended there in favor of smaller gatherings.³

TABLIGH ABROAD

The beginnings of Tabligh activity overseas are precisely remembered by activists today. Thus the first tour in Britain is dated to 1946; in the United States, to 1952; in France, to 1962. The change came under the leadership of Maulana Muhammad Yusuf (1917–65) as the movement's amir, a role he succeeded to upon the death of his father, Maulana Muhammad Ilyas, in 1944. From the very beginning, he encouraged a worldwide vision of the spread of the Tabligh message; that spirit continues, so that even if the traces are slight, it is important to activists that their brethren have traveled everywhere, whether to China or Alaska. It was, however, with the substantial labor, student, and professional migrations to Europe and North America, beginning in the 1960s, that a network of support and a core audience for preaching appeared and substantial Tabligh activity began.

There have, however, been other networks utilized by Tabligh missions (Gaborieau 1993: 17). A key occasion for Tabligh activity has been hajj travel, when the pious use the unavoidable companionship of travel to persuade their fellows; once in the Hijaz, they turn their attention to Arabs and others they encounter. Hence diaspora Muslims might hear the Tabligh message while on hajj or might themselves undertake the pilgrimage as part of a Tabligh mission.

A second network has been that established by students and scholars of Islam, especially those associated with the academy known as the Nadwa-tu'l-'Ulama, located in Lucknow in north India, which has a strong tradition of Arabic scholarship and links to the Arabic-speaking world. Maulana Abu'l-Hasan 'Ali Nadwi (1914–), a distinguished scholar and international Islamic figure, who identified himself for a time with the Tabligh program, has been particularly influential among the Nadwa *'ulama*.[4] Again, this influence has reached beyond the Arab world itself in a variety of ways— for example, in the interest 'Ali Miyan, as Maulana Nadwi is known, took in Muslims in Europe.[5] A third important network has been that established by trading communities, particularly Gujaratis, whose effectiveness in the diaspora may be linked to their previous experience in culturally and religiously plural societies (van der Veer 1994), an experience less true of Pakistanis and Bangladeshis. Gujaratis dominate the European center at Dewsbury (Lewis 1994: 90–94) and are prominent among active participants elsewhere. Tabligh activity has also been stimulated among North African immigrants in Belgium and France who have responded to missions from the Indian subcontinent.

Certain key figures and moments stand out in the history of early Tabligh expansion to the West. One almost legendary figure was 'Abdu'r-Rashid Arshad, a telecommunications engineer from Peshawar (in Pakistan) whose influence spread participation in Tabligh throughout the federal government's Post and Telegraph Department. Arshad not only traveled in the Indian subcontinent but also joined an early mission to England; then, thanks to overseas appointments, he was able to carry his missionary work to Japan, to the United States, and, finally, to Saudi Arabia, where he died in 1963 in an accident (Gaborieau 1992: 9).

Cherished events in the early years of Tabligh activity in Europe include the participation in a mission in London in 1946 of Dr. Zakir Husain, scholar and president of the Republic of India (1967–69), who had come to Britain for a scholarly conference. According to Maulana Muhammad Yusuf's biographer, "because of Dr. Zakir's high rank and his worldwide reputation, people paid attention to him" (Muhammad Sani Hasani n.d.:

257–58). Also significant were the visits to Britain in 1979 and 1981 of Maulana Muhammad Zakariyya Kandhalawi (1898–1982), the author of the movement's guiding books and pamphlets (Metcalf 1993a), at the invitation of his disciples engaged in founding the seminary at Dewsbury (Gaborieau 1992: 20).

Tablighis were not the first organized Muslim missionaries from the Indian subcontinent to spread to America and Europe, however. That role was played by the Ahmadis, a controversial modernizing movement that emerged in the late nineteenth century around the figure of a charismatic teacher, Mirza Ghulam Ahmad (183?–1908). The first mosque in Britain, established at Woking in 1889, was associated with Ahmadi activities for some years (Lewis 1994: 12). Ahmadis continue to be active throughout the world today, at a time when they are severely curtailed in some core Muslim areas because of the Pakistani-generated move in 1974 to label them "non-Muslims" (cf. Haider, this volume). In the United States, many African-American Muslims, who may no longer be affiliated with the Ahmadis, first heard about Islam from Ahmadi missionaries (Beverly McCloud, personal communication). Ahmadis use the same vocabulary for their work as do Tablighis, not least the non-qur'anic term *tabligh,* as did a number of ephemeral movements of the 1920s, however different the content of their teachings.[6]

Although the goal of the Tabligh movement has been to permeate mainstream Muslim life, using all mosques as bases, particular institutions have in fact come to be associated specifically with Tabligh activity. In Britain, the Dewsbury seminary, established in the early 1980s, now has some 300 students, of whom 15 percent are from overseas: the mosque of the seminary dominates the neighborhood of modest row houses, many inhabited by immigrants, in the town (fig. 21). The students follow a six-year course, spending one year at the original center of Tabligh work, the Banglewali Masjid in the Nizamuddin section of New Delhi; a new five-story building adjoining the original mosque was built primarily to house members of overseas missions.[7] The central Tabligh mosque in London, the Markazi Masjid, is housed in a former synagogue, whose interior is wholly utilitarian. In Belgium, a Tabligh association and mosque were formally established in 1975 under the leadership of a Moroccan who had gone to Bangladesh on a mission; a dozen other Tablighi mosques were built during the 1980s (Dassetto 1988: 164). In Paris, the Mosquée Omar, shown in figure 22, is a bustling center of Tabligh activity (Kepel 1987: 192–201). In Canada, the Al Rashid Islamic Institute, set up in 1987, now educates fifty boys and has a Toronto mosque of its own as base (Azmi 1989). In the United States, a recent survey showed some twenty-five mosques under the control of "a group of 'evangelical' missionary Muslims called Jamaati Tableegh" (Haddad and Lummis 1987: 21).

Lack of involvement in politics does not mean that Tablighis wholly

Figure 21. Street in a Muslim area of Dewsbury, Yorkshire, with the Tabligh mosque and seminary in the distance. Photograph by Barbara D. Metcalf.

Figure 22. The Mosquée Omar, rue Jean-Pierre Timbaud, Paris. Photograph by Isabelle Rouadjia.

eschew utilization of facilities offered by the state. They do indeed turn to government at every level, of necessity, to negotiate permits for buildings and meetings, visas for travel, and so forth. In Belgium, Tablighis chose to organize as a voluntary association and have, apparently, wanted to make themselves visible through a council of mosques, claiming a "nonfundamentalist" voice in relation to the state (Dassetto 1988: 165–66). In Britain, Tablighis have utilized the opportunities offered to religious schools to gain local education authority support for instruction in the Dewsbury seminary (Lewis 1994: 91). The Tabligh in the West, given the exigencies and opportunities presented by state recognition, seems to have adopted a higher institutional profile than that common in India or Pakistan.

The first general annual meeting, or *ijtimaʿ*, of the Tablighi Jamaʿat in North America was held in Detroit in 1980, and similar meetings have followed—for example, one in Chicago in 1988, with attendance estimated at 6,000, which would make it the largest gathering of Muslims ever held in North America (Ahmed 1991b).

A major ijtimaʿ was held in Belgium, at Charleroi, in 1982 (Dassetto 1988: 164). The Dewsbury meeting, held each June, now attracts several thousand participants, who are lodged in the main mosque and private homes. In addition to participants from Europe and North America, mission groups come to Dewsbury from countries such as South Africa, as well as from old Muslim areas. Although the proceedings are in Urdu, translation is provided into English, French, and Arabic in various corners of the meetings rooms.[8] When I visited the Dewsbury ijtimaʿ in 1991, I met or heard about British-born Muslims of Indo-Pakistani origin; South and East Africans, mostly of Gujarati background; Indians and Pakistanis; Canadians; British converts; and Americans. I met an African-American U.S. Army sergeant based in Germany who had converted to Islam and to Tabligh activity through the influence of another American Tablighi in Munich: he had adopted the name of one of the humble Mewati peasants won over by Maulana Ilyas in the very earliest days of Tabligh, Muhammad Musa. He was accompanied by his wife, a former Jehovah's Witness from Philadelphia. I also met a large *jamaʿat* of South African men and women on a *chilla,* a forty-day tour that included the hajj, this ijtimaʿ in Dewsbury, and an ijtimaʿ in Los Angeles. Tabligh networks link diverse populations and far-flung geographic areas.

Most descriptions of Tabligh, like Muhammad Raza's above, implicitly define the movement as one of men—for example, by describing missionary tours, residence in mosques, and characteristic dress. In Dewsbury, I joined a gathering of women assembled in the home of a family of active participants located near the mosque where the men were gathered. Bedroom walls had been removed to turn the upper story into a single open space; mats spread on the floor allowed large numbers to gather for sitting, sleeping, and participating in discussions and talks. Women in the diaspora and elsewhere meet regularly—in Dewsbury every afternoon—for the kind of study and prayer shared by men. Women are responsible for guiding their families and other women, and, when I asked the assembled group if they had come to know Tabligh through the men in their families, they were indignant at my failure to recognize how often it was women—dating back to the Prophet's day—who had offered correct guidance to men.[9] Women travel only when accompanied by men and typically stay in homes, while men stay in mosques.

Tabligh involves fundamental reconfigurations of gender boundaries as part of its overall deemphasizing of hierarchy, evident above all in the insistence that every Muslim, poor or rich, learned or not, can participate (Metcalf 1993b). At Dewsbury in 1990, for example, one session was given over to the importance of women's participation. The preacher enjoined men to share child care in order to make this possible, citing a hadith that women were permitted to refuse even to nurse their children. If women could refuse to nurse, he argued, men were not in a position to require them to do anything. Women, therefore, could prefer to do Tabligh rather than care for children. A further mark of changes in social roles is the fact that many marriage contacts were concluded at the ijtimaʿ, presumably blessed for being undertaken on such an occasion (Syed Zainuddin, personal communication). To the extent that this meant eliminating the elaborate gifts, visits, and transactions customarily entailed in celebrating weddings, it also meant a new basis for social relations and a diminution of traditional roles defined by gender and hierarchy.

Tablighis insist on the priority of face-to-face encounters, and relationships, for communicating their message. Even in the West, they eschew the powerful new media, including cassettes and videos, that have been so effective in so many other movements. They do utilize print, however, although they emphasize a narrow range of books and use them, typically, in oral settings. A book publisher and distributor, the Idara Ishaat-E-Diniyat (Institute for Disseminating Works on Religion), adjoining the Banglewali Masjid, has been particularly important in publishing, translating, and disseminating Tabligh-related materials. Visitors to its shop typically find the aisles crowded with crates destined for countries around the world. It translates extensively into English and, to a lesser degree, into Arabic and French (Metcalf 1993a).

In accounting for the effectiveness of Tabligh, the constitution of a new basis for social relationships, perhaps particularly felt in situations of social dislocation like immigration, is clearly significant. Ideally, Tabligh groups operate on principles unlike those of the everyday world, stressing mutuality, a nonjudgmental quality, and intense, yet typically transitory, relationships, as jamaʿats group and regroup in ways that reconfigure customary patterns of hierarchy and gender. Also important to Tabligh success both in old Muslim areas and in the diaspora is the relentless apoliticism of the Tabligh: it is thus inconspicuous and regarded as at least harmless and at most, by some regimes, as beneficial and stabilizing.[10] Keeping aloof from politics has become all the more important with increased international travel and the need to secure visas to countries often suspicious of anyone who even looks like a Muslim.[11] Also powerful is the Tabligh resistance to "Western" culture in favor of presumed authentic Islamic values and imperatives, a resistance that fosters the conviction that ultimately it does not matter where one is.

THREE CONVERSATIONS

Many of these themes are evident in the three fragments of conversations that follow, not least the spatial mobility of many engaged in Tabligh and the spatial conceptions that inform this movement. In the following three anecdotes, for example, the British Bengali funeral director was on the verge of leaving for the annual Tabligh meeting in Tungi, Bangladesh. The Pakistani scientist, while now based in Pakistan, has spent considerable time abroad and is immersed in international networks. The Canadian-born Muslim student had studied for two years in Medina and told me this story in Britain. Although brief, the fragments signal something of the coherence and autonomy of Tabligh conceptions. The first two conversations suggest how readily non-Tablighis (in this case, myself) fail to see this distinctiveness.

Conversation 1

December, 1991. We enter the modest, bustling office of an elderly energetic British Bengali, resident in Britain since he was shipwrecked as a sailor in World War II. Shortly after his arrival, having encountered Tabligh missionaries from the subcontinent seeking a place to pray, he himself became active in Tabligh. I am accompanied by a colleague, a Bangladeshi historian. Our host has dedicated his career to two essentials of Muslim life in the diaspora: halal provisions and Muslim burial arrangements. He described his many tours undertaken for Tabligh, and, being a Californian, I spoke up when he mentioned my home state to ask about the ethnic composition of the tour that went there. (The humor of his answer rests in part on the pride Bengalis typically have in their beautiful, cultured homeland.)

BDM: Were you all Bengalis who went on the tour to California?
Interlocutor: Why do you ask that? Allah said, "I created men and jinn that

they might worship me." He did not say I created Bengalis and Californians! It's not my fault I'm a Bengali.

Conversation 2

July 1991. A comfortable sitting room in a house in a quiet urban residential area. I have come to meet a fortyish scientist who has participated in Tabligh, and whose family, including some in the United States and in Britain, have been active in the movement. He reminds me that we met at a dinner party in Berkeley some ten years back. I am accompanied by a longtime woman friend who is a cousin of this person's wife (who is also a professional). Although all four of us are present, the conversation is largely between myself and the scientist. It is intense and focused on my proposal to write about Tabligh. He challenges my topic on two grounds: first, the implications of writing about a movement whose members do not seek publicity and do not want to be documented, and, second (the point in the exchange below), that as an outsider in a movement that is predicated on experiential, not intellectual, understanding, I cannot be accurate in my presentation.

> *Interlocutor:* Why are you interested in Tabligh?
> *BDM:* Well, for starts, the Tablighi Jama'at is very unusual. It is a transnational institution but communicates something very different from the consumer culture, Westernization, whatever we usually associate with "transnational institutions." I'm interested in countering monolithic views of "Islamic fundamentalism." I'm intrigued by the organization of Tabligh, which is so intrinsic to its goals.
> *Interlocutor:* Then why not study some international social science organization? You are missing the point completely in your analysis. The only appropriate analysis of Tablighi Jama'at puts God at the center and sees that all else rests on His grace.

Conversation 3

The Medina Mosque, a Tablighi mosque, in Toronto. A Muslim graduate student chatting to a young Canadian Tablighi:

> *Student:* How do you feel as a Muslim about living in Canada?
> *Tablighi:* Where I am, there it is *daru'l-islam.*

The three conversations above suggest critical parameters of what could be called a Tabligh apprehension of human society, the Divine presence, and history. The first conversation insists that national and ethnic identities do not matter. The second refuses, inter alia, to conclude as a result that we are dealing with "transnationalism." How can transnationalism be the point if nationalism is irrelevant? What is at stake are issues of a different order completely: the experiential realization of Divine grace. And in the third, what we generally take to be some vision of an Islamically organized society, "the abode of Islam," turns out to be available to any individual who—in any place, in any time—relives the prophetic example of Medina.

BEYOND HISTORY AND THE NATION-STATE

The issues of history and the nation are closely conjoined. If we think of modern history and its implicit assumptions, nothing has been more significant to its shaping than the nation-state. Just look at any college catalogue of courses to see the way historical study is organized in terms of nation-states, typically using that geographical framework for periods long before the nation-state existed. We smile at a book title like *Five Thousand Years of Pakistan,* but what seems implausible on the face of it is only an extreme example of the project of historical writing to shape national identities.

In the 1920s, at a time when politically oriented Muslims in British India were shaping stories about themselves, typically ones that focused on periods of past greatness, current decline, and a vision of progress and greatness once India was free, Maulana Ilyas and those associated with him chose to focus on a different kind of history, one that gave no room to national boundaries (of any kind) or to nationalism. A widespread debate of the period was over which term should be used for Indian Muslims, the chief contenders being *qaum,* with its emphasis on ethnic ties, and *millat,* a term associated with juridical arrangements established by the state. Ilyas's only term for Muslims was the ideal, apolitical *umma,* which includes all Muslims everywhere. It is striking that in letters to Maulana Muhammad Yusuf dating from the early years of work in the diaspora, the writers speak of their homeland—for example, in trying to encourage residents in America and Europe to travel there to participate in missions—as "hind-o-pak," India-Pakistan, as if the area were (still) one country (Muhammad Sani Hasani n.d.: ch. 11). Tabligh history is history without the nation-state and with no concern for worldly progress. It is what has been called "typological" history of nonlinear time created by patterns of moral significance.[12] The issue for Tablighis is not to trace linear change and causality but to identify moments when individuals have followed the pristine example of the Prophet; the goal, then, is to relive his time. All such moments are the same in essence, and contingencies of time and place are irrelevant. The importance of transcending particular space in favor of the umma is the theme of a talk given by Maulana Muhammad Yusuf shortly before his death in 1965: "Remember! The words, 'my nation, my region, and my people' all lead to disunity, and God disapproves of this more than anything else" (quoted in Wahiduddin Khan 1986: 47).

Historians of the Indian subcontinent have in recent years become deeply interested in the themes that have shaped the historical and social thought of subordinate groups who did not themselves write history (Guha and Spivak 1988; Chatterjee 1986; Chakrabarty 1992). In this quest for "subaltern histories" that do not fit the dominant narratives, whether colonial, Marxist, or nationalist, historians have sometimes seemed to search for an untouched or authentic cultural expression. In many cases, however, it is clear that the subaltern voice is in fact responding to and shaped by colonial or nationalist cultural norms.[13] In the case of Tabligh, the underlying assumptions do in fact seem to be fundamentally independent of British or nationalist concerns. At the same time, one must see the extent to which the context of British rule stimulated the movement and the fact that certain assumptions—not least the starting point of Muslim decline, decadence, failure—were shared in common.

Contemporary observers, however, write Tabligh into the dominant narratives. In Muhammad Raza's account above, intended as a value-free catalogue of movements and sects, the word *but* suggests the common criticism that Tablighis do not participate in politics as they should, whether for the sake of the state or the sake of Islam. A recent, insightful scholarly account of Tabligh makes the same judgment: that Tabligh isolates from politics significant segments of the population that might otherwise be drawn to Islamically oriented positions (Ahmed 1991b). Other critics have insisted that whatever Tablighis may think they are doing, they have contributed to ethnic separatism that can be destructive of social goals. The significance of Tabligh is thus weighed in relation to the state, a perspective of no relevance to Tablighis' own view of their activities.

MANZIL-I LEILA: REACHING HEAVEN

Tabligh preaching stresses over and over again how transitory this world is in contrast to the world to come. Thus, in a sermon recorded at the Mosquée Omar in Paris, the preacher sought to turn his listeners away from the ambitions and comforts of this world—perhaps all too scarce for many of them in any case—in favor of remembering judgment and the blessings they could win then:

> There are people who come and say to me, "Brother, they don't let me pray at work!" They don't let you do it, pray, at work? So? Is work God as far as you're concerned? So who provides for you? Well? When you are here, with us, you say, "God," but to your boss [using the French word *chef*] you say,

"Boss! I'll drop praying so you don't get angry!" Well, just wait for the anger of the Lord of the Heavens and the Earth.

And continuing, not about the French boss, but about other Muslims who denounce those who pray, learn the Qur'an, go on missions (*al khuruj fi sabil illah,* expeditions in the path of Allah), call others to faithfulness, and spend their nights in remembering God (*dhikr*) as "dervishes," he says: "Soon, they will learn, they will see the 'dervish' who will be the first to enter Paradise!" And, he adds, the man successful in this life in worldly affairs, will be the first to enter hell (Kepel 1987: 197–98).

But what is most striking about this emphasis on Paradise is the conviction permeating Tabligh discourse that Paradise is not only in the future but now. Maulana Ilyas, the movement's founder, made that promise: "[The servant of God] will find, in this world, the pleasures of Paradise" (Troll 1985: 171). And Tablighis today insist on the same. Thus an academic, currently based in Delhi, who shifted from being a "cultural Muslim" to a faithful Tablighi while doing a Ph.D. in English literature at a British university some ten years back, used exactly that language in describing to me the intensity of the pull to missions—that to go out on them was an analogue of Paradise.

The letters printed in Maulana Yusuf's biography are permeated with the Sufi discourse that turns on the passion of the soul for the Beloved, who is ultimately God. Certain classic stories are allegories of that relationship—for example, that of the Leila referred to in the subheading above, the dark Arab beauty in pursuit of whom Majnun, his very name describing his maddened state, wanders the Arabian desert. In spatial terms, the Sufi quest is a journey, and the goal is a series of *manzil,* or stages. Muhammad Sani Hasani's chapter on the spread of Tabligh to Europe, America, and Japan is introduced with the poetic couplet "O believer, let us show you / A display of the Divine, inside the house of idols" (Muhammad Sani Hasani: 516). Places like America and Europe are houses of idols (*butkhane*), but, just as the young Canadian Tablighi mentioned above insisted, daru'l-islam can be anywhere. Indeed, the greatest and most abiding pleasure, the divine encounter or *manzil-i leila,* may be found in the very context of infidelity, even if one is lured there by the deceptive (*majazi*) beauty of material gain.

The presence of the Divine for those engaged in Tabligh in the diaspora is not expressed abstractly but in terms of extraordinary interventions and experiences. A key teaching of Maulana Ilyas was that the work of guidance was the responsibility, not of learned scholars and Sufi shaikhs alone, but of every Muslim. This radical transformation of the role of religious leaders is at the heart of Tabligh organization (Metcalf 1993b). Moreover, ordinary people now not only fulfill the duties of guiding others but also receive the blessings, including those of "openings" (*kashf*) that, as Tablighis have explained to me, come almost immediately to those who go out on missions, in contrast to those who simply follow a Sufi path and must endure years of effort.

Hagiographies of pious ʿulama are filled with stories of the miracles (*karamat*) God works through them (see, e.g., Metcalf 1982: 176–79). Stories of Tablighis, by contrast, are filled with accounts of miracles worked through everyone. A classic pattern in such stories is that of the English literature professor noted above: people were appalled when he set out on a four-month mission, leaving his ill father behind with inadequate resources; when he returned, the father was cured. Muhammad Sani Hasani begins his account with a story he identifies as a key to the character of Tablighis:

> A small jamaʿat of four people set out for the United States. On ship, they went to ask permission from the captain to give the call to prayer and to pray. He demurred, saying that people would be bothered by the noise. Nonetheless, they did give the azan and pray, and people came and watched them, inviting those on the ship who were Muslims to join them. The captain was very impressed by their ethical teaching. When the ship docked, he said that it was only because of them that God had spared the ship a storm since this was the very first time he had ever sailed that route in quiet weather. (paraphrased from Muhammad Sani Hasani n.d.: 518)

In a classic Sufi account, it would have been a saint's charisma that controlled the elements.

Similarly resonant of the stories of the saints is an account of a terrible car accident that occurred during travel to an ijtimaʿ in Detroit. On that occasion, even with others grievously wounded around him, one faithful Tablighi astonished the ambulance attendants by registering completely normal blood pressure. This was a mark, I was told, of the complete peace, *sukun,* known to participants who put their trust in God. The trope of an outsider dumbstruck at a saint's marvelous achievement is common in the stories of the saints, and here appears in the story of an ordinary Tablighi.

Tablighis cite moments of divine intervention that change the course of everyday life. At the time of the Gulf War in 1991, for example, the African-American U.S. Army sergeant mentioned above was posted in Kuwait. He was deeply troubled about engaging in a war against the Iraqis, his fellow Muslims. He turned to a Muslim elder, also in the army, who advised him to follow his military duty but to pray for help. He "prayed hard." On the verge of crossing the border into Iraq, his tank broke down and remained inoperable for the duration of the fighting. He saw no action in the war.

Travel and migration set a context for such happenings. The accounts of early Tabligh missions in Europe and America reveal an extraordinary opportunity to travel in complete dependence on God, which is always their goal. The missions arrive with no place to go, perhaps only scant knowledge of the language. A characteristic approach has been to proceed to a phone book and seek out Muslim names to set up appointments. As recounted in these letters, both the Tablighis and those they find experience the satisfactions and peace vouchsafed to the spiritually advanced: *sukun, rahat, luzzat, zauq.*

Writing of an ijtima‘ held in Manchester in 1962, one participant recalled that in twenty years of activity, he had never encountered such faith and fear of God as in that week. He described the sight of Manchester filled with Tablighis as a veritable Bhopal (site of many large Tabligh ijtima‘ in India) (Muhammad Sani Hasani n.d.: 525). This same participant was transfixed with admiration for converts; for example, in describing an ijtima‘ in London where there was an American jama‘at en route to Pakistan, including two converts, he said, "Our faith is not one-tenth of theirs" (ibid.: 524). Similarly, a Pakistani, assigned to translate for an Australian convert who had come on a mission to Pakistan, rejoiced in how much he had learned from the convert's faith, as exemplified in a comment he had made. When asked why he had come, the Australian answered, "My home is on fire," an answer the Pakistani still pondered years later. Tablighis in the diaspora and Tablighis in the homelands mutually sustain one another.

CONCLUSION

The worldwide spread of Tabligh has transformed the movement in significant ways. It has reinforced a change in the context of preaching to emphasize Tabligh as a counter to all that is summed up by "the West"—materialism, neglect of family, sexual promiscuity—instead of simply Tabligh as a challenge to Muslims' own forgetfulness. For those resident in Europe and North America, Tabligh insists that, whatever their original motives in coming may have been, they can choose to live out a different story than that of material advancement, assimilation, and identification with a new nation-state. In Tabligh thinking, the very fact that they have traveled is rendered positive. Tabligh assuages the ambiguities associated with materialist motivations, residence in a place associated with a secularism and consumerism they deplore, even the fact that instead of achieving worldly success, they may find themselves unemployed.

What turns out to be at stake is not *space,* the new place where they have chosen to live, but *time,* in which the past and future converge in the present (cf. Schubel, this volume). In Tabligh, participants seek to relive the highest moment of human history, the Prophet's society in Medina, and in so doing to taste the joys of the eternal happiness promised to them in Paradise ahead. Far from being on the periphery, they can make any place a center. Whatever the spiritual links to Nizamuddin may be, it is in the end ideally only the local jama'at, and ultimately the individual alone, that matters. Long ago Maulana Ilyas told Tablighis that each jama'at was to be a "traveling hospice or academy." Instead of travel or pilgrimage to a center, the center is where one is.

Tabligh can be seen as one response, that of drawing boundaries and reasserting absolute truth, in the context of the pluralism engendered by our increasingly integrated global society and ever more intrusive modern states. Tablighis reject the kind of ecumenicism that invites non-Muslims to grace their proceedings: not for them the Lord Mayor at their assemblies (cf. Werbner, this volume). Ideally, non-Muslims are not constituted as an "other" but, ultimately, rendered invisible, although, a Tablighi would insist, treated with respect. The end result, of focusing on one's own and one's community's religious life and avoiding religion in public life, converges with a secular approach to politics and religion.

If Tabligh thus seems able to deal with the problem of cultural and religious pluralism, it also offers an implicit response to the racism and disdain that pluralism often entails. The power of that racism to shape an individual's self-image is shown at its most extreme, in Salman Rushdie's Saladin Chamcha, who wants to be an Englishman, but turns into a goat: "They describe us. . . . and we succumb to the pictures they construct" (Rushdie 1989: 168). Tabligh ideology gives participants in the diaspora a powerful script unlike those the dominant society offers—they are reliving Medina and they are concretely blessed. In embracing that picture, the space they inhabit becomes their own.

NOTES

1. See the forthcoming volume under the editorship of Muhammad Khalid Masud on Tabligh activities throughout the world, in particular, the articles by Marc Gaborieau, on the international spread of Tabligh; S. H. Azmi, on Tabligh in Canada; and Philip Lewis, on Britain. The volume is based on a workshop on the Tablighi Jama'at organized by the Joint Committee on the Comparative Study of Muslim Societies of the Social Science Research Council / American Council of Learned Societies and convened by James Piscatori at the Royal Commonwealth Society, London, June 1990.

2. For general background to the Tablighi Jama'at in the Indian subcontinent, see Haq 1972, Lokhandwala 1971, Metcalf 1982, Nadwi 1948, Troll 1985, and Wahiduddin Khan 1986.

3. For an attempt to use scientific precision in estimating participation at the Raiwind meeting, see Qurashi 1986.

4. In this regard the forthcoming work of two doctoral students is particularly important. Mariam Ghalmi is currently preparing a dissertation at the Ecole des hautes études en sciences sociales on the subject of the relationship of the Nadwa-

tu'l-'Ulama to the Tabligh. Ahmed Mukarram, at Oxford University, is studying Maulana Abu'l- Hasan 'Ali Nadwi himself.

5. See among Maulana Nadwi's writings *Na'i dunya men saf saf baten* (Speaking Plainly to the West) (Lucknow: Majlis-i-Tahqiqat wa Nashriyyat-i-Islam, 1978) and *Muslims in the West: The Message and Mission* (Leicester, Eng.: Islamic Foundation, 1983).

6. For references to other "tabligh" movements, see Siddiqi 1986. On the Ahmadiyya, see Friedmann 1989. Both Khalid Masud and Marc Gaborieau have pointed out that no one has studied the possibility of Ahmadi influence on other transnational movements.

7. I am grateful to Philip Lewis for arranging my visit to Bradford and accompanying me to Dewsbury in June 1991.

8. I am grateful to Syed Zainuddin (Aligarh University, India) and Muhammad Talib (Jamia Millia, New Delhi, India) for their firsthand descriptions of the ijtima' they attended in 1990.

9. At issue in a more extensive study of women participants would be the question of whether women's themes and interpretations differ systematically from those of men. For a study of the differing ideologies of women and men in a (far different kind of) religious movement, see Bacchetta, forthcoming.

10. In the 1960s, for example, President Mohammed Ayub Khan is reported to have directed his officials to cooperate with Tabligh activities, regarding them, unlike those of the politically oriented Islamic movements, as desirable.

11. The inability of Westerners to distinguish among Islamic groups is exemplified by the case of Lieutenant General Javed Naser, an active participant in Tabligh, who was appointed head of Inter Services Intelligence in Pakistan in March 1992, but was removed some months later as part of Pakistani efforts to ensure that the United States, apparently on the verge of declaring Pakistan a terrorist state, did not panic at the sight of his beard (*Newsline,* March–April 1992, p. 97). With thanks to Syed Vali Nasr for this and other clippings.

12. For a study of typological or mythical thinking within the Christian tradition, see Frye 1982.

13. It would, for example, seem plausible to argue that in the late-nineteenth-century chronicle Pandey discusses (1990), the zamindar was in fact very much a product of the colonial culture. We know that he was involved in conversations taking place at the local middle school, and we can speculate, at least, that he was directing his account to local officials and representing himself and his class as the people who had the town's interests at heart. Similarly, the weaver, author of a diary Pandey studies, far from being untouched, is himself the head (*sardar*) of an upwardly mobile crafts group identifying themselves no longer as *julaha* ("weaver," a category so humble that the term is also glossed "blockhead") but as *nurbaf* ("weaver of light," a positive term of Persian, hence learned, etymology).

WORKS CITED

Ahmed, Mumtaz. 1991a. "The Politics of War: Islamic Fundamentalisms in Pakistan." In *Islamic Fundamentalisms and the Gulf Crisis,* ed. James Piscatori, pp. 155–85. Chicago: University of Chicago Press.

————. 1991b. "Islamic Fundamentalism in South Asia: The Jamaat-i-Islami and the Tablighi Jamaat." In *Fundamentalisms Observed,* ed. Martin E. Marty and R. Scott Appleby, pp. 457–530. Chicago: University of Chicago Press.

Azmi, S. H. 1989. "An Analysis of Religious Divisions in the Muslim Community of Toronto." *Al-Basirah* 1, 1 (January 1989): 2–9.

Bacchetta, Paola. Forthcoming. "On the Constructions of Identities in Hindu Nationalist Discourse: The Rashtriya Swayamsevak Sangh and the Rashtra Sevika Samiti." Doctoral dissertation in French. Institut d'études du développement economique et social, Université de Paris I, Panthéon-Sorbonne.

Chakrabarty, Dipesh. 1992. "Postcoloniality and the Artifice of History: Who Speaks for 'Indian' Pasts?" *Representations* 37 (Winter 1992): 1–26.

Chatterjee, Partha. 1986. *Nationalist Thought and the Colonial World: A Derivative Discourse.* London: Zed Books.

Dassetto, Felice. 1988. "The Tabligh Organization in Belgium." In *The New Islamic Presence in Western Europe,* ed. Tomas Gerholm and Y. G. Lithman, pp. 159–73. New York: Mansell, 1988.

Fazalbhoy, Nasreen. 1990. "A Sociological Investigation of Selected Problems in the Study of Islam in an Urban Setting." Doctoral dissertation, Department of Sociology, University of Delhi.

Friedmann, Yohanan. 1989 *Prophecy Continuous: Aspects of Ahmadi Religious Thought and Its Medieval Background.* Berkeley: University of California Press.

Frye, Northrop. 1982. *The Great Code: The Bible and Literature.* New York: Harcourt Brace Jovanovich.

Gaborieau, Marc. 1992. "'Abdu'r-Rahman Mewati," "'Abdu'r-Rashid Peshawari," "Iftikhar Faridi," "M. Ilyas Kandhalawi," "Muhammad Isma'il Kandhalawi," "Muhammad Yusuf Kandhalawi," and "Muhammad Zakariyya Kandhalawi." In *Dictionnaire biographique des savants et grandes figures du monde musulman périphérique du xixe siècle à nos jours,* fasc. 1, ed. Marc Gaborieau et al. Paris: Ecole des hautes études en sciences sociales, Research Group 0122.

Guha, Ranajit, and Gayatri Chakravorty Spivak, eds. 1988. *Selected Subaltern Studies.* New York: Oxford University Press.

Haddad, Yvonne Yazbeck, and Adair Lummis.1987. *Islamic Values in the United States: A Comparative Study.* New York: Oxford University Press.

Haq, M. Anwarul. 1972. *The Faith Movement of Maulana Muhammad Ilyas.* London: George Allen & Unwin. This is largely based on Nadwi 1948 [1983].

Kepel, Gilles. 1987. *Les Banlieues de l'Islam.* Paris: Editions du seuil.

Lewis, Philip. 1994. *Islamic Britain: Religion, Politics and Identity among British Muslims.* London: I. B. Tauris.

Lokhandwala, S. T., ed. 1971. *India and Contemporary Islam: Proceedings of a Seminar.* Simla: Indian Institute of Advanced Studies.

Metcalf, Barbara D. 1982. *Islamic Revival in British India: Deoband, 1860–1900.* Princeton: Princeton University Press.

————. 1993a. "Living Hadith in the Tablighi Jama'at." *Journal of Asian Studies* 52, 3 (August 1993): 584–608.

————. 1993b. "'Remaking Ourselves': Islamic Self-Fashioning in a Global Movement of Spiritual Renewal." In *Accounting for Fundamentalisms,* ed. Martin E. Marty and R. Scott Appleby, pp. 706–25. Chicago: University of Chicago Press.

Muhammad Sani Hasani. N.d. *Sawanih-i hazrat maulana muhammad yusuf kandhlawi.* Lucknow: Nadwatu'l-ʿulama.

Nadwi, S. Abul Hasan Ali [Maulana Abu'l-Hasan ʿAli Nadwi]. [1948] 1983. *Life and Mission of Maulana Mohammad Ilyas.* Lucknow: Academy of Islamic Research and Publications.

———, ed. 1964. In Urdu. *Hazrat maulana muhammad ilyas aur un ki dini daʿwat.* Lucknow: Tanwir Press.

Pandey, Gyanendra. 1990. "Community as History." In *The Construction of Communalism in Colonial North India,* pp. 109–57. Delhi: Oxford University Press.

Qurashi, M. M. 1986. "The Tabligh Movement: Some Observations." *Islamic Studies* 28, 3: 237–48.

Raza, Muhammad S. 1991. *Islam in Britain: Past, Present and the Future.* London: Volcano Press.

Rushdie, Salman. *The Satanic Verses.* New York: Viking, 1989.

Siddiqi, Majid. 1986. "History and Society in a Popular Rebellion: Mewat, 1920–1933." *Comparative Studies in Society and History* 28, 3 (July 1986): 442–67.

Tozy, Mohamed, and Bruno Etienne. 1986. "La Daʿwa au Maroc." In *Radicalismes islamiques,* ed. Olivier Carré and Paul Dumont. 2 vols. Paris: L'Harmattan.

Troll, Christian W. 1985. "Five Letters of Maulana Ilyas (1885–1944), the Founder of the Tablighi Jamaʿat, Translated, Annotated, and Introduced." In *Islam in India: Studies and Commentaries,* vol. 2: *Religion and Religious Education,* ed. Christian W. Troll, pp. 138–76. Delhi: Vikas.

Van der Veer, Peter. 1994. *Religious Nationalism: Hindus and Muslims in India.* Berkeley: University of California Press.

Wahiduddin Khan. 1986. *Tabligh Movement.* New Delhi: Maktaba Al-Risala.

PART TWO

Claiming Space in the
Larger Community

SEVEN

Island in a Sea of Ignorance

Dimensions of the Prison Mosque

Robert Dannin
with photographs by Jolie Stahl

"Islam allows you to look beyond the wall."
—UMAR ABDUL JALIL, 1991

The spatial metaphors in the title and epithet above suggest significant dimensions of the role of Islam in the lives of African-American prisoners. Islam, unlike the "sea of ignorance," offers an autonomous source of education and discipline in all aspects of life. Islam, moreover, situates the prisoner not only in the context of the controlling prison but in a context that reaches, ultimately, worldwide—"beyond the walls." At its best, Islam has provided prisoners with order, community, and purpose.

In 1992, the New York State Department of Corrections (DOCS) counted 10,186 registered Muslim inmates in eighty-two different prisons, annexes, and reception centers, a significant increase over the 7,554 counted only three years earlier. African-American Muslims constitute more than 16.9 percent of the total state prison population of more than 60,000, and more than 30 percent of all incarcerated African-Americans.[1] In other populous states, such as New Jersey, Ohio, Illinois, Indiana, Texas, and California, one can confirm the same trends toward Islamic conversion and its institutionalization in the form of permanent mosques, special dispensations for the faithful, and the professionalization of a corps of Muslim chaplains paid by the state to assist with counseling and services.[2]

Green Haven is a maximum security prison located 80 km north of New York City in the foothills of the Catskill Mountains. Rising from the abundantly lush slopes of upstate farmland to disrupt the traveller's gaze, the fortresslike prison evacuates its surrounding ecology. The rectilinear form signifies an urban intrusion. Once inside its tomblike labyrinth, sectioned by iron gates, one confronts the reality of Foucault's "complex social machine" defined by the principles of labor, detention, and surveillance. According to a former inmate, the prison is designed to subjugate the prisoner totally. He is fixed within an architecturally determinate structure of corridors, yards, blocks, and cells, where all quotidian movements are programmed months or even years in advance.

But if one tries to extend the Foucauldian idea of the prison as a simulacrum of the medieval monastery (Foucault 1979), there is a realization that something has changed, because this architecture conducive to introspection and *Christian* rebirth has increasingly become a place of mosques and communal prayers. The predictable monastic effect has been achieved, but somewhere its content has been subverted. As late as the 1930s, when the access and flow of information could be restricted, it might have been possible to influence the spiritual conduct of inmates and perhaps to limit their acquaintance with anything but the most traditional Western religions. However, by most accounts the Islamic *din* is now entering its fourth decade in American penal institutions. The significance of this is that the ideals of rehabilitation have been changed by those inside prisons. This is a radical departure from previous models of reform by even the most liberal criminologists (Baker 1964; Brody 1974).

Islam offers a counterdiscipline, a *counterforce* to the prison's own ideal of stringent discipline (Cloward et al. 1960). In the words of a young Los Angeles gangbanger:

> Islam has changed my life tremendously. It has caused me to be disciplined to an extent I never thought possible. I came out of a culture that reveled in undiscipline [*sic*] and rebelliousness, so to go the opposite direction was major for me. . . . I firmly believe and see that for the 1990s and beyond, Islam will be an even more dynamic force and alternative for many prisoners, especially the confused youth, who are more and more receptive to the teachings of Islam and the self-esteem it provides them in abundance, not to mention the knowledge.[3]

This attractiveness of the "discipline" of Islam in the context of a repressive mechanism conforms to Foucault's understanding of the fluidity of power—its direction never quite corresponds to the purpose for which it was initially employed. Islam's popularity in the prison system rests in part on the way in which qur'anically prescribed activities structure an alternative social space that enables the prisoner to reside, as it were, in another place within the same confining walls.

MASJID SANKORE: "MEDINA" FOR NEW YORK'S PRISONS

Founded in 1968, Masjid Sankore became the first recognized Islamic institution in a New York prison. Its founders were several African-American converts who in the late 1960s collectively sought assistance from Muslims outside the prison in a crusade to ameliorate their conditions of worship. They turned particularly to the leaders of Brooklyn's indigenous Dar ul-

Islam movement, who soon were making regular visits and offering assistance in negotiating with the prison administration, as well as with the outside world. Eventually, the Muslims won the warden's approval to establish a permanent prayer hall and named their mosque after an ancient African center of Islamic teaching in Timbuktu, Mali.

Sankore rapidly outgrew its initial cramped space, eventually taking over the prison's old tailor shop, a comparatively spacious area with real pillars. The prisoners devoted much time and effort organizing the space into a genuine masjid and a place of refuge from the drab confines of the rest of the prison. "When you walked in there, it was another world. You didn't feel like you were in Green Haven in a maximum security prison. *Officers* [guards] *never came in.* It was like going into any other masjid on the outside; you felt at home," commented Sheikh Ismail Abdul Raheem, one of the first emissaries from the "Dar" movement to visit Sankore. The door to the mosque announced a transition to a different space (fig. 23). Once inside, it provided space for quiet, interaction, and, above all, communal prayer (fig. 24).

Sheikh Ismail also recalled that, in the early years, both the Sunni Muslims and the Black Muslims (Nation of Islam) practiced a cadenced march through the corridors as if to mark out their own militant counterdisciplinary tradition. That was the only thing they shared, however. The Nation sought and demanded its own mosque, which after 1976 became the American Muslim Mission Mosque (fig. 25), known as the Masjid ut-Taubah (the Mosque of Repentance). Today, the American Muslim Mission and the Nation of Islam compete fiercely with the Sunnis for new initiates at Green Haven. Because of official policy, life-sentence prisoners as well as those viewed as potentially disruptive to the prison regime are transferred every few years in and out of the ten different maximum security prisons in the state. Thus as time went on, alumni of Sankore spread their Islamic fervor throughout the correctional system. Simultaneously, the Nation of Islam and orthodox Sunni groups like the Dar ul-Islam Movement won further concessions on behalf of Muslim inmates. In these negotiations with authorities, the Dar's "Prison Committee" used Masjid Sankore as the standard against which Islamic religious freedom in prison was measured.

By 1972, the official status of Muslim inmates was further enhanced by the role they had played during the bloody Attica uprising of the previous autumn. Contrary to their image as militant radicals, the Muslims in Attica protected their guards and used their power as a disciplined, self-governing inmate organization to reestablish order during a period where the entire prison society was threatened with permanent anarchy. For the first time in history, inmates formed a disciplined syndicate, visibly identifiable by their prayer caps (*kufa*) and manicured beards, whose outlook was linked

Figure 23. Door to Masjid Sankore at Green Haven Correctional Facility, N.Y. Photograph by Jolie Stahl.

Figure 24. Friday prayers at Masjid Sankore, Green Haven Correctional Facility, N.Y. Photograph by Jolie Stahl.

Figure 25. The American Muslim Mission mosque, the Masjid ut-Taubah, in Green Haven Correctional Facility, N.Y. Photograph by Jolie Stahl.

neither to the old criminal subculture nor to the rebellious militant ideologies of the epoch. Consequently, the embattled Department of Corrections offered them a modicum of legitimacy and surrendered some of its own power to govern the prison in a tacit alliance with the Muslims.

Following the Attica riot, DOCS designated Green Haven, the scene of similarly explosive tensions, a "program facility," where emphasis was placed on learning and rehabilitation as opposed to punishment. College courses, vocational training, substance-abuse programs, work release, and family-reunion visits resulted directly from a negotiation of inmate demands and the actions of newly appointed liberal administrators. Muslims were situated at the center of these activities and forced the administration to submit to literal interpretations of laws pertinent to religious freedom for prisoners. During this period, they asserted the right to perform daily *salāt,* and they even achieved relative financial autonomy by importing and selling legal commodities from the outside. Masjid Sankore instituted classes in qur'anic instruction and Arabic. Prisoners throughout the state referred to Green Haven's masjid as the "Medina" of the system—a place of *hijra* in the sense of retreat, refuge, and reconstruction. According to records from the Islamic Center, Sankore had more converts to Islam than any other mosque in America during the years 1975 and 1976. Some of

Figure 26. Shu'aib Adbur Raheem, a former imam of Masjid Sankore, and his wife during a family reunion visit at Wende Correctional Facility, N.Y. Photograph by Jolie Stahl.

the converts were outside guests or even corrections personnel, who would often volunteer to work Sankore religious events without pay (Mustafa et al. 1989). Other successful prison mosques were eventually started in Attica, Auburn, Clinton, Comstock, Elmira, Napanoch, Ossining, Shawangunk, and Wende. A family reunion visit at Wende is shown in figure 26.

THE CONVERSION OF BLACK POWER MILITANTS

If Attica provoked a period of liberalization inside these largely uncontrollable institutions, it also stimulated intensification of the covert domestic war led by the FBI against black revolutionaries, who were held responsible for the prison uprisings, as well as for waves of bombings and armed attacks on government targets. In New York, at least a dozen Black Panthers were jailed with sentences of 25-years-to-life. The decapitation of the entire political spectrum of the black movement, including the assassinations of Malcom X in 1965 and Martin Luther King, Jr., in 1968, led to a general crisis of demoralization among urban blacks. Aided by the Islamic conversion of H. Rap Brown, the imprisoned leader of the Student Non-Violent Coordinating Committee,[4] an alternative began to attract numerous revolutionary figures whose apprehensions about religion were assuaged by the teaching that "Islam was not inconsistent with their revolutionary goals." Like Brown, who changed his name to Jamil Al-Amin, they turned their grassroots skills for mass organizing toward Islamic *da'wa* (propagation) and soon began to offer the Qur'an to fellow inmates as a substitute for revolutionary or African nationalist literature. The programs of former militants came to envision personal rebirth as a prerequisite for social transformation, a position supported by the passage, "Verily, never will Allah change the condition of a people until they change it themselves with their own soul" (Qur'an 13:11 or 8:53).

The tremendous effect of these words on Black Power advocates is reflected in the testimony of a member of the Black Liberation Army, sentenced to life imprisonment in 1973:

> I was a very determined socialist when I was placed in jail with another black leader. He had already accepted Islam, and I was confronted by his daily prayers. At first I could not understand why he was praying to a god who, I felt, had abandoned black people. We argued and battled, but eventually Islam helped me become more relaxed. It relieved a burden because I had become frustrated by the failure of the political movement. And then you read the *ayat* in the Qur'an where Allah told the Prophet, "Maybe we might show you a victory in your lifetime. Maybe we won't, but you must keep striving." So then you start to see things in a broader perspective, outside of yourself as an individual. It was then that I realized that black revolutionaries didn't suffer a major defeat, but that we were part of an ongoing process that would eventually culminate in victory.[5]

Prison, it can be argued, is a bizarre and violent "university" for those who reach maturity behind bars. There the brutality and corruption of the street are magnified to gargantuan proportions. Even to the extent that he complies with the rules of incarceration, the prisoner becomes entangled in a world of material desires and moral prostitution. From the lowly prisoner up to the warden, by way of the prisoners known as "big men," snitches, guards, program instructors, and bureaucrats, prison is a pathological society asserting a unique institutional order. This regime codifies various methods used to alter and perhaps destroy the inmate's physical and psychological integrity. It forces him to regiment his personal habits and behavior in accordance with the social ecology of the prison. In preparation for his eventual release on parole, the inmate studies a "curriculum" of ruse and discipline. He learns few of the many skills necessary to lead a law-abiding life back on the street. Even worse, as part of his daily transactions in the prison environment, the prisoner is subjected to a hierarchy of physical brutality, psychological manipulation, and frequent homosexual rape. The prison is an administrative-bureaucratic space that marks every aspect of the inmate's existence unless he can use his minimal rights to circumscribe an autonomous zone whose perimeter cannot officially be contested.

A NEW PEDAGOGY OF THE INCARCERATED

Acting through the principle of freedom of worship, Islam meets these conditions and shows a remarkable capacity to redefine the conditions of incarceration. A new Muslim repeats the attestation of faith, the *shahada,* before witnesses at the mosque. His Islamic identity then means a fresh start, symbolized by the choice of a new name, modifications in his physical appearance, and an emphasis on prayer. He is linked to his Muslim brothers worldwide, as suggested by frequent representations of Mecca in the mosque's decor, for example in the mosque shown in figure 25 above. More immediately, he is linked to his fellow Muslim prisoners. Inmates like those at Masjid Sankore, thanks to communal prayer, qur'anic and Arabic scholarship, and invocation of *sharʿia* have been able to exercise significant group control over their fellows. Historically, Christian prison reformers envisioned conversion as *cloistered* reflection or *silent* prayer. Islamic teaching, however, changes self-image and social relationships primarily through *communal* prayer and qur'anic *recitation,* which establish ties of identification and action between the Muslim believers and the sacred texts of the Qur'an and Sunna. Through religious practice,[6] the prisoner distances himself from the outside world, conceptualized as *dar al-harb,* and migrates (*hijra*) toward the ideal of *dar al-Islam,* defined not by territory but by Islamic practice. The greater the capacity of the prison *jamaʿa* (congregation) to establish the privilege of congregational prayer, the greater the potential effect upon the individual Muslim. It is an impressive sight to see 50 or 100 prisoners bowing and kneeling in prayer in the middle of a prison exercise yard or in a room isolated within a maze of corridors and cells, as in figure 24, above. Since 1973, after consulting the Islamic Center in New York, DOCS has recognized four holidays: Hijra (New Year's Day), Maulid al-nabi (the Prophet's birthday), ʿId al-fitr (feast commemorating the end of the Ramadan fast), and ʿId al-adha (feast of the sacrifice). During the Ramadan fast, Muslims can requisition *halal* meat and are permitted to use the kitchen to prepare *iftar* meals. For breaking the fast, they are also permitted exceptionally to take some of the food back to their cells.

The Muslim's cell can be recognized by the absence of photographic images and the otherwise ubiquitous centerfold pinups of naked women. When a man becomes a shahada (convert), he gradually learns the proper etiquette for a Muslim inmate. To reorganized personal space corresponds a changed attitude toward his body for the new Muslim. He tries to avoid pork and other non-halal foods; some prisoners even object to the use of utensils that have touched forbidden foods. The issue of providing halal diets to Muslim prisoners in New York State has been in litigation for many years, with the state now using the excuse of budgetary constraints to refuse. The convert also becomes concerned with *wuzu* (ablution), here transformed into a code of personal cleanliness and grooming. In addition to their *kufa* (skullcaps), beards, and *djellabah* (long shirts), the Muslims are usually well scrubbed, and, as advised in the orientation booklet, often wear aromatic oils when entering the mosque. The use of personal toiletries defines the Muslim's body as different from the sweaty, disciplined body of the ordinary prisoner. Cigarette smoking is also frowned upon among orthodox Muslims.

In respect to a prisoner's repressed sexual desire, the Islamic regime acquires double significance in its strict opposition to homosexuality. Certainly, it upholds qur'anic injunctions and encourages the sublimation of desire into a rigorous program of study and prayer. More subtly, however, a man's adherence to these injunctions illustrates counterdisciplinary resistance to one of the more overt dominance hierarchies encountered in prison life. Sexual possession, domination, and submission represent forms of "hard currency" in prison. Thus by asserting the distinction between halal and haram, between what is permitted and what is forbidden, the Muslim community simultaneously follows Islamic law and negates one of the defining characteristics of prison life.

The most contentious issue regarding the prisoner's body involves surveillance and personal modesty. For example, during the 1970s, the Prison Committee worked with the state to arrange special times for Muslims to shower as a way to ensure privacy. Eventually, DOCS designated Thursday nights for Muslims to coordinate showers among themselves. A related yet unresolved issue is the "strip search," when men are forced to strip naked and submit to an inspection of their body cavities. Many prisoners refuse to undergo this procedure. Consequently, they file grievances, risk being "written up," sent to the "hole," or even beaten if they refuse too vehemently. Lawsuits have been filed, but the courts have backed up the wardens, who insist that security issues take precedence over freedom of religious expression.[7]

The Muslim community generates a certain degree of physical, emotional, and even biological relief from the grinding prison discipline. This extraordinarily synthetic capacity to alter the cognitive patterns of an inmate's world may even carry over into the realm of taste (halal diet), sight (reverse-direction Arabic script, calligraphy, absence of images, geometrical patterns, etc.), and smell (aromatic oils, incense). By staking out an Islamic space and filling it with a universe of alternative sensations, names, and even a different alphabet, the prison jama'a establishes the conditions for a relative transformation of the most dreaded aspect of detention—the duration of one's sentence, the "terror of time." No other popular inmate association has proved itself capable of redefining the prison sentence in such a long-term way, for in its most successful manifestation, Islam has the power to reinterpret the notion of "doing time" into the activity of "following the Sunna of the Prophet Muhammad."[8] Prisoners spend much of their time engaged in qur'anic study, conducted according to a nationwide curriculum, moving through various levels from elementary instruction in beliefs and behavior (*'aqida* and *adab*) to advanced scholarship in law, qur'anic commentary, and theology (*fiqh, tafsir,* and *kalaam*). There is even a course in leadership training to prepare prisoners for their roles as imams in other jails or on the street.

Materials for these classes, including cassette and video tapes and books, were initially donated by concerned Muslim organizations, but for the past ten years, Muslim inmates themselves have earned surprisingly large amounts of cash through their monopoly of the distribution and sale of aromatic oils, incense, and personal toiletries throughout the prison system. These funds are also used for the elaborate carpentry and calligraphic painting that is done in their mosques, as well as for the catering of ritual feasts for the Muslim 'Id-al fitr and 'Id al-adha holidays. They contribute to the sponsorship of intramural cultural events, which are often staged for the purpose of da'wa. Sankore even published a critically acclaimed newsletter, *Al-Mujaddid* (The Reformer), which has found its way to important readers throughout the Muslim world sparking international concern for Sankore's inmates, as well as donations in the form of Qur'ans and other literature, from Saudi Arabia, Egypt, and Pakistan. Sheikhs, diplomats, and other emissaries from Muslim countries traveled to Green Haven to visit Sankore. Even the late Rabbi Meir Kahane, founder of the Jewish Defense League, met with Green Haven's Muslim community to thank them for the hospitality extended to a Jewish inmate who was welcomed to conduct Hebrew prayers in a corner of the mosque after being ostracized by his own synagogue. The prison mosque is not only the center of religious instruction but also serves as an alternate focus of authority within the prison. Its power is determined mainly by its large membership, who legitimize the influence of their chosen leaders with respect to the larger inmate hierarchy, encompassing representatives of powerful ethnic gangs such as the Mafia and the Chinese triads, or white fascist parties such as the Aryan Brotherhood and the Ku Klux Klan.[9] For example, in the late 1970s, Sankore's inmate imam was Rasul Abdullah Sulaiman, who came to prison already possessing some of Malcolm X's charisma because he had been a prominent member of the latter's entourage. He quickly rose to such a powerful position within the prison that he had his own telephone and traveled around the place at will, accompanied by a corps

Figure 27. The Majlis ash-Shura, or high council, of Masjid Sankore at Green Haven Correctional Facility, N.Y., with the author, 1988. Photograph by Jolie Stahl.

of surly bodyguards. He arranged the visits of outside Muslim dignitaries, brought family and friends of the prisoners into the masjid for prayer every Friday, and reportedly even constructed a network of small bunks inside the mosque for conjugal visits after *jum'a* (Friday prayer).[10]

This was the period when Sankore achieved its reputation as the most important center for Islamic da'wa in America. Before his release in 1980, Rasul married the mother of a fellow inmate, and his new "stepson" was elected imam. This union resulted in the effective and orderly transition of power in the mosque after Rasul's release on parole. "Sheiks" who study tafsir, fiqh and Hadith, moreover, use these skills to play a role in councils (*majlis*) to resolve conflicts and keep the peace (fig. 27). They challenge the secular jailhouse standard of status based on physical strength or a manipulative intellect.

It is possible to explore the deeper implications of the Islamic pedagogy of African-American prisoners if we look at the process of Islamization as a negotiation between the prison authorities and the Muslim inmates where the state's logic of institutional order meets the fundamentalist doctrine of Pax Islamica, according to which the world consists of only two domains, the dar al-Islam, literally, the House of Peace, and the dar al-harb, the House of War, which is identical with non-Muslim territory. The reorientation and purification of personal space is made possible for the

Muslim prisoner through a serious counterdisciplinary regime. Once he is known as a Muslim, the prisoner has little choice but to follow this new set of rules or else he risks at least the disapprobation of his fellow inmates and possibly a physical lashing. Non-Muslims who have been around long enough to understand the alternative set of rules will even admonish the novice convert (*mubari*) if he is derelict in performance of his obligations.

As enforced by the incarcerated community in general, the *shar'ia* becomes an autonomous self-correcting process administered by and for Muslims. "A Muslim's blood is sacred. We will not allow anyone to shed a Muslim's blood without retaliation. The prison population knows this and would prefer for us to handle our situation."[11] So widespread is the fierce reputation of the incarcerated Muslim that the most ruthless urban drug dealers carefully avoid harming any Muslim man, woman, or child lest they face extreme prejudice during their inevitable prison terms.

If this capacity to purify and control Islamic space is remarkable in its consistency, it is not without problems. Inmates may come to Islam merely for protection, not to find a new life. Or they may mistakenly believe that they can absolve past misdeeds and change themselves simply by changing their names and reciting the *kalima shahada*. They then give the outward appearance of devotion but end up returning to prison having committed the same crimes. Generally, however, low recidivism rates and success in the rehabilitation of drug and alcohol addiction, win tolerance, even approval, for Muslims (Caldwell 1966).

The numbers of practicing Muslims remain significant and their influence continues to rise among the transient populations who fluctuate between prison and the devastated streets of America's urban ghettos. This calls to mind a comment to the effect that all African-American youths have at least some familiarity with Islam, either through a personal encounter, a relative, a friend, a fashionable item of apparel, or, as is more frequently the case today, in the form of rap music poems.[12] Islam constitutes a cultural passport, whose bearer may exercise the option to depart the anomic zone of ghetto life for destinations mapped out by the Qur'an and Sunna. Nowhere is this option more evident than inside a maximum security prison, where the literal interpretation of the Prophet's hijra functions as a utopian itinerary and an alternative vision of truth and justice. It insulates the prisoner against the dulling experience of incarceration by inducing him to a regime of five daily exercises (salāt), consisting of a series of obligatory prostrations, that not only transforms the physical relationship to his immediate personal space but also restructures time according to a daily, weekly, and annual calendar of rites that correspond neither with the prison nor with American society at large.

In this sense, Islamic pedagogy has an invigorating effect upon the prison convert. The Qur'an becomes his instructional manual of counter-

discipline. Its study opens more than new scriptural potentials and interpretive traditions, more than simply a new grammar, phonetics, and vocabulary (Arabic), but also an impenetrable code whose messages elude all
but the most devout. As a consequence, this counterculture is not simply a
ritual of distraction but an ontological reconstruction occurring within a
well-defined space, dar al-Islam, characterized by a common set of sensory
values evident in smell (aromatic oils, incense); sight (elimination of literal
and plastic art forms, elevation of figurative and stylized forms); sound
(qur'anic recitation), taste (halal diet) and touch (promotion of strict in-
terpersonal modesty). New intellectual values focus upon the Islamic sciences, particularly fiqh, and new ideas about geopolitics and history from
an Islamic perspective.

These values have compelled many African-Americans to review traditional interpretations of their ethno-history, literature, and folklore.
Through the prism of Islam, the African-American Muslim invokes a new
hermeneutic of power: historically captured, enslaved, and transported to
the New World, then miseducated and forced to live an inferior existence,
the African-American must enshrine powerlessness even in the act of remembrance, celebration of, or reverence for his ancestors. But his conversion to Islam adds new dimensions to that history, particularly as it emphasizes the presence of African Muslims and nonslave populations, as well as
evidence of resistance to Christianization.

Islam symbolizes the aggregate value of authentic African-American culture. In the past, dance, music, fashion, narrative, and even certain forms
of Christianity (e.g., Afro-Baptism) have served to mediate, if not transcend, social, racial, and economic oppression. As revealed through the
experience of prison da'wa, Islamic discipline has the power to effect this
ontological transformation through a series of counterdisciplinary measures. In terms of social relations, Islam teaches that those who lack the
power to transform their material conditions need only reflect upon the
ideal qur'anic past in order to see themselves as contemporary actors in a
world whose rules of social distinction are neither tangible nor fixed unless
they are divine. In this way, Islam deals with class, ethnic, and racial differences—even those as widely divergent as between freedom and incarceration—by collapsing the past, the present, and the future into a simultaneity
of space and identity. To the extent that Islam succeeds in America's prisons, it offers a closed but definitive response to the modern dilemma of
justice in an unjust world.

By instituting a strict code of behavior and by networking with other
prisoners, the Sunni Muslims established a unique identity. While they are
predominantly African-American in membership, there are now a few Ara-
bic- or Urdu-speaking prisoners, and more recently a handful of Senegalese Muslims. Green Haven today, however, as noted above, is divided

between two mosques, Sankore and ut-Taubah. The Muslims at ut-Taubah have pledged bay'a to Warith D. Muhammed, whose imams are always the civilian chaplains appointed by DOCS.

In Attica Prison, the Muslim communities united in 1985 under the aegis of a strong Sunni presence, but there, too, the administration is seen as fomenting disputes, and the community remains unstable because of ongoing differences between Sunnis and members of Farrakhan's resuscitated Nation of Islam. The Sunni Muslims, who labored to unify Islam under a homogeneous practice, are seeing their space fission once again. "The Nation of Islam has recently been restructured and separated from the Sunni community. . . . There are approximately three hundred Muslims in the facility" (Rahman 1989). Less than twenty-five miles from Attica at Wende Correctional Facility, similar issues plagued the unified jama'a (Raheem 1991).[13]

For all these problems, the goal has always been to create a territory that is neither "of the prison" nor "of the street" but a "world unto itself" defined by the representational space that is common to Muslims worldwide. The profundity of this spatial vision is evident in the metaphor, quoted in the title above, used by one prisoner serving a 25-years-to-life sentence: "In here the Muslims are an island in a sea of ignorance." Islam's attraction for prisoners lies in its power to transcend the material and often brutally inhuman conditions of prison. Although it may seem to some just another jailhouse mirage, the Muslim prisoner sees entry into that space as a miracle of rebirth, and one that may even spread from the prison to the street.

NOTES

1. The prisons we visited during this study with their 1992 Muslim populations (1989 in parentheses) were Sullivan 84 (112), Green Haven 348 (286), Auburn 310 (234), Attica 388 (327), Wende 125 (74), and Eastern 175 (135). We did not include Riker's Island, with its active Muslim missionary activity, nor the some 305 Muslims registered among female inmates at various institutions.

2. There are an estimated one million African-American Muslims in the United States today.

3. Letter from Mujahid al-Hizbullahi, 1991.

4. By the late 1960s, SNCC was militant and advocated armed revolution despite its name. H. Rap Brown was the alleged author of the famous phrase, "Violence is as American as apple pie." He was hunted down and shot by New York police under the same conspiracy law that produced the famous Chicago 7 trial.

5. Interview with Sheikh Albert Nuh Washington on April 11, 1988.

6. Our formulation of the notion of "counterdiscipline" relies on the ideas expressed by De Certeau, especially his discourse on the impact of scriptural recitation.

7. One might argue that the prevalence of advanced electronic detectors, used

especially to screen incoming visitors to the prison, obviates the need to continue the strip search unless it is being retained for its general disciplinary effect of symbolic submission and acknowledgement of the state as the ultimate authority over a prisoner's body.

8. Such formulas are not uncommon in our own secular experience. For example, the practice of substituting an odometer (which measures distance or space) for a chronometer is common during long-distance commercial air travel. An airline pilot rarely mentions travel time. Usually, he refers to time only immediately after takeoff and just prior to landing. On the other hand, he may refer to visual landmarks periodically throughout the flight as a way of representing the distance traveled. Obviously, this practice evolved as a way of easing the journey by relieving the passengers of the "terror of time."

9. Ironically, the KKK has become a model for cooperation between white prisoners and guards. It is often referred to as the guards' "labor union."

10. In the course of this study, we have met at least three children who were conceived inside Green Haven prison.

11. Remark by Jalil A. Muntaqim, a former member of the Black Liberation Army and *akhbar* (secretary of information) of Sankore.

12. A sampling of the fusion of Islam, the prison experience, and early rap music can be heard on tracks such as "Blessed Are Those Who Struggle" (The Last Poets, *Delights of the Garden* [New York: Celluloid Records, CEL 6136, 1987]), "Oh My People" and "Hold Fast" (The Last Poets, *Oh My People* [New York: Celluloid Records, CEL 6108, 1987]), and "Time" (The Last Poets, *The Last Poets* [New York, Celluloid Records, CEL 6101, 1984]). Another recording, *Hustler's Convention* (New York: Celluloid, CEL 6107, n.d.), develops the classic prison "toast," the prisoner's autobiographical narrative.

13. For background on the Nation of Islam, see Marsh 1984; Jamal 1971; Malcolm X and Alex Haley 1966; Perry 1991.

WORKS CITED

Baker, J. E. 1964. "Inmate Self-Government." *Journal of Criminal Law, Criminology and Police Science* 55, 1: 39–47.

Brody, Stuart. 1974. "The Political Prisoner Syndrome." *Crime and Delinquency* 20 (April): 102–11.

Caldwell, Wallace F. 1966. "A Survey of Attitudes Toward Black Muslims in Prison." *Journal of Human Relations.*

Cloward, Richard A., et al. 1960. *Theoretical Studies in the Social Organization of the Prison.* New York: Social Science Research Council.

De Certeau, Michel. 1984. *The Practice of Everyday Life.* Berkeley: University of California Press.

Foucault, Michel. 1979. *Discipline and Punish: The Birth of the Prison.* Translated by Alan Sheridan. New York: Pantheon Books, 1977. Reprint, New York: Vintage Books.

Jamal, Hakim. 1971. *From the Dead Level: Malcolm X and Me.* New York: Random House.

Malcolm X, and Alex Haley. 1966. *The Autobiography of Malcolm X.* New York: Ballantine Books.

Marsh, Clifton. 1984. *From Black Muslims to Muslims.* Metuchen, N.J.: Scarecrow Press.

Mustafa, Khalil, et al. 1989. "Overview Revealing the Premeditated Overthrowing of the Sankore Masjid Green Haven Correctional Facility and Those Similarly Situated Throughout New York State Correctional Facilities." Unpublished report.

Perry, Bruce. 1991. *Malcolm.* Barrytown, N.Y.: Station Hill.

INTERVIEWS

Raheem, Sheikh Ismail Abdul. 1991. Interview with the author, Brooklyn, N.Y. February 12.

Raheem, Shu'aib Abdur. 1988. Interview with the author, Alden, N.Y. November 26.

Rahman, Da'ud. 1989. Interview with the author, Attica, N.Y. July 17.

EIGHT

A Place of Their Own

Contesting Spaces and Defining Places in Berlin's Migrant Community

Ruth Mandel

In a mosque in Berlin, located in a cavernous, unheated former textile factory, now subdivided and shared by a dozen migrant families, a Turkish Sunni *hoca* (religious leader, teacher, or preacher) told me that he and many other migrants intend to remain in Europe until the last European Christian has converted to Islam. This vision of the transformation of Europe to a landscape populated with Muslims and ruled by Islamic law is not, however, the only one held by migrants from Turkey. For example, some of the minority Alevis from Turkey, in radical contrast, extol the virtues and tolerance of their newfound European homes. These two divergent visions of "place" have created in Kreuzberg—the so-called Turkish ghetto of Berlin—a highly variegated ecology of Muslim experience. For some, Christian Europe is a land of infidels, and most certainly experience religious hardship there. For others, Europe is, rather, a land of opportunity. In this essay, after describing Kreuzberg, I address the complex expressions of Islam among Sunni and Alevi migrants, and discuss some of the ways in which these expressions change as a result of migration.[1]

DEMOGRAPHY, ZONING, AND SQUARE METERS

German discourse about the "foreigner problem" often claims that the high Turkish birthrate will eventually overwhelm Germans demographically, particularly given the negative birthrate among the native German population.[2] Berlin's foreign population remains the highest in Germany. West Berlin experienced a decline in population over the fifteen years encompassing the early 1970s to the mid 1980s, with the number of residents falling from 2,268,718 in 1973 to 2,156,209 in 1986. However, West Berlin's foreign population grew from 178,415 to 257,916, about 12 percent of the whole. Despite alarmist rhetoric, however, Turks in Kreuzberg made up only 19.3 percent of the quarter's legal residents in 1983: of a total population of 139,590, 28.7 percent, or 40,025 residents, were foreigners, of whom 26,952, or 67.3 percent, were Turks. In the next three years Kreuzberg's foreign population barely changed, standing at 40,087 in 1986, compared to 110,490 Germans (West Berlin Municipal Government 1986). By 1992, the population of West Berlin was 2,163,040. However, German/German unification drove the figure for the new, united Berlin up to 3,456,891 in 1992, of whom 3,070,980, or 88.8 percent, were German. Of the 11.2 percent who were registered foreigners in 1992, 138,738, or 36 percent, were Turks, who thus comprised 4 percent of the city's total population.

There are far more Turks in Kreuzberg than official figures indicate, and their number would no doubt be larger but for restrictive zoning laws regulating the whereabouts of foreigners. These laws, enforced by the Ausländerpolizei (Aliens Police), identify three quarters of the city—Kreuzberg, Wedding, and Tiergarten—as off-limits to the least desirable foreigners (those from the Third World). These are the three districts with the highest percentages of Turkish residents, with 19.3 percent, 13.7 percent, and 10.2 percent respectively. This restrictive regulation has been only partially successful. Informal restrictive covenants effectively prevent foreigners from renting housing outside these three neighborhoods, forcing them to circumvent the zoning laws. Housing has thus been a perpetual problem for the Turks of Berlin, with people shifting among several occasional and illegal residences. A Turk may be registered with the Ausländerpolizei at an address in a quarter that is not off-limits, perhaps the home of a sympathetic friend or relative, while actually living in Kreuzberg in a flat legally registered to others.

Turks also suffer because of the legally required minimum number of square meters per inhabitant in every flat set in 1977 (Castles 1984: 79).[3] Turkish families commonly fail to meet this requirement, based as it is on German, not Turkish, habits. Turks resort, therefore, to some form of false residency registration. It is not uncommon for a Turkish family of, say, seven, perhaps including three generations, to live, eat, and sleep in two rooms. Turks often sleep on *dösek*, futonlike mattresses, laid side by side at night and folded up and stacked in a corner by day, when the room becomes the living and dining room.

A visitor usually can ascertain if indeed this is the sleeping arrangement in a Turkish home by the presence or absence of the telltale alarm clock on a low shelf of the requisite huge breakfront in this multipurpose room. (Many migrants work very early shifts on construction jobs or in factories and rely on alarm clocks to waken them at 5:00 A.M.). The breakfront is considered a highly desirable piece of furniture in migrant homes, and is used for displaying china, souvenirs, plastic flowers, family photographs—particularly wedding photos—and countless knick-knacks. In front of the sofa, often used for sleeping at night, there will generally be a long, low table, around which the family gathers for meals. Several adults and children might sleep side by side on the floor of one such room. Moreover, space can always be made for guests. Reactions from the Turks to the space requirement range from confusion to embarrassment, as they realize that they are being legally—and morally—sanctioned for what they take to be normal behavior.

LANDSCAPES OF KREUZBERG: THE STRUCTURAL, THE SOCIAL STRUCTURAL, AND THE ANTISOCIAL

It is no accident that Kreuzberg, the "Turkish ghetto," is the least-renovated district in western Berlin. In the former West Berlin, it was surrounded on three sides by the Berlin Wall. Today, in Germany, Turkey, and indeed in many circles throughout Europe, the name Kreuzberg connotes a very specific set of images and associations, which revolve around its reputation as "Kleine Istanbul," Little Istanbul. However, its notoriety was already established long before the Turks' arrival in the 1960s, for Kreuzberg has been politically marked for centuries (cf. Spitalfields: Eade, this volume). In the seventeenth century, French Huguenot refugees found asylum there. In the nineteenth century, indigent, landless immigrants from Silesia, Pomerania, and eastern Prussia came in search of work. At the turn of the last century, the district served as home to industrial workshops and small factories, as well as to the workers employed in them. A particular form of building structure was erected to serve these working and living needs. This multilayered, structurally dense and complex configuration was known as the *Hinterhaus* (back/rear house, or building), designed around a series of *Hinterhöfe* (back/rear courtyards). This living/working arrangement distinctly delimited a highly stratified social ordering, in brick and mortar, of classes and functions. The rear buildings, unlike those in front, were built of plain brick, lacked direct access to the street and to sunlight, had no private toilets, and were invariably noisy and crowded.

Thus, although they lived in contiguous structures, different social classes experienced vastly different lifestyles. Large courtyard buildings, typically about six stories, opened up to secondary and sometimes tertiary and even fourth courtyard buildings. Sometimes an additional building might jut off one of the sides, or stand free in the middle of the courtyard; this might be a factory or workshop. The spacious sunnier apartments facing the streets were reserved for the wealthy workshop and factory owners. Often these apartments would consist of an entire floor of the building—in other words, the four sides of a square, constructed around the inner courtyard. The workers' flats in the *Hinterhäuser* behind the main building and courtyard were smaller, darker (in an already dark city, with fewer sunny days than most in Europe) and hidden from street view.

These are the buildings in which Berlin's Turkish migrants typically live. Many of their mosques, community, and political organizations are located in such buildings as well (fig. 28). Today, most of the flats have been repeatedly subdivided and allowed to fall into disrepair. Although many façades, and some interiors, have been beautified in a public renovation project undertaken in Kreuzberg in the past decade,[4] in the courtyards beyond the often grandiose entrances, the inner Hinterhaus of run-down, dark, dank buildings remains. These façades are not decorated with elegant *Stücken* (decorative stucco reliefs) like the adjacent streetside buildings, but instead stand in quasi-ruin, occasionally still pockmarked with bullet holes from World War II.

For many migrants from Turkey, the space of the inner courtyards, where children play and adults socialize, defines their social life. Some apartment houses are known for the regional homogeneity of the residents. Upon entering some of these unrenovated apartment buildings, one is often confronted with the lingering odor of urine emanating from *Aussentoileten,* tiny shared "water closets" located in the stairwell between floors. In many, there is no central heating, no hot water, and only one cold-water tap. Coal dust in the air settles on clothing, under fingernails, and, of course, in the lungs.

The Germans who live in Kreuzberg are themselves among the powerless: elderly pensioners; alcoholics; the indigent; visual and performing artists seeking loft space for studios, theaters, or cinemas; or other members of counterculture groups, who fall into roughly two categories, the punks and the *Alternativen,* the latter being the remnants of the *Acht-und-sechziger*—the "sixty-eighters," an expression that refers to the politicized radical activists of the highly charged times surrounding 1968, now closely associated with the Green Party, health food, and communes.[5]

Although for many it is the thriving alternative scene that has lent Kreuzberg its notoriety, for others it is the presence of the Turkish *Ausländer* (foreigners)—people brought to Germany as *Gastarbeiter* (guest workers)—that defines Kreuzberg's identity as Kleine-Istanbul. The large number of Turks who ride the subway into Kreuzberg have given it the sobriquet "Orient Express." The train's final stop is a few blocks from Mariannenplatz, a large park favored by Turkish women and families for picnics. Nicknamed *Turken-wiese,* the "Turkish pasture" or meadow, this park lies in front of a former children's hospital, since transformed into Kreuzberg's Künstlerhaus Bethanean, an artists' center, often catering to the local Turkish community, which sponsors exhibitions, concerts, theater, and a Turkish children's library. In addition, it provides studio space

Figure 28. A Berlin mosque seen through a *Hinterhof* courtyard. Photograph by Ruth Mandel.

to local artists and housing and studio space for temporary foreign artists-in-residence. Mariannenplatz is a popular site for summer outdoor concerts and festivals—alternative art and music fairs, "foreigner festivals," and the like. Political posters and notices of demonstrations are commonplace. Although Kreuzberg may no longer mark an international frontier, the Turks who live there regularly cross a perilous divide separating two different worlds. They navigate between their worlds, not only when they make the annual vacation trip to Turkey each summer (Mandel 1990), but daily when they leave the Turkish inner sanctums of their cold-water flats, their Turkophone families and neighbors, their Kleine-Istanbul ghetto to enter the German-speaking work world and marketplace, where the characteristic economic relations between "First" and "Third" worlds are linguistically, socially, and cultural reproduced.

LITTLE ISTANBUL

Both Sunni and Alevi migrants from Turkey take great care to prevent the moral contamination that they believe threatens them in Germany particularly in the form of *haram* (forbidden) meat, pork. *Helal* (that which is obligatory or permitted) dietary laws, nearly unconscious in Turkey, have moved to the forefront of concerns in *gurbet* (exile). Clever entrepreneurs have used the fear of haram to their advantage and have had great success with their helal industries, which sell everything from "helal" sausage to "helal" bread. Elsewhere (Mandel 1988), I have discussed the explicit association many Turks make between pork and promiscuity, which lends still greater fervor to the conspicuous avoidance of German food, restaurants, grocery stores, and butchers. The result has been a proliferation of shops catering nearly exclusively to Turks. Like the British fish-and-chips shop pictured in figure 2, Turkish food shops in Germany typically put the word *helal* on their signboards, or even post a certificate guaranteeing helal meat.

One of the central Turkish commercial districts is near Schlesisches Tor, the terminus of the subway. The area boasts dozens of Turkish-owned and -operated businesses, carrying Turkish products for Turkish customers: bakeries, tailors, coffeehouses catering exclusively to Turkish men (for card-playing, gambling, drinking), butchers, greengrocers, grocery stores, restaurants, video rental shops, and Turkish travel agencies, some of which also perform several other functions, such as those of insurance agency, realtor, and translation bureau. There is a storefront office housing the Turkish branch of the German Social Democratic Party. Several "Import-Export" shops sell items such as the coffee cups and tea glasses favored by Turks, colorful shiny fabrics, assorted knickknacks, electronic goods, music cassettes, and jewelry. Some of these shops do an excellent business in items for the dowry and *baslik,* the brideprice.

German-owned shops close promptly at the legal time, whereas Turkish shops have gained a reputation for staying open late. This is widely appreciated, not only by Turks, but by working Germans as well. Furthermore, Turkish greengrocers have acquired a reputation for produce of much higher quality than that offered by their German counterparts. For example, the greengrocer (*manav*) I patronized received shipments of good fresh produce twice weekly from Turkey. Many Turks in Berlin, and, increasingly some Germans as well, shop at the weekly Friday Turkish open market (*pazar*) at the Kottbüsser Tor neighborhood of Kreuzberg, winding several blocks along a canal. Stands sell produce, dairy products, meat, flowers, bread, and spices, as well as olives, feta cheese, Turkish tea, and pork-free Turkish sausages. A major social event, this weekly outdoor market is reminiscent of markets held in Turkish towns and cities. Shoppers exchange news, gossip, glances, recipes, and information, and the mood is one of noisy chatter, bargaining, and busyness. Not far from the market are several mosques. In recent years, attendance at mosques has escalated, and after Friday prayers, the streets around them are filled with Turkish men, many identifiable as Muslim by their skullcaps or hats and characteristic beards.

The oldest mosque in Berlin is not in the heart of Kreuzberg, however. Founded in the nineteenth century, Turk Sehitliki Camii served Berlin's

Figure 29. Minaret at Berlin's oldest mosque and cemetery complex. Photograph by Ruth Mandel.

small Muslim community as a house of worship and a cemetery, now over-flowing to a huge adjacent area. Even so, many prefer to repatriate bodies for burial "at home." Figure 29 shows the mosque's minaret rising above the burial ground.

Islamic organizations and parties coexist with the mosques and businesses in Kreuzberg. For example, Refah (Prosperity), Turkey's main religious party, maintains an active storefront shop and local headquarters in the heart of Kreuzberg. It looks like a bookshop from outside, its windows stocked with books and pamphlets in Turkish on subjects like "Marriage and Wedding in Islam"; "Youth and Marriage: A Marriage Guide"; and "How to Pray" (a manual for children). Juxtaposed with this literature are banners and busts won in sports competitions by the organization's teams. Inside, a few young men may be milling around drinking tea in the book-filled front room, some wearing Refa lapel pins. A heavy curtain separates the front room from an inside room, which is set up for meetings and lectures, with a large Turkish flag in the front.

GURBET: CINEMA AND EXILE

Given this physical setting, how do Turks view their life in Germany? In the mid 1980s, a very popular film called *Gurbet* told the story of the religious, obedient daughter of a migrant family who always wore total "Islamic" dress (*kapalı*), complete with large head scarves and long coats. She associates with Germans, however, who introduce her to liquor, drugs, and miniskirts and rape her. Meanwhile, one of her brothers has become involved with organized crime and is shot. Another brother tracks down the wayward sister; the girl, afraid of what he will do to her, jumps from the top of a high building and kills herself. Germans are made out to be cold, indifferent, calculating, inhuman, and abusive as employers of Turkish workers. They are immoral and sexually promiscuous. The close-up camera work focuses on crucifixes, the breasts of braless German disco dancers, thighs of German girls in miniskirts, and the like. The entire migrant enterprise is portrayed as fraught with tragedy and shame. The Turks do ultimately return to Turkey, but they return either in their coffins, or bitter in mourning for their dead relatives, cursing the day they left their homeland and villages.

Frequent exposure to movies such as this surely play a role in the Turkish viewers' fears of and attitudes toward Germans. The fear of foreignness reflected in *Gurbet* is, however, anything but novel. Rather, it is only a new variation of an old theme. Hundreds of similar movies made in Turkey depict nearly identical narratives; the only difference is that Istanbul, instead of Germany, is portrayed as the corruptor of innocence. The ratio expressing the cultural topography is: Turkish village : Turkish city :: Turkey : Germany.

The same values of home, safety, morality are associated with either one's village or one's homeland, and stand in sharp contrast to the immorality of *gurbet*, represented either as the evil city or Germany. Turkey is the village, and Germany the city writ large. Yet Germany is not Turkey and offers constraints and opportunities that shape religious and ethnic life in ways that may also be seen as positive.

EXPRESSIONS OF ISLAM ABROAD: ALEVIS AND SUNNIS

For the migrants from Turkey, well-entrenched networks sustain an international movement of personnel that fosters what are seen as competing Turkish and Islamic identities. For example, a bilateral agreement permits the Turkish Ministry of Education to send Turkish teachers to the Federal Republic of Germany to teach public school courses in Turkish history, culture, and civics. These teachers have generally tended to be staunch supporters of Kemalism—by definition, laicists.[6] A lively competition for control of the indoctrination and education processes of the second generation has thus ensued, compounded in 1987 by a major scandal linking key officials in the Turkish government to Saudi Arabian funding of the export of Islamic religious education to Germany.

Many Turks in Germany already were observant Muslims before migrating. However, for others it is the foreign, Christian, German context that provides the initial catalyst for active involvement in religious organizations and worship. In part, this increased identification with Muslim symbols and organizations is a form of resistance (on women and head scarves, see, e.g., Mandel 1989: 27–46) against the prevailing norms of an alien society commonly perceived of as dangerous, immoral, and *gavur* (infidel).[7] The migrants' marginality provides the context for explicitly religious expressions and concerns that might not be relevant were they part of society's mainstream.

Migrants also have opportunities to participate in organizational, preaching, and educational modes that would be illegal in Turkey. All are free from legal constraints on religious activities. The minority Alevis in particular find in the diaspora an environment conducive to expressing their Alevi identity, free from what they perceive as the pressures of a repressive Sunni-dominated order in Turkey.

Repatriated Sunni migrants in Turkey frequently told me that it was in Germany that they had become religious (*dinci, dindar*); only there had they begun wearing head scarves and attending mosque. Anti-Alevi prejudices migrate along with Sunni Gastarbeiter. Direct contact may overcome some of these, but friendships between the two groups are generally thought of as exceptional. Sunni beliefs about the alleged immorality, ritualized incestuous practices, and impure nature of the Alevis are deeply ingrained. The second-generation young people thus rarely marry outside sectarian boundaries.

HEAD SCARVES AND ALEVIS

The official government position is that the majority, perhaps 80 percent, of Turkey's nearly sixty million citizens are indeed Muslim and identify on some level with the Hanefi branch of Sunni Islam. However, it is estimated that approximately 20 percent of the population, some ten million, adhere to the "heterodox" sect of the Alevis.[8] Although the Alevis share many dogmatic tenets with Shi'ism, they do not identify with the Iranian Shi'a, the Syrian 'Alawites, or any other Shi'a group. For decades in Turkey, the Alevis have had reputations as leftists and communists of various persuasions.

Many, if not most, of the anti-Alevi allegations revolve around morality and women. In Germany, one of the symbolic markers of religious affiliation that has grown in importance is the head scarf. The closer the scarf is to a totally covering veil, the higher its piety/prestige value. Therefore, one mode used by observant Sunnis to differentiate themselves from the Alevis is by the type of headgear one wears or has one's wife and daughter wear, since a woman's public appearance directly reflects on her male relatives. Many observant Sunnis are offended by Alevi practices. They speak disparagingly of Alevi women and girls parading about without this symbolic barrier of cloth, an ostensible protector, announcer, and definer of morality.

Alevi women in Germany frequently do not wear scarves. This is especially true of those who were born in Germany or who came as children. Their middle-aged mothers might wear kerchiefs (loosely tied, revealing hair) on the street, but never a complete three-layer semi-veil. This lack of concern for scarves resonates with the Alevi belief system, which privileges inner qualities over external practices and display such as dress. Indeed, the Alevis, like the Shi'a generally, practice *taqiya,* dissimulation (in relation to sectarian affiliation). Following the doctrine of dissimulation, Alevi women need not keep their scarves on to keep their identity intact.

Interestingly, the act of shedding the scarf, an act not particularly significant to Alevis, becomes imbued with meaning for some Germans. This is because the Turkish women's head scarf has entered German discourse as an important symbol, signifying the will and capacity to integrate (cf. Bloul, this volume). Conservative advocates of repatriation point to the head scarves as proof that Turks are fundamentally incapable of fitting into German society. Others, some of whom might defend the continued presence of Turks on German soil, see the scarf as a marker of backward, patriarchal oppression of women, and try to persuade the wearers to change in order to fit in. A minority among this latter group of German liberals are aware of the differences between Sunnis and Alevis. They are quick to appropriate the Alevis for their own political project and to use them as an example of Turks who "successfully integrate." Thus, both wearing and not wearing scarves are political and polysemic statements in both German and Turkish societies (Mandel 1989).

ALEVIS AND SUNNIS: SEPARATE SPACES IN A SHARED WORLD

The migrant diaspora context does little to alleviate the already deep-set antagonisms, suspicion, and animosity between Sunnis and Alevis. In fact, if anything, many Sunnis become still more hostile toward Alevis. The unchecked politicization of mosque-centered religious preaching that proliferates in Germany is often directed against infidel immoral Germans, communists, and, by extension, Alevis. Abroad, located as they are in an environment that is characterized as haram, it is easy for anti-Alevi Sunnis to make the association that these heretical Muslims would not only join forces with Germans of the political left but adopt German moral codes as well. Berlin supports dozens of mosques, which focus sectarian identity. The Mevlâna mosque (fig. 30), for example, is located in a modern Berlin-style high-rise, shared with numerous doctors' practices and residential apartments. Named for the Mevlevi dervish order founded by Jalal ud-din Rumi, a medieval Persian poet who settled in Konya, this mosque is associated with Sufi devotional practices. The signboard depicts Rumi's mausoleum in Konya.

The Sunnis and Alevis generally live and operate in very different social circles. It is rare for individual Sunnis to be invited to an Alevi wedding or circumcision celebration—or vice versa. When a Sunni friend of mine in Berlin was asked by an Alevi friend and neighbor to be the *kivre* (circumcision sponsor; godfather) of his son, the novelty generated quite a bit of gossip. Alevis try to do as much business as possible at Alevi-owned establishments, a preference reinforced by regional identity for both Alevis and Sunnis. In Berlin in 1990, for example, a large group of Alevi families collectively pooled their resources in order to open a private wholesale store. Some claimed that they had been excluded from similar Sunni-owned ventures and therefore wanted their own. Both in Istanbul and in Berlin, I often was astonished at the extent and intricacy of how the Alevi networks functioned. Particularly in Turkey, since Alevis are the minority group, they are more sensitive than Sunnis to the subtle clues and signs that indicate who is who.

Alevis may conceal their identity, as did Haydar, a young Alevi man from eastern Turkey in trying to appeal to Sunni customers in his video shop. In 1985, approximately seventy Turkish video rental shops in West Berlin catered to tens of thousands of clients demanding new films several times a week.[9] At Haydar's shop, the clientele ranged from young children not tall enough to reach the counter to fatigued working people on the way home from work to single young people congregating to socialize. Relatives and friends of the shop's owner often dropped in, including several young male cousins and their friends, who would sit in the shop learning to play the lutelike *saz*, associated with Alevi mystical poetry, under Haydar's tutelage.

Figure 30. Concrete apartment/office block with names of
residents (several doctors' practices) and the Mevlâna Camii
mosque, Berlin. Photograph by Ruth Mandel.

At times when he had to work at a second job, his wife, Havva, ran the
store.

During the Şeker Bayramı holiday (celebrated at the end of Ramadan),
Haydar had a bowl of the conventional candies to give to customers, as
well as *limon kolonyasi* (lemon cologne) to squirt on their hands.[10] Although Haydar offered me some candy, he and his cousins refused to par-
take of it, his nephew explaining, "We don't celebrate it—it's not our holi-

day. Kurds don't observe Şeker Bayramı." When I asked, he admitted that he had meant Alevis, not Kurds. Perhaps he thought that I, a foreigner, might know what Kurds were but not Alevis.[11] He may have been testing me; or, he may have preferred not to implicate himself and his relatives as Alevis.

The very act of providing Bayram candy for Sunni customers was telling. Not only would it please them, it was a good business practice. Consonant with the Alevi practice of dissimulation, Haydar could "act" Sunni; he feared that had he not tried to "pass," he might have lost customers, who would have taken their business to a Sunni.

FROM RITUAL TO REVOLUTION

Alevi and Sunni attitudes to their stay in Germany seem to differ. More Alevis appear to stay. Not only have Alevis left behind their minority religious status, they also have left a particularly difficult political and economic situation. Many are from the poor eastern, Kurdish regions that have been under martial law and suffered protracted civil war. Thus Alevis tend to see themselves as staying in Germany indefinitely. They are more apt than Sunnis to invest in nicer and costlier flats, while Sunnis might stick to a slum and a simple diet of beans, rice, and bread in order to save their money for investment in property or a business in Turkey. I contend that Alevis, by virtue of their historical tenacity in the face of centuries of repression, massacres, and discrimination, see in Germany, not a land of infidels whose influence is to be feared and avoided, but rather a land of opportunity and tolerance, neither of which they have found in Turkey.

Today, in Europe, several Alevi groups conceive of themselves in explicitly political—and national—terms. Perhaps the most extreme, a group calling itself "Kızıl Yol" or Red Path, advocates the founding of "Alevistan," or a nation of Alevis. Taking its model from the struggles of Kurdish separatists for the establishment of an independent Kurdistan, these followers of the Red Path are criticized by some on the grounds that Alevilik (Aleviness) is a religion, not a nationality. Most Alevis would not support this nationalist expression of Alevilik, and Kızıl Yol is far from representative. Nonetheless, the notion of "Alevistan" is compelling, for it suggests the emergence in the diaspora of a consciously discrete identity that gravitates around a fantastic center.

Thus, it is precisely because of their absence from Turkey and their presence in gurbet, in diaspora, that some Alevis have begun to refashion their identity. Moreover, this condition has afforded them the political and conceptual freedom in which to imagine a nation-state for themselves. In terms of notions of place, it is important to note the influence of the discourse of Western nationalisms, and particularly the idea of the nation-state. For what is perhaps the first time, Alevis have begun to conceptualize themselves in terms of *place,* in a jargon borrowed from the West—*territory.*

In Turkey, anti-Alevi repression is felt in multiple realms, in explicitly political activity, and also in the religious domain. In particular, the Alevi practice of their central communal ritual, the *cem* (pronounced "gem"), was until recently outlawed.[12] The cem is the secret communal Alevi-Bektasi ritual of solidarity and "collective effervescence," involving song, music, and dervish trance dancing, as well as a reenactment of the martyrdom of Husain (cf. Schubel, this volume). As part of Atatürk's secularization policies, a law enacted in 1925 closed down all *tarikats*—religious, often dervish, orders—and forbade their ceremonies and practices. Even prior to this ban, the Alevis were forced to practice the rite of cem in secret. The clandestine nature of the cem is not only suggestive of a restrictive and oppressive political and social climate but resonates as well with the dissimulation condoned and practiced by the Alevis. In addition, the ceremony itself reproduces an identification with the oppression and martyrdom of ʿAli, Hasan, and Husain.

In this diaspora, the celebration of the cem ritual provides a collective grounding for displaced Alevis. Similarly, it offers a familiar and emotionally charged mytho-historical charter, providing and suggesting an associated code for conduct. In recent years it has been celebrated approximately on an annual basis, although in a novel form and setting. A cem that I attended took place in a run-down working-class district of Berlin whose population boasts a high proportion of foreign—primarily Turkish—residents. It was held in a large hall, deep in a complex of large, old *Hinterhäuser* (like that in fig. 28), now converted and rented out for discos, parties, and the occasional religious ritual.

This cem was attended by about three hundred people, fairly evenly divided among genders and generations. It was complete with the sacrificed animal, divided, cooked, and eaten together. All presented *niyaz* offerings of food to the presiding *dede.* Several musicians played the *baglama,* or saz, throughout the ceremony. After the emotionally charged dousing of the candles (for the twelve imams and martyrs) came the *semah,* a type of music and dance associated not only with the Alevis but with dervishes generally. There are many varieties of semah, and the men and women who rose to dance to saz music represented stylistic and regional variants. The music is highly rhythmic, begins slowly, then speeds up as the dancers enter a *dervish,* or ecstatic trance state.[13]

The ritual and the feast are geographically movable. The organizers had brought the proper decor and affixed it to the wall behind the *pirs* (who are members of holy lineages). This consisted of pictures of Ali, Hasan, Husain, the other imams, Haci Bektash, the Bektashi Pir Ulusoy, and, to be safe (again, dissimulation), there was a large portrait of Kemal Atatürk. Above all these hung the Turkish flag.

Not only did this Berlin cem occur in an unconventional space, the time continuum was radically transformed as well by the addition of a novel element: video. Three video cameras had been set up, with blinding lights, all operated by amateur cameramen. No one thought it peculiar or paid the cameras any heed. The multiple recordings of the ritual on videocassette offer new meaning to the concepts of participant, observer, and event. For example, a few days after the cem, I was in an Alevi home, and someone suggested they watch it on the VCR. It was put on, but after about five minutes the father of the family demanded that it be turned off. He could not tolerate the children laughing and playing in one part of the room and his cousins on the sofa next to him gossiping about what some of the people in the video were wearing. For him, the only way to watch it was to recapture the intensity and sober ambiance of the ritual itself.

Despite the warehouse environment and the foreign context, it is at events such as this cem that Alevi identity renews itself for the migrants and their children. Much of the novelty lies in the very composition of the group participating—for example, the juxtaposition of pirs from diverse regions of Turkey, all seated at the place of honor, the *post*, with the officiating dede—some of whom had only become acquainted with one another at the cem itself. Until very recently, such a cem probably would not, could not, take place in Turkey.[14] Yet in the diaspora, highly effective informal networks forge a community of a sort that has never existed at home, as it attempts to worship and celebrate in concert.

Conversely, in the diaspora context, some leftist Alevi activists have again reinterpreted the meaning of the cem. A young leftist Alevi man in Germany explaining the cem in terms of the progressive nature of Alevilik said to me, "Without women there can be no cem; without women there can be no revolution." Thus, the cem becomes the metaphor and template for social change. Quintessentially polysemic, the cem emerges as a ritual act, either reactionary or revolutionary,[15] depending on the context and interpretation. In its very practice, then, it assumes historical importance as an expression and assertion of an identity that must struggle to survive against odds at home and abroad. In that assertion, historical meanings and relations are assimilated and reinterpreted in a new, contemporary context— for example, "revolution."

Migrant Alevis have in many ways successfully reversed their hierarchical subordination to Sunni Turks. While steadfast in their Aleviness, they identify with and admire many aspects of German society that Sunnis find threatening. Modeling themselves on certain German, Western modes, they pride themselves on how modern they are, as opposed to the "backward" Sunnis. They point to what they see as their more "democratic, tolerant, and progressive" stance, and to the "marked" village clothing many Sunni women wear: flowing *salvar* pants, head scarves, and so on. Finally, Alevis tend to be more politically engaged in leftist politics and syndicalism than Sunnis, and, through such activities, have greater contact with Germans. This greater contact with Germans reinforces their self-image as "tolerant."

The differences between Sunni and Alevi attitudes can be seen in the way the two groups speak of Germans. Alevis referring to Germans will say, for example, "They're people, too," whereas Sunnis tend to be critical and dismissive of Germans, commonly disparaging them as *gavur.* Although still peripheral with respect to Sunnis, the Alevis may be slightly *less* marginal than Sunnis in relation to mainstream German society. As a consequence of their greater acceptance *of* German ways and people, they have become more accepted *by* Germans than are many Sunnis. The status of Alevis is also raised in the eyes of Germans by the fact that they characteristically do not attend mosque, and perhaps also by some aspects of the practice of dissimulation.

While Alevis abroad are doubly marginal, with respect to both Germans and Sunni Turks, their relative position vis-à-vis Sunnis has undergone a transposition. In Germany, Sunni dominance has become less and less relevant as a reference point. Alevis had traditionally defined themselves primarily in opposition to Sunnis, and always in relation to them; now, in Germany, they have in some respects gradually replaced Sunnis with Germans as their salient other. Whereas some Alevis in Germany have taken advantage of Western freedoms to adopt a more inward, communal orientation, unfettered by past political and social constraints, others have opted for an ecumenical stance, and still others choose to dissociate themselves from anything they perceive as religious.

CONCLUSION: TOPONOMY, ALMANYALI, AND NEW IDENTITIES

The migrants' experience of Kreuzberg both derives from and helps to shape its physical reality. Ultimately, despite their presence in "Gavurıstan," the land of the infidel, surrounded by all sorts of things profane and haram, the Turks manage to create and define a world for themselves. The world they construct lies on frontiers ranging from culinary to linguistic, from sartorial to domestic. These markers serve as functional borders delimiting a new center, which, differentially and subjectively interpreted, defines the meaningful expressions of Turkish identity abroad.

This essay has been concerned with the ways migrants from Turkey fit into the existing urban social and physical structures, and have helped to refashion, challenge, and revalorize the German definitions. Paralleling the defining German nicknames "Little Istanbul," "the Orient Express," and "Turkish pasture," some Turks have their own code names for parts of Berlin as well. Istambulis sometimes use the names of the Istanbul neighborhoods for functionally analogous neighborhoods of Berlin: "Cağaloğlu" for a section of Kreuzberg that has Turkish printers, publishers, and bookstores; "Bebek" for the elegant Grünewald neighborhood of Berlin; and Kreuzberg itself might be referred to as Turkey or Istanbul; and "Beyoğlu" serves as the nickname for the main shopping district in Berlin; an old, out-of-commission covered train station, now converted to Turkish shops, advertises itself as "Türkische Bazaar." An indoor shopping area in Kreuzberg calls itself Mısır Çarşısı—Egyptian Market—the Turkish name for the famous spice bazaar in the old part of Istanbul.

The ability to name itself or be named by others is not the only measure of control over the construction of a community or the definition of group boundaries. In the process of creating and recreating itself, the community does so, on the one hand, in implicit opposition to the German context—in defiance of the official definition of Germany as a nonimmigration land, one implicitly unsuitable for pluralism—and, on the other, against pressures to assimilate. By redefining, or renaming parts of the German urban environment, these Turks are staking a claim and appropriating it for themselves—and on their own terms.

The extensive degree of commercial self-sufficiency is another way the migrants have recreated the place for themselves, and in their own terms. Thus, one need not know a word of German to buy insurance; rent a video; buy pide bread, olives, or helal meat; talk to a child minder at a day-care center; deal with a travel agent; and so on. Thus the motivation for many of the migrants to learn German remains minimal. In addition, the prevailing ideology that most everyone shares remains the "myth of return." For many, if not most, migrants, Kleine Istanbul is not home. They dream of their final return to Turkey, plan for it, save for it, talk of it. And in their summer vacations, they rehearse it, returning for a month or five weeks.

When they arrive in Turkey, however, they are greeted with an ironic appellation; they are called *almanyalı,* "German-like." The dream of going home proves to be an impossible one, since they are no longer accepted as they once were. In fact, many migrants are relieved to return to Germany after disappointing summer trips. Once back "home" in Germany, they can find sympathetic friends with whom they can complain about this bitter experience, and recall that Germany is so much cleaner, more efficient, and the bureaucrats more honest. After a quarter century in Germany, the idealized dream of Turkey becomes distorted; in its stead, whether they are willing to admit it or not, Germany has begun to come to the conceptual fore.

In this new place, by their own actions and decisions, they are setting new precedents, as they project an agency of their own design, reshaping the Kreuzbergs of Europe into novel and heterogeneous communities. It is in the recognition of an alternately constructed center that the Turks are able to seek positive identifications. Paradoxically, however, this center is located in a peripheral place vis-à-vis Turkey, the original affective orienting center. Thus, the longer the migrants live in the "peripheral center," the greater its prominence and the more of a competing threat it poses to the traditionally central role occupied by Turkey.

In the 1980s, the Turkish-German "second generation" came into its own as a resident "ethnic" group—albeit in a country that denies this categorical possibility. The likelihood of repatriation is rapidly diminishing for this young Turkish-German population, and the prospect of living their lives as Turkish-Germans in Germany has come to seem more normal to them. Many of them who attend vocational school and university will be productive workers in German society; others, who had the misfortune to be shuttled back and forth between Anatolia and Germany as children, are more marginal and are now bilingual but illiterate young adults. Some have joined Kreuzberg's growing street gangs and have in that way become involved either in crime or in defending against neofascist Germans who assault Turks, or in both. In a sense, this defending of their turf by Turkish gangs symbolically affirms their right and intention to remain in Germany.

In this "peripheral center," the Islamic dimension of Turkish life is far from a mere changeover from the migrants' previous experience. For many, religious behavior and symbols are new or infused with new meaning, whether as a mark of the new ethnicity thrust on them, as a response to the change from rural to urban life, as resistance to German culture, or, for some Alevis, as a claim on that culture. The conceptualization of this space is anything but homogeneous, whether articulated as gurbet or as a potential *dar al-Islam* (House of Islam). Embedded within Kreuzberg's variegated social ecology are the seeds from which alternative expressions of Islamic identities may bloom.

NOTES

1. The information presented here reflects the rapidly changing situation in 1988–90. Some place names, statistics, and so forth, may therefore be out of date.

2. Germany's highly restrictive abortion law, an important part of the Federal Republic's pro-natalist policy, contrasts sharply with that of the former East Germany. In the "five new states," eastern German women have been reluctant to accept the imposition of the anti-abortion policy by the west. This has been one of the most highly charged issues surrounding unification.

3. Bund-Länder-Kommission, *Zur Fortentwicklung einer umfassenden Konzeption der Ausländerbeschäftigungspolitik* (Bonn: Bundesministerium für Arbeit und Sozialordnung, 1982).

4. This citywide urban renewal project, International Bauaustellung, sought to dislocate as few people as possible and to allow residents to decide the nature of alterations. Thus, poorer residents were able to opt against central heating and to retain their coal ovens, for example, to keep costs down. Stephen Castles et al. discuss "the old assertion that the 'German Federal Republic is not a country of immigration' " and remark that some have suggested ameliorative steps such as granting residence and work permits, monitoring the school attendance of the migrants' children, and requiring "adequate" dwelling space (Castles et al. 1984: 79).

5. In the years since unification, Kreuzberg has undergone further gentrification, and now areas of eastern Berlin have emerged as centers of countercultural bohemian and artistic life, assuming the role once played by Kreuzberg.

6. Not all European host countries follow Germany's example. The Netherlands, for instance, refuses to admit Turkish textbooks and teachers into its school system in favor of its own texts taught by resident Turks. The Dutch claim that the official books and teachers export objectionable political propaganda. West Berlin also commissioned a controversial new set of Turkish textbooks for grades one through eight. They were written and illustrated by Turkish writers and artists residing in West Berlin and contain a great deal of literature and many references that were banned in Turkey.

7. *Gavur* (or alternatively, *kâfir*) is an extremely pejorative term for non-Muslims, embodying strong moral condemnation and unambiguously asserting the user's superiority. Technically, it only refers to peoples who are not "of the book": Jews and Christians are thus not *gavur*. However, in common usage, it refers to all non-Muslims, and often to Alevis, as well. Pious Muslims used—and use—this word for Mustafa Kemal Atatürk, the architect of Turkish secularism.

8. Non-Muslim minorities live in Turkey as well. There are, for example, ancient communities of Christians—Armenian, Greek Orthodox, Levantine Catholic and Protestant, and Assyrian. A Sephardic Jewish community, with roots in fifteenth-century Spain, lives primarily in Istanbul. In the far east of the country, there are small groups of Kurdish-speaking Yezidis, as well as Shafi Muslims.

9. In the late 1980s, cable had begun to arrive in Berlin, and with it a Turkish station. It is likely that this will have an affect on how much video will be viewed in the future.

10. Lemon cologne is regularly used in the context of hospitality and more generally when one comes in from outside. A generous amount is squirted into the cupped palms, then rubbed on the hands and face. It is also used in homes and commonly on intercity buses in Turkey, squirted by a young boy hired to assist the bus driver.

11. Haydar's and most Alevi families in Berlin are from eastern Turkey. Many of these Alevis speak a Kurdish language called Zaza (others speak Kurmanci). Alevis from western Anatolia for the most part speak only Turkish and claim only the slightest affiliation with the Kurdish Alevis.

12. Although illegal, cems have always taken place in Turkey. Moreover, an Alevi revival has been gaining momentum in recent years. On the national level, Alevi assertiveness can be seen in the massive attendance at events such as the August Haci Bektash festival; a celebration of Pir Sultan Abdal that ended in tragedy, with

an arson attack that killed many celebrants; and, finally, several days of rioting in Istanbul in March 1995, provoked by an attack on Alevis.

13. For the Sunnis, the phrase "to put out the candle"—*mum söndürmek*—is an expression that directly refers to this ritual. It is a far from neutral expression and has long gained notorious popular colloquial currency in Turkey, implying the common Sunni belief in the moral inferiority of the Alevi community. Specifically, it is a metaphor referring to the Alevis' allegedly engaging in scandalous, immoral activities. The Sunnis would have the Alevis committing ritualized incestuous orgies when "the candles go out" at the cem. This is consistent with Sunni logic, which finds joint participation of women and men in cems offensive and sinful.

14. In view of the liberalization in Turkey vis-à-vis the Alevi population in recent years, cems are again taking place.

15. Some Alevis, cynical about "reactionary, feudal-like" abuses of power alleged against some religious leaders, scorn the dedes and cems.

WORKS CITED

Berlin. Senat. 1994. *Bericht zur Integrations- und Ausländerpolitik*. Berlin: Ausländerbeauftragter des Senats.

Castles, Stephen, Heather Booth, and Tina Wallace. 1984. *Here for Good: Western Europe's New Ethnic Minorities*. London: Pluto Press.

Mandel, Ruth. 1988. "We Called for Manpower but People Came Instead: The 'Foreigner Problem' and Turkish Guestworkers in West Germany." Ph.D thesis, University of Chicago, Department of Anthropology.

———. 1989. "Turkish Headscarves and the 'Foreigner Problem': Constructing Difference through Emblems of Identity." *New German Critique* 46 (Winter): 27–46.

———. 1989. "Shifting Centres and Emergent Identities: Turkey and Germany in the Lives of Turkish *Gastarbeiter*." In *Muslim Travellers: Pilgrimage, Migration, and the Religious Imagination,* ed. D. Eickelman and J. Piscatori, pp. 153–71. London: Routledge.

West Berlin. Municipal Government. 1986. *Miteinander leben: Bilanz und Perspektiven*. Der Senator für Gesundheit, Soziales und Familie Ausländerbeauftragter, Berlin; and Statistische Berichte, Berliner Statistik, Melderechtlich registrierte Einwohner in Berlin (West), December 31.

NINE

Stamping the Earth with the Name of Allah
Zikr and the Sacralizing of Space among British Muslims

Pnina Werbner

Twice a year, winding their way through the drab dilapidated streets of Birmingham, Manchester, or London's immigrant neighborhoods, processions of Muslim men celebrate anniversaries of death and rebirth. As they march, they chant the *zikr*, the remembrance of God. This chanting not only purifies their hearts and souls, but also sacralizes and "Islamizes" the very earth, the buildings, the streets and neighborhoods through which they march.

The two events celebrate Eid-Milad-un-Nabi, the anniversary of both the Prophet's birth and death, and the Urs, the anniversary of a Sufi saint's death and his final unification with the Prophet and God. The Urs starts with a *julus* (procession) and culminates in a *du'a*, or supplicatory prayer, delivered on behalf of the whole community of worshippers. Here I am concerned mainly with the significance of the procession, as movement in and through space, and the performance of zikr as part of the procession.

URS: MIDDAY, BIRMINGHAM, MAY 1989

We arrive from Manchester, a coachload of men, a minibus of women, a few private cars. The men congregate at the gates of a park, not far from the Dar-ul-Uloom, Birmingham, the religious center of Sufi Abdullah, who is head of a Naqshbandi regional cult in Britain. He is the leading deputy, or khalifa, of Pir Hazrat Shah, known throughout Pakistan as Zindapir, the "Living Pir." Zindapir in turn is the most illustrious disciple and deputy of Hazrat Muhammad Qasim, Baba Qasim, a renowned saint of the Naqshbandi order who arrived from Afghanistan and established his lodge headquarters, Mohara Sharif, in the Muree hills in the late nineteenth century. The anniversary of Baba Qasim's death (in 1943) is being celebrated today.

Zindapir founded his own lodge, known as Darbar-e-Alia Ghamkol Sharif, in 1951, in the barren and lonely Kohat hills, in the North-West Frontier Province of Pakistan. He has built it up, during the past forty years, into a vast regional cult focused on the lodge headquarters in Kohat, and stretching from Karachi in the south to Abbotabad in the north, and from Lahore in the east to Birmingham and Manchester in the far west.

JULUS

The men congregate at the entrance to the park. Venerable elderly men with graying beards and turbans, energetic young men, teenage boys, and little children, all wearing white traditional Pakistani clothing and green caps (fig. 31). They come from all over Britain, as well as from Birmingham itself. As in other processions described in this volume (Slyomovics, Schubel), participants carry banners with written texts. In this case, each group carries a green or black banner inscribed with golden Islamic calligraphy, usually with the *kalimah* ("God is one and Muhammad is his Prophet") or other verses from the Qur'an. Leading the procession are several cars elaborately decorated with green, gold, and red tinsel, carrying Islamic insignia on a green background. There is a palanquin of cloth on the roof of one of the cars. Another car carries a loudspeaker, to the blare of which the assembled men respond:

> "Nara-i takbir" ["Say: He is Greatest"].
>   Response: "Allahu akbar" ["God is Greatest"].
> "Nara-i risalat" ["Say: Prophethood"].
>   Response: "Ya Rasul allah" ["O Prophet of God"].
> "Zindapir" ["The Living Saint"]!
>   Response: "Zindabad" ["Live forever"]!
> "Mera pir" ["My Saint"].
>   Response: "Zindabad!"
> "Tera pir" ["Your Saint"].
>   Response: "Zindabad!"
> "Islam zindabad" ["Islam live forever"].
>   Response: "Zindabad!"
> "Darbar-e-Alia Ghamkol Sharif" ["The Lodge Ghamkol Sharif" (Zindapir's headquarters)].
>   Response: "Zindabad!"

Leading the procession is a group of some seven or eight khalifas, deputies of Zindapir and of Sufi Abdullah, venerable sages with flowing beards. Each khalifa wears a black robe, a *juba*, a gift from the shaikh in Pakistan, over a new white cotton robe. Heading the procession is Sufi Abdullah himself, one of the most prominent Sufi saints in Britain today. He is a giant of a man, his head held high, his massive white beard covering his

Figure 31. Sufi Abdullah and other khalifas leading the procession on Eid-Milad-un-Nabi, Birmingham, England, 1989. Photograph by Pnina Werbner.

face. It is the face of a man who has known the heavy toil of twenty-five years' work in the iron foundries of the Midlands. He carries a long cane and strides ahead of the procession, looking for all the world like a latter-day Moses, a biblical shepherd leading his flock.

It is time to start. I follow the procession in my car, accompanied by the women who have come with me from Manchester, and who are as keen as I am to witness the march (in which women do not participate). In front of the procession and flanking it on either side are English policemen who accompany the march, redirecting the traffic and clearing the way ahead of the marchers. We move past the Dar-ul-Uloom and continue through Small Heath and Sparkbrook toward the Birmingham Central Jamia Mosque. As the men march they recite the zikr. Melodiously, "La-ilaha-il-Allah," ("Allah is God") or, more stridently, "Allah-Hu, Allah-Hu" ("God is present"). Now and then the chanting is interrupted by the same loud, high-pitched calls of the loudspeakers on the cars, to which the marchers respond with answering refrains.

The men march through the streets of Birmingham, through Asian commercial areas, shabby, run-down but teaming with life (fig. 32). Grocery stores advertising ritually slaughtered halal meat, their vegetables and fruit piled high outside on the pavements, sari and clothes stores stocked with shining silks and colorful synthetics, Asian traditional jewelry stores with their delicately designed gold earrings and necklaces, Asian sweet

Figure 32. The Urs procession, displaying written texts, Birmingham, England, 1989. Photograph by Pnina Werbner.

shops with their sweets piled high in perfect conical towers, Muslim banks, travel agents, restaurants and takeaways. Aromas of cumin, cloves, and cinnamon follow us as the men turn the corner and march into a residential area, tall three-story terrace houses overlooking narrow streets. Curious bystanders stare at us as we pass, English residents and shoppers, Pakistani women carrying their babies, young men idling on the sidewalk. Now we move into a second commercial area. Then, once again, back to terrace-lined neighborhoods. The procession itself extends for some half a mile, several hundred men of all ages marching along, three or four abreast. It is a three-mile walk. Finally, over the crest of the hill, we see the Central Birmingham Mosque. Set somewhat apart from other buildings, flanked by a busy thoroughfare, its minarets beckon the tired marchers. We reach the mosque, the march is over. The women are waiting at the mosque together with the cooks of the *langar,* the ritually prepared and blessed food offered freely to all those attending the Urs. It is food cooked in the name of God by pure men who perform zikr as they cook; it is *tabarruk,* blessed. Like all actions at the Urs—the procession, the prayers, the praises of the Prophet, the reading of the Qur'an—the giving of food is a source of merit, *sawab.*

The traders have also arrived and have set up their stalls in the courtyard, displaying a colorful variety of wares: bottles of scent from Saudi Arabia and Pakistan, cassettes of famous devotional singers (*qawwal*s), recorded *khutba*s (sermons) of venerable Muslim sages, hagiographies of saints and other books in Urdu and Arabic, pictures of famous saints, Qur'anic and Sufi calligraphy in bold gold lettering, framed in golden frames and ready for hanging in the terrace houses we have just passed. There are food stalls selling tea and bottled drinks. The traders are there for the profit; they need not be followers of Sufi saints, although many are. They come twice a year, on the Urs and Eid-Milad-un-Nabi.

At the steps to the mosque, the lord mayor of the City of Birmingham awaits, together with several Muslim city councilors and the Pakistani vice-consul, who is based in Birmingham. The end of the julus is also an occasion for the leaders of the order to honor local notables and public figures, who, in turn, dignify the festivities with their presence. Despite its cultural and religious specificity, the celebration thus allows for the creation of a shared institutional space where Muslims and non-Muslims can assert common public values. The presence of the lord mayor signals the order's identification with civic institutions and its interest in cooperating with them. Indeed, the chairman of the order's management committee is closely tied to the Labour Party in the city, and the order has been a recipient of a major grant to build a community center on its premises.

The Maulvi opens the proceedings with a prayer, followed by the Pakistani chairman of Sufi Abdullah's Dar-ul-Uloom Committee, a jovial, blue-eyed, spectacled accountant, who makes the opening statement. He thanks the guests for having come on the procession, despite arriving home late last night after participating in an anti-Rushdie demonstration in London the previous day. His opening speech is followed by short speeches by the lord mayor, the vice-consul, and two councilors. Finally, the pir stands up and raises his hand in du'a, supplicatory prayer. The congregation below the crowded steps raise their hands silently as he prays. This is the first supplication, which seals the julus and opens the mosque proceedings. The second and culminating du'a late tonight will seal the Urs as a whole. That second prayer would be attended, I was told, not only by the living congregation present at the Urs but by the living souls of all those *auliya*, saints, who have reached and merged with God and the Prophet, including Hazrat Muhammad Qasim, the departed saint in whose name the Urs is being held.

URS: GHAMKOL SHARIF, KOHAT, PAKISTAN, OCTOBER 1989

Preparations for the Urs have been going on for several weeks. As the time of the Urs approaches, more and more *murids* (disciples) of the shaikh arrive to help with voluntary labor. The lodge nestles in the valley, climbing the slope of a hill, surrounded by hills on all sides, a series of stone buildings with internal courtyards, walled enclosures, walled orchards of apples, oranges, and lemons, well-tended vegetable gardens, and cattle and goat pens. Surrounding it is a perimeter wall, running along the slopes of the hills, protecting the lodge from the leopards that come down from the mountains during the winter snows. It is a lovely, prosperous, tranquil scene. The courtyards of the houses and hospices are surrounded by green lawns and bordered with flower beds and shady trees. The beautiful mosque is elaborately decorated in white, green, and dark red, its three domes and delicate minarets set against the blue skies and the hills beyond. Two fountains of pure water splash into pools on either side of the entrance to the vast open courtyard, shaded by a giant banyan tree. All is quiet apart from the sound of zikr echoing in the mountains and the splashing of the water fountains. Because of the beauty and the abundance, visitors and Zindapir himself have associated Ghamkol Sharif with paradise (P. Werbner 1990b: 271–72).

It was not always thus. When the shaikh arrived here in 1951, there were only the bare mountains. The *darbar* contains several key landmarks of the pir's settlement in this "jungle" (wilderness). Of these, one is the cave in which the pir first settled, sent by the Prophet, where he spent three days and three nights without eating or drinking. Then God said to him: "I have not sent you here to close yourself up inside a cave. Go out and meet the people." This cave, now just beyond the perimeter wall, has been preserved as it was, apart from a lone electric bulb lighting the interior. It has become something of a shrine, and pilgrims to the lodge climb the hill and leave pledges of their requests in the form of pieces of cloth tied to the thornbushes outside the cave. From here, the pilgrim has a perfect view of the lodge and the valley below.

A second landmark is another cave at the heart of the lodge, which towers above the mosque and all the other buildings on the slope of the hill. The cave is reached by a steep staircase and has been converted into a windowless room. Its floor is covered with Persian carpets and its whitewashed walls are decorated with pictures of the Ka'ba in Mecca and a chart of the spiritual genealogy of Sufi saints leading to Zindapir. Outside this cave is the rock on which the shaikh sat and preached to his disciples for many years before the mosque was built.

There were no roads, no orchards, no cattle, no electricity, at that time. Water was carried several miles from a spring on the other side of the hills on donkeys. Before the shaikh came, the area was the abode of a famous dacoit from the fierce Kabaili tribes that live beyond the hills. He was said to have robbed the British and stored his booty in one of the caves in the valley.

It has taken almost four decades to build the lodge to its present state of perfection. Virtually all of the labor that went into this building has been voluntary. Even the electricity and the digging of the well were provided by the government free of charge. They were not asked for, they were simply given. But a good deal of the building work, the construction, the extension of water pipes, electricity, and sewage lines, the building and decoration of the mosque, the planting of orchards—all these have been achieved gradually, year by year, during the weeks preceding the annual Urs.

The khalifa who runs these arrangements has taken over the job from his father before him. He is also the *darban*, the gatekeeper of the shaikh, who handles the guests and decides how long they will spend with him. He carries the keys to all the locked buildings, storehouses, and gardens, supervises the preparation of the langar and meals for the guests and the feeding of people during the Urs, and, indeed, all the preparations for the Urs.

The murids arrive in groups, many of the helpers about three weeks before the Urs. There is a good deal of building going on, and rocks are being broken with sledgehammers by hand and carried in baskets on the workers' heads from the rocky hillsides. This year the murids are in the process of building a watchtower on the periphery to guard the lodge. The khalifa supervising the building work is an ex-army man from Jhelum District. Another khalifa, from Faislabad and also an ex-army man, is supervising the decoration of the lodge buildings and hillsides with elaborate colored lights and neon signs, as well as the various extensions needed for the new buildings. Some of the lighting is already in place from Eid-Milad-un-Nabi, which was celebrated last week. There are chains of moving flashing colored lights, brightly lit colored signs, spinning neon spoke wheels and the Arabic inscription "Allah-Hu" extending across the hillside. Most spectacular, perhaps, is the decoration of the mosque, each of the three domes being lit with chains of light, which spin around it. Teams are setting up broad metal *chapati* grills and giant *tandur* pits for baking *nan*, clearing the ground of rocks and stones for sleeping spaces, connecting new electricity and water lines, extending sewage lines and building sumps, and clearing areas for the coaches carrying the pilgrims. The mosque is being cleaned and redecorated, and the elaborately designed iron gates are being repainted with blue and red flowers by a local "artist," another murid. One of the fountain pools flagging the entrance to the mosque is being whitewashed.

People at the lodge perform zikr at all times of the day and night. Even as they work, they perform the zikr. Some, especially the khalifas supervising the arrangements, have not slept for many nights, yet still they continue with this labor of love, performing the zikr as they work (cf. Lings 1971: 18–19, on North Africa). The hills echo with the melodic sound of "La-ilaha-il-Allah," "La-ilaha-il-Allah." The shaikh comes out to inspect the work's progress, accompanied by a group of khalifas. Nothing happens in the lodge without his knowledge. He is the ultimate planner and decision maker.

We meet two young men from Birmingham, here to attend the Urs. They have many wonderful tales of the *karamat,* miracles, associated with the shaikh. One tells a story about the zikr:

> The people here do zikr all the time. Even when they are working they do zikr. When I came here the first time, I insisted that I wanted to do some work. So they gave me an area to clean. I was cleaning one of the rooms when I heard someone doing zikr in one of the other rooms. But when I looked into that room there was no one there. But still I kept hearing the zikr. Then I looked up and saw that there was a pigeon sitting on the edge of the roof doing zikr. I had heard that the pigeons do zikr here.

The house we are staying in, a two-room house with a bathroom, running water, and sewage line surrounded by a walled garden, was built last year for the English Pakistani pilgrims led by Sufi Abdullah who attended the Urs as a group. The house is beautifully furnished, with a three-piece suite, coffee tables, Persian carpets, and European beds—for this is, after all, what British Pakistanis have come to expect as normal, and the shaikh provides only the best in hospitality for his guests.

The preparations continue. More and more murids arrive and join the work, speaking of their great love of the shaikh, of his devotion, his purity, his dedication. He never sleeps and barely eats; all he does is pray day and night and devote his life to God. The cooking areas are being prepared with great pots, towers of utensils, and wood piled high. Another guardroom is being built outside the women's quarters. Canvases are extended over the whole area, so the women are screened from onlookers on the hills. The organizers rush around madly, making sure everything is working. People are arriving in buses and trucks. Some carry banners, which they place around the pir's courtyard, and they put banners on the colorful tents they set up too. Decorated in green, white, and red, the tents are secured on tall bamboo stakes, with wide gaps between the walls and the roofs. On the ground, they lay thin rugs. Although it is October, it is very hot in the sun, and it is getting very dusty.

Everywhere zikr is being sung. People sing zikr on the trucks when they arrive, sometimes fast—"Allah-Hu," "Allah-Hu"—sometimes slow and melodious—"La-ilaha-il-Allah," "La-ilaha-il-Allah." What they sing also depends on the driving speed or the work tempo. From time to time, other prayers are blared over the sound system, but the sermons have not started in earnest yet.

The groups continue to arrive. They come from all over Pakistan. Some have been traveling for forty-eight hours, a thousand miles. A city of tents arises in the arid valley inhabited by 60,000–100,000 men, women, and children, an enormous crowd brought in by convoys (*qafilahs*) from every

Figure 33. The final *du'a* at the Urs at Ghamkol Sharif, North-West Frontier Province, Pakistan, October 1989. Photograph by Pnina Werbner.

big town in Pakistan and many of its villages. All have come to attend the Urs and receive the pir's blessings; they will share in his final du'a (fig. 33). There are no processions. They have traveled great distances in the name of Allah, traversing the length and breadth of Pakistan, singing zikr all the way.

HIJRA AND THE SACRALIZING OF SPACE

Sufism is conceived of as a journey along a path (*suluk*) leading toward God. The central ritual practice on this journey is zikr, the remembrance of God. Those who continuously practice zikr find their lower selves (*nafs*) and their very bodies transformed. A young khalifa of Sufi Abdullah's, alluding to complex Naqshandi cosmological theories, explained to me:

> There are seven points of energy in our body through which the spiritual power of Allah enters the body. If you do zikr correctly, and in my case it didn't take long, then your heart starts doing zikr all the time, every moment of the day and night, even when a person is doing other things. Like now, when I'm talking to you.

This merging of body and cosmos are the means of purifying and transcending the vital self, which is recovered as the eternal soul (see also Subhan 1960: 61–71).

But Sufi Islam is not only a journey within the body and person, conceived of as a journey toward God. It is also a journey in space. The sacralizing of space is not, it must be stressed, simply a coincidental feature of Sufi cultic practices. It is a central, essential aspect of Sufi cosmology and of Sufism as a missionizing, purificatory cult. Beyond the transformation of the person, Sufism is a movement in space that Islamizes the universe and transforms it into the space of Allah. This journey or migration (*hijra*), which evokes the migration of the Prophet to Madina, empowers a saint, just as it empowers the space through which he travels and the place where he establishes his lodge.

The journey is twofold: on the one hand, into the wilderness, the "jungle," beyond human habitation, a place of capricious jinns and dangerous outlaws, of predatory nature beyond civilization; on the other hand, toward the land of infidels, *kufristan*, of idolaters, hypocrites, backsliders—the "unbelievers." It is these dangerous journeys that endow a Muslim saint with his charisma. He who stays home and grows fat on the land may be rich and powerful; he will never be the founder of a Sufi regional cult, he will never be revered and worshipped as one of God's chosen friends. It is the divine transformation in space that is the ultimate proof of the divine transformation of the person.

About a week after the Urs in Birmingham, Sufi Abdullah came to Manchester to celebrate the *gyarvi sharif*[1] with the congregation at the Dar-ul-Uloom there. After the celebration and the shaikh's final du'a, he received supplicants with various problems and ailments seeking his advice and blessings. I went in to see the pir with several other women. When my turn came, we talked first of the Urs and Islam and he turned to me and added:

> You ask about the julus. It is written in the Qur'an [and here he quoted a qura'nic verse in Arabic] that you must do zikr [remember God] when you are standing, when you are walking, when you are lying down. According to the Hadith, when you walk along saying zikr, then everything, including people and objects and things of nature, will be your witness on the Day of Judgement that you have performed zikr, yes, even the stones and buildings.
> *Werbner: "Even the earth?"*
> Yes, it is said in the Hadith that once you have said zikr stamping on the earth, the earth will wait for you to come back again.

Sufi Abdullah came to England in 1962. He had known Zindapir when he was still in the army, when he first became a pir, and he had shared with him some of the arduous experiences of the wilderness of the Kohat hills during his long leaves from the army. In the late 1950s, there were many among the shaikh's disciples, especially ex-soldiers, who were going to England to seek their fortunes. It is said by some that Sufi Abdullah approached the shaikh and asked him if he could go to England. Reluctantly, the shaikh agreed to part with him, and appointed him to be his first khalifa in England. According to a British Pakistani visitor to the Urs in Gham-kol Sharif, however, when it came to actually leaving his shaikh, Sufi Abdullah had "cried and wanted to stay, but the shaikh told him he must go."

Zindapir told me that he had sent Sufi Abdullah to England because the people there, the Pakistani labor migrants, did not even know how to pray, they did not celebrate Eid, they did not fast on Ramzan, they did not perform the zikr, they had forgotten Islam. They needed a spiritual guide to lead them on the path of Allah. Before Sufi Abdullah left, Zindapir made him his khalifa. He was one of his earliest khalifas and most trusted companions.

One of the speakers at the Urs in Birmingham talked of this mission fulfilled by Sufi Abdullah and men like him:

> It is all because of those God-loving people who started the movement to raise the religious consciousness in you [the people present at the Birmingham mosque gathering] years ago, and enabled you to raise the flags of Islam, not only in the U.K. but all over the world, and especially in *kufristan* [the land of the infidels] of Europe.

Whether it is to the land of infidels or into the wilderness, the saint's journey is a lonely journey, filled with hardship. It constitutes the ultimate ordeal. This is why the followers of an "original" saint like Zindapir or Sufi Abdullah speak somewhat dismissively of the *gaddi nashin*, the descendants of illustrious founding saints and guardians of shrines, whose charisma is derivatory and who are seen to benefit materially from the cults their glorified ancestors founded. They respect them greatly, but they are not "real" saints. A true friend of God is a man who endures incredible hardship. Zindapir told me:

> When I first came here, the land was barren and hostile, and it had never witnessed the name of Allah. Yet look at it today, a green and pleasant land [*abad*—cultivated, populated], all owing to the faith in Allah of one man. No one had ever worshipped here since the creation of the world, it was a wild and dangerous place, a place of lions (my own son saw a lion). Now the earth is richer in religion than many other places. One man is the cause of it all. One man came here and did zikr, and this place became a place of habitation.

In his final sermon on the last day of the Urs, Zindapir elaborated on the transformation of the wilderness and especially on Allah's favor to the graves of the pious. One of the guest speakers at the Urs in Ghamkol Sharif stressed this relation between the love of God and the sacralizing of space in the course of his sermon:

> When a man starts loving Rasul-i Pak [the Pure Messenger, Muhammad] then everything starts loving him. Every part of the universe—the water, the

flowers, the morning dawn, the moon, the roses, the green plants—everything starts loving that man. And this is the love of Rasul-i Pak, which has
given beauty to the flowers and beauty to the whole of the world. And whatever is present here is due to the love of Rasul-i Pak and the love of Allah.

THE SUFI SAINT AS TAMER OF THE WILDERNESS

Zindapir and other speakers at the Urs repeatedly evoked the trope of the
Sufi saint as tamer of the wilderness, a trope related closely to another, that
of the Sufi saint as bringer of natural fertility. Zindapir's story is of the
successful overpowering by the Sufi saint of the devil, on the one hand,
and of wild animals, wild men and the bare wilderness itself, on the other.
It is the mastery of the soul's own lower self (*nafs*) and its wild, animal-like
passions, its desires and temptations. The way to the valley of the cave is
thus a concrete embodiment of the battle of the nafs, the inner *jihad* (see
Schimmel 1975: 4, 98, 119; Rao 1990: 19; Nicholson 1989: 108–9; and
Attar 1990: 158, 164, 273).[2] The jihad is replicated externally in wilderness
settings (see, e.g., Nizami 1955: 36, 114). The control of nature is an important feature of a Sufi saint's claim to charisma.

The centrality of a Sufi saint's power over the earth and nature is explicitly personified in Sufi theosophy by the mystical rank of *abdal,* part of the
esoteric set of beliefs regarding the ranked community of saints. According
to this set of beliefs, there are at any one time forty living saints in the
world who are abdals. These saints, I was told, make the grass grow, give
food to birds, and ensure the fertility of the earth (see also Nicholson
1989: 123–24).

Just as saints are internally ranked, as well as being intrinsically superior
to ordinary human beings, so, too, *places* in Sufism are ranked. Their ranking corresponds to the ranking of the saints who are alive or are buried
there. Thus another speaker, a well-known maulvi, speaking in Urdu, told
the congregation:

[To] the people who are resident in Pakistan and the friends who have come
from outside Pakistan: I would like to say clearly that nothing in the universe
is equal. Everything has its own status and honor. . . . Even the piece of land
where we are sitting now has different honors. For example, not every peak
of a mountain is the peak of Tur [Mt. Sinai]. And not every piece of land is
the land of Madinah Sharif. And not all stones have been honored to become
the House of Allah, the Ka'ba [in Mecca]. And not every domed mosque is
Al Aqsa [the Dome of the Rock in Jerusalem]. And not all hills could be the
hills of Ghamkol Sharif. People may wonder why the people of Pakistan and
people from outside Pakistan have come here after obtaining visas and
spending a great deal of money? What have they traveled so far for? All the
speeches have been made. What are they waiting for? I know that they have

all come here only to share in the du'a of Khawaja Zindapir . . . wherever Khawaja Zindapir has placed his foot on the earth, he has turned it into a garden and flower bed. . . . When love makes its place in the heart of man, the world is changed altogether.

. . . I request all of you to place your hearts at the feet of Muhammad Mustafa (P.B.U.H.) so that they be cleaned of sins and desires. Because when my Lord, the sacred Prophet, came on this earth and placed his feet here, the whole land was declared a pure and orderly place—East and West were cleansed [purified]. We, the Muslims, have been allowed in the absence of water to do ablution with sand or dried mud. Before the coming of the Prophet, no person was allowed to do his ablutions with sand or mud and no one was allowed to pray on the earth anywhere they chose. When my Lord Muhammad (P.B.U.H.) put his sacred feet on the earth, the earth was declared a pure place and we were allowed to say our prayers wherever we liked, and to do our ablutions with sand and dry mud. How was this permission given? It is clearly written in the Qur'an: You may do ablution with dry mud. This earth became pure, not because we cleaned it with soap but because of its relation with the feet of the Prophet (P.B.U.H.)

. . . And, O audience, if the prayer of a person is accepted because of his contact with the dust that touched the feet of Muhammad (P.B.U.H.) I say to you that all the murids who have come to Ghamkol Sharif should come once a year, if you could, you should come daily, because in the hijra of Ghamkol Sharif there is a lover of the Prophet Muhammad.

THE SPATIAL DIMENSIONS OF SUFI MUSLIM INDIVIDUAL IDENTITY

The spirituality of a Sufi pir is embodied in the space he has sacralized. His divine blessing purifies his spatial dominion and endows it with sanctity. For Sufi Muslims in Britain who are followers of Sufi Abdullah, Darbar-e-Alia Ghamkol Sharif is the center of their symbolic universe. The separation and distance between Kohat and Birmingham or Manchester are overcome in their symbolic imagination to create a single, unitary cosmic order. As Muslims and "brother-disciples" (*pir-bhai*) within a single regional cult, they are united in their expression of love for two men: Sufi Abdullah in Britain and Zindapir in Pakistan. Their religious identity as Muslims and Sufis is particularized through this love and loyalty and revitalized periodically through pilgrimage and celebration at the spaces these holy men have sacralized by their religious activity.

I stress that they are members of a single "regional cult" rather than simply of a Sufi "order" (R. Werbner 1977: ix). The distinction is important. The Naqshbandi order stretches from Iraq and Turkey in the west through Persia and Afghanistan to the whole of South Asia. It is only in theory a unitary organization. As a distinct order, it recognizes slight variations in Sufi mystical practice on the path toward unification with the

Prophet and God. The regional cult built up by Zindapir is, by contrast, an active organization with a known hierarchy of sacred centers and sub-centers and recognized chains of authority. It is a known universe of specific communities linked together in devotion to a single man.[3] For disciples living in Britain, their various communities are united with all the other communities centered on Ghamkol Sharif, even though the majority of these communities are, of course, located in Pakistan itself. Regional cults are not contiguous, spatially *bounded* territorial organizations; they are spatially discontinuous, interpenetrating organizations linked together through a common connection to ritually sacred centers and subcenters (see R. Werbner 1989: 245–98).

The great regional cults in Pakistan today were founded recently (see Gilmartin 1979; Hafeez ur-Rehman 1979), and some of today's vicegerents will ultimately found new centers, which in time may become the foci of viable new cults, whose moral and religious excellence may outshine the tired inheritors of present-day shrines. It is, above all, the "living pirs," those who venture beyond the established order, even as far as Britain, who endow Sufi Islam with its continued vitality.

JULUS AND HIJRA

I have argued that the charisma of a holy man is objectified, and thus proved, through its inscription in space. The saint has inscribed his charisma on the new place he has founded, and this very act of inscription constitutes the ultimate proof that he is, indeed, a saint. But there is a further question that needs to be asked if we are to understand the significance of movement through space for British Pakistanis: why is it that for these immigrants, the holding of the julus in Britain seems to represent a radical departure from previous practices, a new movement imbued with deep subjective experiential significance?

To answer this question we need to recognize that the julus embraces a plurality of meaningful acts.[4] It is, of course, above all a religious act, in which the name of Allah is ritually inscribed in the public spaces Muslims march along. Through the chanting of zikr, British Pakistanis Islamize the urban places where they have settled.

Historically, the holding of Muslim public processions can be seen as constituting a radical shift in the terms in which Muslim immigrants have come to present and represent themselves to the wider society. During the initial phases of migration, the only public religious signs of an Islamic presence in Britain were the stores and mosques immigrants built or purchased. Outside mosques, ritual and religious activities took place in the inner spaces of homes, which were sacralized through repeated domestic Eid and communal Qur'an reading rituals (see P. Werbner 1990a, chs. 4

and 5; Qureshi, this volume). Sacred Islamic spaces were thus confined within fortresses of privacy, whether mosques or homes, and these fortresses protected immigrants from external hostility (McCloud, this volume). When Sufi Abdullah first held a julus in Birmingham around 1970, he was warned that such an assertion of Islamic presence might expose marchers to stone throwing and other attacks. Sufi Abdullah, not a man easily intimidated, went ahead with the procession anyway. Over the years, it has sometimes been the target of attacks, mainly verbal, from outsiders, but the organizers of the processions take pride in the fact that these events have never become the scene of trouble or violence.

Marching through immigrant neighborhoods, the processions not only inscribe the name of Allah on the very spaces they cover—they also call Muslims back to the faith. The julus is, as one khalifa told me, above all an act of *tabligh,* of publicly saying to other Muslims, Look at us: we are proud of being Muslims, we are willing to parade our Muslimness openly in the streets, we believe that Islam is the last and best religion, containing the true message of God, the whole message, including even its hidden truths; and we are not afraid to show our pride in our religion openly and publicly. But, he explained, we are also making clear that if you want to be a good Muslim, you have to choose; you can't be a part-time Muslim.

The processions specifically assert the legitimacy of a particular Islamic approach—that focused on saints and their shrines—which has come under attack from other reformist movements in South Asia. In Britain, they represent an act of assertion in a struggle between different Islamic approaches, all competing for local hegemony. They also attest to the ascendancy of a particular Sufi regional cult in a city. In Birmingham, Sufi Abdullah holds the processions, to which all the other Sufi orders are invited. In Manchester, the procession was, until 1991, dominated by members of the Qadri order, whose khalifa controlled the central mosque.

As in Toronto and New York, processions literally address non-Muslims as well (cf. Schubel, Slyomovics, this volume). Although the banners carried in the Birmingham processions I observed were in Urdu and Arabic and inscribed mainly with verses from the Qur'an, in Manchester in 1990, by contrast, banners in English made implicit references to the Rushdie affair, demanding a change in the blasphemy laws. Other banners in English declared that Islam was a religion of peace, implicitly referring to the association in the public mind of Muslims with violence, which the Rushdie affair generated. The banners in English are thus part of the missionizing activity of Muslims in Britain. They appeal to an English audience of potential converts—people who feel that Christianity or secularism have somehow failed them, and who are seeking a new religious truth. Whatever the nature of the procession itself, in both cities, the meetings held either before or after the procession included invited English dignitaries and officials, and the speeches made in them referred openly to the current political concerns of Muslims in Britain (for a detailed analysis, see Werbner, forthcoming).

The processions are open to anyone. Many of those who march are members of the Muslim underprivileged or working class. By marching, they assert their pride in Islam, their self-confidence and power. Whether explicit or implicit, once people have marched openly in a place, they have crossed an ontological barrier. They have shown that they are willing to expose themselves and their bodies to possible outside ridicule for the sake of their faith. Once they have organized a peaceful procession, they know they are capable of organizing a peaceful protest. Such processions can thus be seen as precursors to more overt (democratic) political protest. Marching through the streets of a British city, then, is in many different kinds of way an assertion of power and confidence. This is, I think, why the holding of the processions seems to have a deep subjective experiential significance for those who participate in them.

Finally, and most simply, the julus is an expression of the rights of minorities to celebrate their culture and religion in the public domain within a multicultural, multifaith, multiracial society. Seen thus, Muslim processions do not differ significantly from Chinese New Year lion dances, public Diwali celebrations, St. Patrick's Day processions, or Caribbean carnivals. They are part of a joyous and yet unambiguous assertion of cultural diversity, of an entitlement to tolerance and mutual respect in contemporary Britain. Through such public festivals and celebrations, immigrants make territorial claims in their adopted cities, and ethnic groups assert their equal cultural claims within the society.

CONCLUSION

This essay has shown the importance of space in Sufi practices generally. It has also demonstrated that as Pakistani Muslim migrants have migrated beyond the boundaries of their natal countries to create Muslim communities in the West, they have also created fertile ground for new Sufi cult centers. In Britain, all saints are "living" saints. Through hijra they have become the original founders of a new order in an alien land. In marching through the shabby streets of Britain's decaying inner cities, they glorify Islam and stamp the earth with the name of God. If, like Sufi Abdullah, they are powerful vicegerents of a great saint, they retain their link to the cult center, they pay homage to it, go on pilgrimage to visit it, marvel at its beauty, and share in the powerful godliness of its keeper.

Once a year, pilgrims from Britain led by Sufi Abdullah meet pilgrims from Pakistan, led by Zindapir, in Mecca on hajj. Zindapir provides free food to all needy pilgrims on the hajj, and it is Sufi Abdullah's responsibility to organize the langar, the cooking and distribution of the food. The two men, friends and companions of old, who have been separated for a quarter of a century by five thousand miles of land and sea, thus meet annually at the sacred center of Islam, part of what has become, through the process of migration, a global sacred network generated by a belief in and love of one man, following a divinely ordained mystical path.

NOTES

This paper is based on research on Sufi cults in Pakistan and their extension into Britain conducted during 1987–91. I wish to thank the Economic and Social Research Council (U.K.) and the Leverhelme Trust for their generous support. A version of this chapter appeared in *Cultural Anthropology* 11, no. 2, and I would like to thank the journal for permission to republish parts of the article in the present volume. I am deeply indebted to Zindapir, Sufi Abdullah, and all their murids in Manchester, Birmingham, and Ghamkol Sharif for their generosity and interest in the research. I also owe special thanks to Bashir Muhammad, who guided me patiently and selflessly along the path to knowledge, to Rashid Amin, and to Nyla Ahmed, my assistant in Britain, whose support and understanding of Islam have been invaluable. The paper was presented at the SSRC conference on Spatial Expressions of Muslim Identity in the West at the Harvard Middle East Center in November 1990; at the Oxford History Seminar; and at the Department of Anthropology, Queen's University, Belfast. I would like to thank Judith Brown, Terence Ranger, Hastings Donnan, and the other participants for their perceptive comments. I am also particularly grateful to Barbara Metcalf for her very stimulating editorial comments on an earlier version of this text.

1. This is the Urs of Shaikh Abdul ul-Qadir-Gilani, the great saint of Baghdad (d. 1166).

2. Legends of North African saints' miracles also evoke the mastery of the wilderness. See Goldziher 1971: 270; and see also Eickelman 1976: 33–34; Meeker 1979: 229–30.

3. Trimingham (1971: 67–104) calls such "regional cults" *ta'ifa*, but the name does not appear to be commonly used by Pakistanis.

4. The cultural and political significance of public processions varies widely. The display of dominance in official state processions may be contrasted with potentially explosive religious-communal processions, such as those in Northern Ireland. There are pilgrimage processions (see, e.g., Sallnow 1987), annual ritual processions (see Fuller 1980), English miners' processions, memorial processions, and processions that form part of broader rituals of revitalization, such as carnival processions before Lent. Although all processions may be said to constitute existential displays of power and territorial occupation/demarcation, their significance differs widely in different cultures and localities, and at different historical moments.

WORKS CITED

Ahmad, Aziz. 1969. *An Intellectual History of Islam in India.* Edinburgh: Edinburgh University Press.

Attar, Farid al-Din. 1990. [1966]. *Muslim Saints and Mystics: Episodes from Tadhkirat al-Auliya'.* Translated by A. J.Arberry. London: Arkana.

Eickelman, Dale F. 1976. *Moroccan Islam.* Austin: University of Texas Press.

Evans-Pritchard, E. E. 1949. *The Sanusi of Cyrenaica.* Oxford: Oxford University Press, Clarendon Press.

Eaton, Richard M. 1984. "The Political and Religious Authority of the Shrine of Baba Farid." In *Moral Conduct and Authority: The Place of Adab in South Asian Islam,* ed. Barbara D. Metcalf, pp. 333–56. Berkeley: University of California Press.

Fuller, C. J. 1980. "The Divine Couple's Relationship in a South Indian Temple: Minaksi and Sundaresvara at Madurai." *History of Religions* 19: 321–48.

Gilmartin, David. 1979. "Religious Leadership and the Pakistan Movement in the Punjab." *Modern Asian Studies* 13, 3: 485–517.

———. 1984. "Shrines, Succession, and Sources of Moral Authority." In *Moral Conduct and Authority: The Place of Adab in South Asian Islam,* ed. Barbara D. Metcalf, pp. 221–40. Berkeley: University of California Press.

Gilsenan, Michael. 1982. *Recognising Islam: Religion and Society in the Modern Arab World.* New York: Pantheon Books.

Goldziher, Ignaz. 1971 [1889–90]. *Muslim Studies,* vol. 2, ed. S. M. Stern. London: George Allen & Unwin.

Hafeez ur-Rehman. 1979. "The Shrine and Lunger of Golra Sharif." Diss., Quaid-i-Azam University, Islamabad.

Jeffery, Patricia. 1981. "Creating a Scene: The Disruption of Ceremonial in a Sufi Shrine." In *Ritual and Religion among Muslims in India,* ed. Imtiaz Ahmad, pp. 166–94. Delhi: Manohar.

Lapidus, Ira M. 1984. "Knowledge, Virtue, and Action: The Classical Muslim Conception of *Adab* and the Nature of Religious Fulfillment in Islam." In *Moral Conduct and Authority: The Place of Adab in South Asian Islam,* ed. Barbara D. Metcalf, pp. 38–61. Berkeley: University of California Press.

———. 1988. *A History of Islamic Societies.* Cambridge: Cambridge University Press.

Lings, Martin. 1971. *A Sufi Saint of the Twentieth Century.* London: George Allen & Unwin.

Meeker, Michael E. 1979. *Literature and Violence in North Arabia.* Cambridge: Cambridge University Press.

Nicholson, Reynold A. 1921 [1967]. *Studies in Islamic Mysticism.* Cambridge: Cambridge University Press.

———. 1989 [1914]. *The Mystics of Islam.* London: Arkana

Nizami, K. Ahmad. 1955. *The Life and Times of Shaikh Farid-Ud-Din Ganj-i-Shakar.* Aligarh, India: Muslim University History Department.

Rao, Aparna. 1990. "Reflections on Self and Person in a Pastoral Community in Kashmir." In *Person, Myth and Society in South Asian Islam,* ed. Pnina Werbner, pp. 11–25. Special Issue of *Social Analysis* (July).

Schacht, Joseph, and C. E. Bosworth. 1974. *The Legacy of Islam.* Oxford: Oxford University Press.

Sallnow, Michael J. 1987. *Pilgrims of the Andes: Regional Cults in Cusco.* Washington, D.C.: Smithsonian Institution Press.

Schimmel, Annemarie. 1975. *Mystical Dimensions of Islam.* Chapel Hill: University of North Carolina Press.

Subhan, John A. 1960. *Sufism: Its Saints and Shrines.* Lucknow, India: Lucknow Publishing House.

Trimingham, J. Spencer. 1971. *The Sufi Orders in Islam.* Oxford: Oxford University Press, Clarendon Press.

Werbner, Pnina. 1990a. "Introduction." In *Person, Myth and Society in South Asian Islam,* ed. Pnina Werbner, 3–10. Special Issue of *Social Analysis* (July).

———. 1990b. "Economic Rationality and Hierarchical Gift Economies: Value and Ranking among British Pakistanis." *Man,* n.s., 25, 2: 266–85.

———. Forthcoming. "Diaspora, Islam, and the Millennium: The Political Imaginaries of British Pakistanis."

Werbner, Richard P. 1977. "Introduction." In *Regional Cults,* ed. Richard P. Werbner, pp. ix–xxxvii. ASA Monographs, 16. London: Academic Press.

———. 1989. *Ritual Passage, Sacred Journey: The Process and Organization of Religious Movement.* Washington, D.C.: Smithsonian Institution Press.

TEN

Karbala as Sacred Space among North American Shi'a

"Every Day Is Ashura, Everywhere Is Karbala"

Vernon James Schubel

Karbala holds a place of central importance in the piety of Shi'i Muslims. As the place where the Prophet Muhammad's beloved grandson Husain was martyred in 680 c.e., Karbala is simultaneously the site of a particular historical tragedy and the location for a metahistorical cosmic drama of universal significance. In the United States and Canada, the ritual evocation of Karbala helps Shi'i Muslims construct a unique and meaningful identity in the midst of an "alien" environment. By creating spatial and temporal arenas for the remembrance of Karbala, the Shi'a consciously adapt and accommodate existing institutions such as lamentation assemblies and processions in ways that allow them to claim space through the expression of central and paradigmatic symbols.

This essay explores the role of Karbala as a "sacred center" for Shi'i Muslims in the context of a particular North American community. The research was conducted primarily at the Ja'ffari Islamic Center in Thornhill, Ontario, in July and August 1990.[1] The Ja'ffari Center is a Shi'i institution whose buildings are located on a major traffic artery in the Toronto suburbs. It serves the spiritual needs of a large community of Urduand Gujarati-speaking Shi'a, consisting largely of immigrants from East Africa.[2] The community's members live dispersed throughout the Toronto area. The community is relatively affluent, the majority of its members having successfully made the transition to become suburban residents in the modern Canadian "ethnic quilt" (cf. Qureshi, this volume).

Living as members of a religious minority group is nothing new for the Shi'a. In most parts of the Muslim world, the Shi'a constitute a religious minority who live their lives physically surrounded by other communities who reject many of their beliefs and practices. The Shi'a of the Ja'ffari Center are also an ethnic, as well as a religious, minority, a situation familiar to the Gujarati Khojas, the majority of members of the center, who migrated from East Africa. They must decide which elements of the cultures of their countries of origin they will preserve. For most, their Shi'i identity is primary.

The remembrance of the battle of Karbala as a significant historical and religious event is crucial to the way in which Shi'i Muslims maintain their unique identity within the larger *ummah*. The importation of rituals for the remembrance of Karbala has also facilitated the community's adaptation to the Canadian environment. The remembrance and re-creation of Karbala allows the Shi'i community to claim space in North America that is both North American and Islamic: they thus Islamize elements of North American culture while creatively adapting Islam to the North American environment.

THE NATURE OF SHI'I PIETY

Shi'i piety is firmly oriented toward a historically focused spirituality that seeks to understand the divine will through the interpretation of events that took place in human history. Important events in the early history of Islam, such as the battle of Karbala, are understood as "metahistorical," in that they are seen to transcend and interpenetrate ordinary reality, providing definitive and dramatic models for human conduct and behavior. While this is true to some degree for all Muslims—as well as for Jews and Christians—the Shi'a place a distinctive emphasis on this aspect of piety, evident in rituals like the one described below.

Shi'i Islam can be described as the Islam of personal allegiance and devotion to the Prophet Muhammad. As one important Shi'i thinker in Pakistan explained it to me, whereas both the Sunni and the Shi'a accept the authority of the Prophet and the Qur'an, the Shi'a believe that the Qur'an is the Book of God because Muhammad says that it is, and he can never lie; in contrast, the Sunni believe that Muhammad is the Prophet of God because the Qur'an identifies him as such (Waugh et al. 1991; Schubel 1993).[3] Thus, although Sunni Islam emphasizes obedience to the Qur'an as the fundamental basis of Islam, the Shi'a, who also fully accept the authority of the Qur'an, categorically reject Umar's statement at the deathbed of the Prophet that "For us the Book is sufficient." The Shi'a argue that the Qur'an can only be properly interpreted by Muhammad and his family (Ahl al-bayt), who specifically include the Prophet's daughter Fatima, his son-in-law 'Ali, their two sons Hasan and Husain, and, for the Ithna'ashari majority of the Shi'a, a series of nine more imams (the first three being 'Ali, Hasan, and Husain), culminating in the hidden twelfth imam, who will eventually return to establish justice in the world. For them, Islam requires allegiance, not only to Muhammad, but also to the twelve imams, to whom God has given divine responsibility for the interpretation of the Islamic revelation.

The Shiʿa also typically claim to be distinguished by their special emphasis on the necessity of love for the Prophet. Muhammad is the beloved of God (Habib Allah). Thus, if one wishes truly to love God, one must also love the Prophet whom God loves; one must further demonstrate that love by expressing love and allegiance for those whom the Prophet loved. This is particularly true of those closest to the Prophet in his own lifetime—Fatima, ʿAli, Hasan, and Husain. For the Shiʿa, the events of their lives form the ultimate commentary upon the Qurʾan.[4] These events carry with them a reality and a meaning that transcends and encompasses all of human and spiritual history.

The most important of these events is undoubtedly the martyrdom of Husain at the battle of Karbala. Vastly outnumbered and cut off from food and water, the last remaining grandson of the Prophet was brutally slain in combat at Karbala, having first watched his close family members killed by the troops of Yazid b. Muʿawiyah, the man who claimed to be the rightful caliph of Islam. Husain, who as a child had climbed and played upon the back of the Prophet, was decapitated; his body was trampled on the desert floor. The women of his family, the surviving witnesses to the slaughter, were marched in shackles before Caliph Yazid in Damascus. Husain's head was carried into Damascus on a pole. Given the atrocities committed against the Prophet's family, from the Shiʿi perspective, the community of Islam divided once and for all at Karbala between those who accepted the necessity of allegiance to the Ahl al-bayt and those who rejected it.

The importance of Karbala for the Shiʿa finds its fullest articulation in numerous rituals that orient the community toward the events that took place there. Indeed, many South Asian cities contain areas called "Karbalas," in which ritual objects such as *taʿziyeh*s (replicas of Husain's tomb) are buried. Annual commemorations of Husain's martyrdom at Karbala during the first ten days of Muharram are essential to Shiʿi piety. These include mourning assemblies (*majlis-iʿaza*) and processions (*julus*). Such activities, collectively known as ʿ*azadari*, are occasions for the ritual re-creation of Karbala. Karbala is ritually portable, and South Asian immigrants have carried it with them to the North American environment.

Karbala is linked both to a place and an event. As such, its re-creation involves the transformation of both time and space. The re-creation of the place of Karbala is typically accomplished through the establishment of buildings dedicated to Husain called *imambargahs*, which are community centers where a number of functions are carried out, including devotional rituals, community education, and the preparation of the dead for burial. The re-creation of sacred time is accomplished by the cyclical commemoration of important events in the lives of the Ahl al-bayt as they appear on the Shi'i calendar through rituals of *zikr* (remembrance) and *shahadat* (witness).[5]

As Professor Abdulaziz Sachedina—an important figure in the community—stated during a *majlis* in Toronto, the Shi'a believe that it is incumbent upon Muslims to remember the *ayam-i allah* (Days of God).[6] For the Shi'a, of course, these *ayam* include the days of Karbala. Optimally, the remembrance of Karbala should be integrated into the everyday lives of the Shi'i community. From the Shi'i perspective, the whole world continuously participates in Karbala; it is as if the events of Karbala are always taking place just below the surface of ordinary reality. Devotional ritual allows devotees to cut through the veil that separates them from Karbala so that they can actually participate in it. "Every day is Ashura, and everywhere is Karbala," banners carried in the Muharram processions in downtown Toronto declare.

The ritual re-creation of Karbala creates an environment that in Clifford Geertz's terms can "establish powerful, pervasive, and long-lasting moods and motivations in men by formulating conceptions of a general order of existence and clothing those conceptions with such an aura of factuality that the moods and motivations seem uniquely realistic" (Geertz 1973). But Shi'i devotional activities not only, ideally, instill the assurance that the "system of symbols" encountered in Shi'i ritual is a "uniquely realistic" model of and model for reality, they can also challenge believers to compare the state of their lives and their society with the paradigmatic actions of Husain and his companions at Karbala. Thus encounters with Karbala serve as opportunities for individual and communal reflection. Devotional activities serve not only to reinforce the unique authority of Shi'i Islam but also to encourage the creative adaptation of the community to changing circumstances.

THE IMAMBARGAH AS "SACRED SPACE"

Imambargahs in North America serve both to evoke Karbala and to publicly claim space by creating an Islamic presence in the midst of the alien "West." Imambargahs are tied to Karbala as a sacred place by decorative symbols that draw one's attention to God, the Prophet, and the Ahl al-bayt. When imambargahs are established in buildings originally designed for other purposes, only the interiors of these buildings are transformed into recognizably Islamic places.

On the other hand, when a community has the opportunity to build its own structure, it must decide to what extent the building will participate in a "Western" aesthetic. In the case of the Ja'ffari Center, which was built in 1978, an architect was hired with explicit instructions to construct a recognizably Islamic building, and yet one lacking such characteristic features as domes and minarets, which might make it stand out too abruptly from the local architecture (cf. Haider, this volume). The completed building is a remarkable edifice, which is recognizably Islamic and yet part of the Canadian architectural landscape. It represents an Islamization of local architecture that mirrors other attempts by the community to find ways to Islamize the local environment—for example, using English in majlis. Imambargahs are therefore places where an indigenous North American Islamic aesthetic is being created.

The Ja'ffari Center is situated amidst other religious edifices, including a Chinese Buddhist Temple and a Jewish synagogue—both of which provide extra parking for the center during Muharram. On its main level, the center contains a large hall for majlis, called the Zainabia Hall, and a *masjid* (mosque). Upstairs are a library and a large room for women with children. Women can participate in majlis from a large room located downstairs.

The centrality of spiritual history and allegiance to the Ahl al-bayt are clearly evident in the architecture and decoration of the building. The very names of the component parts of the structure evoke the presence of the Ahl al-bayt. For example, the majlis hall is named for Husain's sister Zainab. This is significant, since the hall is used for the purpose of bearing witness to the events of Karbala just as Zainab, as a survivor of Karbala, bore witness to the generation of Muslims immediately following those events. A sign notes that the foundation stone was laid by Dr. Abdulaziz Sachedina on the day of Ghadir Khumm, which commemorates Muhammad's designation of 'Ali as his *mawla*, which may be considered the founding of Shi'ism itself.

The importance of sacred names and words is evident throughout the building. The majlis hall is flanked on one wall by ten glassed-in arches. The rear wall contains four more—two each on either side of a large arch-shaped window—for a total of fourteen. When I first saw the structure in 1982, these arches held bare glass. Within the past few years, stained glass bearing the word "Allah" in Arabic script and one of the names of the fourteen *masumin* (those protected from error)—Muhammad, Fatima, and the twelve imams—has been installed at the top of each arch. This hall is laid out towards the *qiblah* (the direction facing Mecca). At the end of the hall closest to the qiblah, there is a large archway connected to a skylighted alcove, which forms an open boundary between the hall and the masjid.

Recently, ornate pieces of Arabic calligraphy have been installed in the center. At the *mihrab,* there is a piece containing many of the ninety-nine names of God. In the hall itself, on either side of the archway leading to the masjid, there are two large pieces of calligraphy. One depicts the *hadith* in which the Prophet designated 'Ali as his successor, the other a qur'anic verse reputed to refer to Husain. During the first ten days of Muharram, the *zakir,* or person who delivers the majlis, sits upon the *minbar* (a wooden

Figure 34. The *majlis* hall at the Jaʿffari Center in Toronto,
showing *minbar* flanked by calligraphy. Photograph by
Vernon Schubel.

staircase of about six or seven steps that serves as a pulpit near the qiblah)
between these two signs of the Ahl al-bayt's authority to deliver his majlis
(fig. 34).

At one end of the hall, there is a room labeled *zari*, which contains
replicas of the tombs of the imams (*taʿziyah*s) and other pictures and objects evocative of the Ahl al-bayt. There are also containers for making
monetary offerings in the name of the imams, ʿAli, or the Ahl al-bayt.

All these features serve to evoke the central paradigm of Shiʿi piety—
allegiance to the Ahl al-bayt. The physical environment of the building

continually draws one's attention to the necessity of that allegiance by constantly evoking Karbala in both the spatial geometry and the decoration of the center. Karbala is thus always present within the imambargah. During the first ten days of Muharram, the presence of Karbala is intensified through the performance of devotional rituals.

MUHARRAM 1411: DEVOTIONAL ACTIVITIES AT THE JA'FFARI CENTER

Large crowds of people came to the center for the Muharram activities—an estimated three thousand people attended on Ashura day, the tenth, alone. They came to attend the religious performance called majlis, when people gather to remember and mourn in a structured way the deaths of the Ahl al-bayt. Majlis may be held quite frequently, but they are most intense during the first ten days of Muharram immediately following the evening prayer. The crowd assembles in the majlis hall facing the minbar. Immediately before the actual majlis, poetry (*marthiyah*) recalling Husain is recited in Urdu.

The zakir's sermon from the minbar seeks to inspire his audience with a sense of mournful devotion to the Ahl al-bayt. The majlis begins with the quiet communal recitation of Sura Al-Fatiha, the first chapter of the Qur'an. This is followed by the *khutba,* a formulaic recitation in Arabic consisting of praise of God, the Prophet, and the Ahl al-bayt. At the center of the majlis is the zakir's presentation of a religious topic. This portion of the majlis generally begins with a verse from the Qur'an, with the rest of the zakir's discourse acting as an exegesis of that verse.

The last portion of the majlis is the *gham,* or lamentation, recitation of an emotional narrative of the sufferings of the family of the Prophet. During each of the first ten days of Muharram, the content of the gham is traditionally linked to a specific incident at the battle of Karbala, which is recounted by the zakir. For many people, the gham is the most important portion of the majlis. Members of the congregation begin to sob and wail at the beginning of the gham. The mourning becomes more and more intense as the incidents of Karbala are recounted. People may strike their chests and foreheads. The gham ends with the zakir himself overcome with tears and emotion.

On certain days, the gham is followed by *matam,* the physical act of mourning. The performance of matam is exceedingly emotional. From the seventh through the tenth of Muharram, the matam is prolonged. Rhythmic and musical variations of poetry are sung by young men standing near the minbar, while the crowd joins in a calling pattern of repetition. The rhythm of the matam is carried by the metrical striking of the hands against the chest.

On the last four days of these rituals, the matam is preceded by small julus, or processions, within the imambargah itself. Symbols that evoke the stories of the martyrs of Karbala are carried through the crowd in the majlis hall. These take many forms: coffins draped in white cloth colored with red dye, as if bloodstained; a cradle representing the infant martyr ʿAli Asghar; a standard bearing the five-fingered Fatimid hand, representing both the severed hand of the martyr Abbas and the five closest members of the Prophet's family—Muhammad, Fatima, ʿAli, Hasan, and Husain. The matam concludes with the recitation of *ziyarat* (visitation), in which the entire congregation turns in the directions of the tombs of the Ahl al-bayt and recites salutations to them. *Ziyarat* is the word used for pilgrimage to the tombs of the imams. As used here, however, it refers to Arabic recitations that serve as metaphorical visits to the tombs of the Imams. This is often followed by the communal sharing of food and drink before the congregation disperses.

These rituals focus the attention of their participants on the Ahl al-bayt and the necessity of allegiance to it. The didactic portions of the majlis are reinforced by the emotional power of the gham, matam, and julus, which follow. Through the gham, the community emotionally enters into Karbala. The fact that the ritual concludes with a metaphorical ziyarat, or visitation, of the places where the Ahl al-bayt are buried is significant. The majlis creates an actual encounter with Karbala and challenges the community to live up to its standards.

On this occasion, Ashura coincided with the 1400th anniversary of the events at Ghadir Khumm. The community commemorated the event with the publication of a book on the subject containing articles by a number of scholars (including Dr. Sachedina, who was serving as zakir). The importance of Ghadir Khumm in Shiʿi history prompted a good deal of discussion within the community around about the meaning of Shiʿi identity.

The main majlis was presented by Dr. Sachedina, himself a member of the East African immigrant community of Indian origin. Dr. Sachedina's majlis made continual reference to Ghadir Khumm, as well as to Karbala. He presented his majlis primarily in English. Some of the content of the majlis dealt with topics that were seen as controversial in the community; at times his positions seemed to provoke some dissension. In response, Sachedina noted during his *majalis* that the minbar on which he sat was not his, but rather the twelfth imam's—thus he believes that what he says as a zakir must conform to the message of the Ahl al-bayt, even if it makes members of the community uncomfortable. Since the majlis is presented in the memory of Karbala, it should challenge the community, just as the original incident at Karbala challenged the ummah.

Aside from the main majlis presented by Sachedina, there were earlier majlis by other zakirs and specific women's majlis. A tent was erected adjacent to the masjid for special English-language majlis for the children and youth. A second tent was established to the west of the center that was used by the local Arabic-speaking Shi'i community, consisting of Muslim immigrants from Arab countries, for their majlis. During the main majlis, men were seated upstairs in the main hall, whereas women were seated in a room below, facing closed circuit television sets, on which the majlis was broadcast.

The seating of men and women is a source of contention within the community. Sachedina several times raised the issue of gender partition from the minbar, which prompted much discussion after the majlis among members of the community. A member of the community told me that there was a time when men and women sat together for majlis; however, when other members of the community arrived from East Africa, where it was customary for the majlis to be fully segregated, they were shocked by this and demanded that there be a partition dividing men and women within the imambargah (cf. Qureshi, this volume). I was told that a *fatwa* (legal opinion) had been sought from the late Iranian Ayatollah Khui on this issue, and he had replied that if men and women dressed modestly, there was no need for segregation in the majlis hall. Those opposed to partition point out that whereas most of the women in the community practice some degree of modest dress, few practice full segregation except in the imambargah. If the imambargah becomes the only place in which *purdah* is practiced, it suggests that it is the function of the imambargah to preserve an East African identity rather than to create a North American Shi'i one. More important, they argue, if the imambargah cannot be used to instill a sense of propriety of interaction between men and women, where will the youth of the community gain the training and discipline necessary to live in a larger society where they must interact with the other gender?

Another point of controversy in the community concerns the use of English as the language of the majlis. Sachedina made the decision to present the majority of his majlis in English, except for the gham, which he read in the traditional Urdu—which has long served as a lingua franca for South Asian Muslims, and has long been the language of the majlis for the Khojas who make up the majority of the congregation. Urdu is both a popular and a scholarly language with a highly developed literary tradition. The issue of the proper language for the majlis has been debated in the community at least since 1981. Many in the community believe that the majlis must be presented in Urdu, as English cannot convey the proper emotional timbre. Others argue that, since so few of the children can speak Urdu, an English majlis is a necessity if the majlis is to have any value for them. One concession to this has been made through the establishment of a children's majlis in English.

Sachedina's decision to present the entire ten days of the main majlis in English was in fact one that he felt he had to justify from the minbar. He argued that the topic of his majlis was more appropriately dealt with in English, even though it was on a theme aimed at adults rather than young people. Interestingly, teenagers tended to attend Sachedina's majlis until the beginning of the gham. Then they would go outside of the hall either simply to gather in small groups or to listen to the English-language youth majlis. Sachedina had previously expressed the opinion in a series of majlis in 1981 that Urdu was not originally an Islamic language: it only became one as Muslims used it. He argued that English will only become an Islamic language when it is spoken by North American Muslims in religious contexts (see Note on Transliteration, this volume).

The controversies over language and gender partition both point to a central dilemma of this immigrant community: is the purpose of the center to preserve a particularly South Asian and East African form of piety within the community or to facilitate the emergence of a uniquely North American articulation of Islam? The younger generation are fluent in the popular culture of North America. They watch *In Living Color* and *The Simpsons* and are as fascinated by them as any other young people in North America. At the same time, they are drawn to the majlis both as a devotional ritual and as a way of making sense of their identity as Muslims in North America. Pride in Muslim identities was clearly evident, particularly in the instances when teenagers brought non-Muslim school friends with them to observe the majlis. The attendance of non-Muslims at the majlis underscores the value of the English majlis in creating common ground between the members of the community and other Canadians. Because of the emphasis on the ethical content of Shi'ism, which resonates strongly with elements of Christian and European ethics, the English majlis simultaneously creates a common ground for Muslims and non-Muslims visitors within an explicitly Muslim arena.

Young people seemed especially interested in Sachedina's approach to Islam, which takes the classical tradition very seriously while simultaneously recognizing the unique challenges of articulating Islam in the presence of modernity. Since discussions about the development of a distinctively North American articulation of Islam are not without controversy, the majlis provides an arena for discussions that might otherwise be too sensitive and divisive outside of the ritual confines of "sacred structure."

THE BLOOD OF HUSAIN

In addition to majlis, the re-creation of Karbala took other dramatic forms, such as the annual blood drive. Blood is an important symbol connected with Muharram. Husain is linked by blood to Muhammad, and the spilling of his blood on the field of Karbala is an act that is seen by the community as essential to the salvation of Islam. In South Asia, acts of ritual flagellation, called *zanjir ka-matam,* are commonplace; however this spilling of blood in remembrance of Husain is seen as problematic in the Western context.

Recent fatwas have shown that flagellation—while considered permissible—is nevertheless an act that is allowed only with the provision that it not be done in such a way as to bring embarrassment to Islam. Zanjir ka-matam is conspicuously absent from processions in North America. When I attended Muharram observances in 1986 at an imambargah located near a fast-food restaurant in New York City, the private practice of matam drew a large crowd of confused North Americans. The initial derision and amazement of American students when I lecture on this subject has demonstrated clearly to me the problem of explaining zanjir ka-matam in the West. Some of the people I talked to at the Ja'ffari Center stated that they believed that such a practice was illegal in Canada. In any event, zanjir ka-matam was not performed at the center.

Instead, East African communities both in Pakistan and North America have engaged in an interesting transformation of blood-shedding in the memory of Husain. For many years, they have encouraged people to shed blood by donating it to blood banks. At the Ja'ffari Center on the day of Ashura, the community set up a Red Cross blood bank and donated over 163 units of blood. Many more people were turned down because in view of the AIDS crisis, the Red Cross would no longer accept blood from people from sub-Saharan Africa.

One of the most interesting discussions within the community addressed from the minbar had to do with the issue of whether or not this blood could be given to non-Muslims. Sachedina argued on the basis of hadith that the imams had given water and food to people in need without asking first if they were Muslim or non-Muslim; thus blood donation to non-Muslims was allowable. The majority of the community seemed to share his opinion.

"THIS IS KARBALA"

During the Ashura period, a scale model of Karbala was erected outside along the rear wall of the center building (fig. 35). I was told that this custom had recently become popular in Tanzania and had made its way to North America in the past few years. The model battlefield was laid out in a wooden box filled with sand. A trench was dug through the sand to represent the river Euphrates. The tents of the forces of Husain, as well as those of Caliph Yazid's general, 'Umar, were erected in the relevant locations and marked with signs. Toy soldiers and horses were placed in different

Figure 35. Model of Karbala outside the Ja'ffari Center. Photograph by Vernon Schubel.

positions on different days to represent the changing circumstances of the combatants. Signs identifying the location of important events of the battle such as "Martyrdom place of Imam Hussein, Son of Ali and Fatema, Grandson of the Holy Prophet," "Place of Amputation of the Left Arm of Hazrat Abas Ibne Ali," and "Place where Ali Ashgar was Buried" were placed on the model battlefield. A roof was erected over the entire area, and a sign was hung over the model battlefield that stated "This is Karbala." A large map on the back wall of the model showed the route Husain and his followers took from Mecca to Karbala.

On the last three nights, a cassette recording of Sachedina explaining the events of Karbala was played in the background. On Sham-i Ghariban, the night commemorating the struggles of the survivors of Karbala as they were marched toward Damascus, the model tents of the women were burned to re-create the actual burning of the tents, and wooden camels were arranged in a caravan to replicate the prisoners' long march to Damascus. This model was primarily for the children, who in fact took a large part in arranging it. They seemed quite fascinated by it and could often be seen crowding around it.

PUBLIC RITUAL: JULUS IN TORONTO

The remembrance of Karbala not only serves to educate the community (particularly the younger generation), it also provides for the education of outsiders, as a means of calling them to the "true" Islam—the Islam best exemplified in the lives of the Ahl al-bayt. Thus, acts of ʿazadari occur both within the center, primarily for the spiritual benefit and education of the community, and outside the center, for the education of the larger community. From the perspective of the participants, Karbala speaks to the humanity of all people, drawing them not only to ethical action, but also to the eventual acceptance of Islam. To this end, the community stages a yearly procession through downtown Toronto.

The julus was held on the 6th of Muharram. It began at roughly 3:00 P.M. on a Sunday afternoon, when the community gathered at Queen's Park. Most of the community members, especially the women, were dressed in black. People carried banners and staffs, distributed water and other beverages, and handed out literature. In many particulars, the julus in Toronto mirrored similar processions in Pakistan, with a few important exceptions. There was no matam, and there was no horse representing Dhuljinnah, Husain's mount; there were also no taʿziyahs or coffins. However, standards and banners similar to those found in Pakistan were present. Women marched separately from the men, at the rear of the procession, whereas in Pakistan women generally do not participate in processions. (The increased presence of women in community activities is a common theme throughout these essays.)

As in South Asia, the julus serves a number of important and interrelated functions. It enables the community both to reenact the Karbala paradigm and to display its religion to outsiders through such acts as distributing water, food, literature, and the presentation of speeches bearing witness to Karbala and its meaning. In Canada, this audience of outsiders is not only non-Shiʿa, but non-Muslim as well (cf. the processions described by Slyomovics and Werbner, this volume). Witnessing to this audience is problematic, given the ubiquitous stereotypes about Islam in American culture. The Muslim community is well aware of these stereotypes and the general lack of knowledge concerning Islam that produces them. It was no coincidence that the banner that led the procession read "Islam Stands for Peace," a clear rebuttal of Western stereotypes about Islam as an inherently militaristic religion (fig. 36). As a matter of fact, despite the attempts of the community to use the julus for education about the religion of Islam, the press seemed more interested in asking questions about their reaction to the attempted Islamic coup that had just taken place in Trinidad. They were seemingly uninterested in the religious significance of the procession.

The use of julus as an act of public ritual illustrates an interesting junc-

Figure 36. Banner proclaiming "Islam Stands for Peace" in a Toronto procession.
Photograph by Vernon Schubel.

ture between Shiʻi and North American culture. The julus has its origin in
the Muslim world, and yet the act of people marching with banners in the
downtown of Toronto seemed curiously familiar. In many ways, the julus of
the Shiʻa could be seen by outside observers as simply another version of a
secular activity, the parade. On one level, the community was simply bringing a ritual to Canada, but on another it was Islamizing the already familiar
North American ritual of ethnic groups parading. This was even more obvious later in the week when the annual Caribbean Festival parade went
through the streets of Toronto, with a distinctly different intent and atmosphere (cf. Slyomovics, this volume).

As a part of the educational function of the julus, members of the procession passed out a pamphlet entitled *Islam: The Faith That Invites People
to Prosperity in Both Worlds,* which was clearly aimed at non-Muslims with
little or no knowledge about Islam or Shiʻism. It stressed the notion of
peace in Islam and emphasized the common elements of the three mono-
theistic religions of Judaism, Christianity, and Islam. It clearly elaborated a
Shiʻi perspective, noting the need for an "authoritative leader in Islam who
will guide the believers on the right path." It further stressed the necessity
of people rising in defense of God's laws on earth, even to the point of

martyrdom if necessary. The paradigmatic example of this martyrdom is, of course, that of Husain: throughout Islamic history, as a result of the battle of Karbala, "When rulers became oppressive, Muslims arose following the examples of Imam Husayn to demand Justice."

This pamphlet presents its argument in a manner common in Shi'i polemics; that is, it appeals to the universal human values expressed in the incident at Karbala. The root paradigms (Turner 1974) at the heart of the Karbala drama include such virtues as courage, honor, self-sacrifice, and the willingness to stand up against injustice and oppression. There is the conviction that the universality of these virtues may ultimately attract people to embrace Islam.

The procession, briefly diverted to avoid a gay and lesbian rights parade, made its way to a central downtown square, where a grandstand had been erected, from which speeches were read. There were few non-Muslims in attendance, but the ones who were there watched somewhat bemusedly from a distance. The presence of black-clad, modestly dressed women bearing a huge banner proclaiming, "Every day is Ashura, everywhere is Karbala" was, from the standpoint of non-Muslim Canadians, strikingly juxtaposed against the ultramodern architecture of downtown Toronto.

As with the majlis, the julus contained elements that made it clear that Karbala is not viewed as a past event that holds no meaning outside of its own time. One of the speeches that took place at this gathering deserves special mention in this regard. One of the speakers at the rally was a young black man who referred to himself as a Muslim who loved the Ahl al-bayt. He made a special point of noting that Husain had died to protect the rights of minorities and drew the community's attention to the events at Oka, where Mohawk Indians had laid siege to a commuter bridge to protest the sale of their sacred lands for the construction of a golf course. The speaker called on the community to see the connections between Karbala and Oka and to send the food gathered at the annual food bank to the besieged Indians.

While the collection and distribution of food is a traditional part of the Muharram observance, the whole issue of giving charity to non-Muslims was controversial. It was addressed several times from the minbar, particularly with regard to the issue of blood donations. A taped telephone message at the center recorded before the julus not only gave the timings for various events but reminded community members to give to the food bank. It assured Muslims that the food would be distributed that year only to Muslims. Following this julus, however, an announcement was made before one of the majalis that a portion of the food would be sent to the Mohawks. This is only one example of the way in which the recollection of Karbala reveals courses of action in the present space and moment. From the Shi'i perspective, the history of the Ahl al-bayt gives direction to the community in its present Karbala.

CONCLUSION

One night while I sat waiting for the majlis to begin, I overheard a small boy running into the center and shouting to a friend, "Karbala is here. It's really here; it's out back." On one level, he was simply referring to the model of the battlefield outside of the center; but on another level, what he was saying was quite profound: the devotional activities at the center during Muharram indeed seek to re-create Karbala. For this child, a lifetime of participation in the paradigm of Karbala had begun.

The re-creation of Karbala allows Shi'i Muslims to focus their attention on the necessity of allegiance to the Ahl al-bayt. For them, Karbala resonates as a beacon in what would otherwise be spiritual darkness, challenging all who encounter it. The ethical life of the community is continually measured against the lives of the participants in Karbala. For example, the first page of a pamphlet promoting a plan organized by the community for sponsoring orphans in the name of Hazrat Zainab states:

> In the name of the great lady who looked after so many children under so much pressure after the event of Karbala, let us fulfill some of our duties as Muslims by actively helping one particularly needy child to enjoy the basic opportunities of life. As Muslims our struggles must go on. Helping the needy is one of the struggles whose results are satisfying. If we remember, "Every day is Ashura and every place is Karbala," then we will not forget the needy.

Karbala in this context not only serves as a point of reference for the maintenance of group identity, it is also a continuous call to creative ethical action. The Shi'i community faces a number of problems common to all religious groups in North America: the impact of secularism, the temptations of materialism, and the often uncaring individualism of a capitalist economy. Majlis functions as a kind of Islamic revival meeting, calling people back to an ethical standard exhibited by Husain and his companions in the battle of Karbala.

Sachedina noted that because the imambargah can convey both cultural tradition and religion, there is always the danger that the former will take precedence over the latter. From his perspective, the imambargah is not a place for sentimental attachment to the customs of "home": it is, rather, a place for spiritual regeneration. As places for the remembrance of Husain, imambargahs are in some sense "sacred spaces." But as Sachedina told the community from the minbar in Toronto, there is, in actuality, no such thing as a specifically "sacred space" in Islam. The purpose and intention of Islam is to bring all of human activity into conformity with the Divine Will. If the imambargah becomes the only place where people encounter Karbala, then it fails to serve its purpose.

The imambargah succeeds in its purpose when people leave it having internalized Karbala. Since the imambargah is dedicated to Husain, Sachedina warned that if the community fails to use it in the proper way, then on the Day of Judgment, the very stones of the building will speak to pass judgment on the community. In a sense, "sacred spaces" such as the Ja'ffari Center are problematic: for the very act of creating a sacred environment carries the risk of thoroughly secularizing the world outside of that space. The real "sacred space" in this interpretation of Shi'ism is Karbala itself, as it is continually encountered in the hearts and lives of each succeeding generation. This focus on the creation of an inner ethical and spiritual life, fostered above all by devotional assemblies, proves to be a common thread in the religious lives of many of the diaspora communities described in this volume.

NOTES

1. The Ja'ffari Center was originally called the Muhammaddi Islamic Center, but its name was changed to honor the sixth Shi'i imam, Ja'far As-Sadiq, thus publicly reflecting the Shi'i identity of the community.

2. This was my second trip to visit this community. I had previously attended Muharram activities in 1982 in preparation for a year of research among Shi'i Muslims in Karachi, Pakistan. Some thoughts on that previous visit can be found in Schubel 1991. The past eight years have seen a number of important developments in the community, some of which are discussed in this essay.

3. I am indebted to Professor Karrar Hussein of Karachi, Pakistan, for this insight.

4. The Shi'i ritual calendar makes special note of these occasions as days of remembrance: the Prophet's naming of 'Ali as *mawla*; the victory at Khaibar under 'Ali; the Prophet's meeting with Christians at Najran; Fatima's confrontation with Abu Bakr over Faydak.

5. Although zikr in the form of the repetition of the names of God is usually associated with Sufi devotions, it is also a part of Shi'i piety.

6. Dr. Sachedina is not only a scholar of great renown in his community, but also a professor in the Religious Studies Department at the University of Virginia. He is also a frequent zakir at the Ja'ffari Center.

WORKS CITED

Geertz, Clifford. 1972. *The Interpretation of Cultures*. Chicago: University of Chicago Press.

Schubel, Vernon J. 1991. "The Muharram Majlis: The Role of a Ritual in the Preservation of Shiʿa Identity." In *Muslim Families in North America,* ed. Earle H. Waugh, Sharon McIrvin Abu Laban, and Regula Burckhardt Qureshi. Edmonton: University of Alberta Press.

———. 1993. *Religious Performance in Contemporary Islam: Shiʿi Devotional Rituals in Pakistan.* Charleston: University of South Carolina Press.

Turner, Victor. 1974. *Dramas, Fields, and Metaphors: Symbolic Action in Human Society.* Ithaca, N.Y.: Cornell University Press.

Waugh, Earle H., Sharon McIrvin Abu Laban, and Regula Burckhardt Qureshi, eds. 1991. *Muslim Families in North America.* Edmonton: University of Alberta Press.

ELEVEN

The Muslim World Day Parade and "Storefront" Mosques of New York City

Susan Slyomovics

The Muslim World Day Parade and the "storefront" mosque both present images of Islam in the city of New York, illuminating political and organizational activities that promote symbolic modes of expression for an emerging Muslim community.

New York City dwellers are nationally famous for their use of collective gatherings such as public parades to enact complex social relations of ethnicity, religion, and power (Kasinitz and Friedenberg-Herbstein 1987; Kelton 1985; Kugelmass 1991). One day each year since 1986, city streets and urban neighborhoods have temporarily reflected festive images of Muslim community solidarity. Similarly, numerous "storefront" mosques (parallel to "storefront" churches and temples) constitute a specifically Muslim reusage and makeover of the quintessential urban venue, the commercial storefront: a first-floor space facing on the street, its entrance flanked by glass windows for merchandise display, that is generally owned or rented by a business for use as a shop. In the terminology of vernacular architecture, the term *storefront* is extended to housing stock, such as apartments, suburban homes, or lofts, when it is transformed into markedly different spaces and new uses—in this case, to sacred space functioning as a mosque.

The storefront mosque comes under the rubric of "non-pedigreed architecture," a label designating the "vernacular, anonymous, spontaneous, indigenous" constructions of the informal, undocumented sector (Rudofsky 1964). So too a parade can be considered as vernacular street drama whose social context, like the storefront mosques, mirrors the changing demographics of the city. In addition, the Muslim World Day Parade explicitly draws upon the iconography of the mosque, not only as a form of self-representation, but also as an image for non-Muslim audiences to interpret.

THE MUSLIM WORLD DAY PARADE

The oldest continuous civic parade in New York City is the Irish-American St. Patrick's Day Parade, which celebrated its two hundredth and thirty-first year in 1993. Many of the subsequently established one hundred and sixty-eight annual ethnic day parades currently marching in downtown Manhattan borrow from the Irish prototype the established "grammar" of parade enactment: floats, marching bands, forward military-like march formation, related community groups, local politicians, banners, and so forth (Kelton 1985: 104). The recently inaugurated Muslim World Day Parade has added the performance of mosque architecture, Muslim procession, and prayer to the visual repertory of parade display.

The Muslim World Day Parade begins with the marchers transforming the intersection of Lexington Avenue and Thirty-third Street into an outdoor mosque (fig. 37). The mosque is, literally, a *masjid,* "a place where one prostrates oneself [before God]," in the context of canonically fixed movements and verbal repetitions. Strips of plastic are laid down diagonally along Lexington Avenue so that participants and worshippers face the northeast corner of the two intersecting streets. The parade thus begins with an outdoor collective ceremony that demarcates the Muslim community and represents the primordial and recurrent moment of the sanctification of the community and the world by a prayerful gathering for which no specific architectural setting is necessary.

Floats, a necessary feature of New York City parades, here take the form of scale models of the three holiest mosques of Islam, concrete expressions of the faith. Parade organizers present these mosques as cultural symbols to teach historic and religious values. First, the Ka'ba, the holiest shrine in Islam, is identified as the "House of God, located in Makkah [Mecca], Saudi Arabia." The second site, that of Muhammad's heavenly ascent, is also identified by place: the Dome of the Rock, which "is" Jerusalem (al-Quds, the name of the mosque and the city). The third, the Masjid Al-Haram, is identified by its location in Medina and its role as the burial place of the Prophet. The information conveyed about these floats is presumably for non-Muslims.

Indeed, a significant characteristic of the Muslim World Day Parade that contrasts with other parades is the visual importance and legibility of banners and signs. Parading banners or carrying the word of Islam becomes the parade's most noteworthy feature and one that points, at the same time, to the omission of other classic parade entertainments: scantily clad females, women on display in floats, dancers, and so forth. Signage identifies specific Islamic organizations and sites unknown to the spectators, who thus acquire knowledge of New York's newer religious groupings by reading the unfolding documentation of the breadth of Islam in the world or

Figure 37. The 1991 Muslim World Day Parade: Lexington Avenue and Thirty-third Street becomes an outdoor mosque. Photograph by Susan Slyomovics.

even of its local co-ethnic permutations (e.g., the Islamic Society of Staten Island, the Chinese Muslim organization, and PIEDAD, the acronym for the emerging Hispanic Muslim community).

Muslim marchers also carry their message by means of banners largely in English with quotes explaining Islam and specifically targeted to non-Muslims: "THE QUR'AN IS THE GUIDENCE [*sic*] FOR ALL MANKIND" (fig. 38). Bystanders literally read ambulating sacred texts as if cinematic subtitles were translating the gestures of the marchers to the viewers. Signs proclaim, "There is no God but Allah the One, the Absolute, the Almighty, One Creator, One Humanity," followed by signs bearing the names of Jewish and Christian prophets recognized by Islam, with Muhammad as the last seal of prophecy: "Noah, Abraham, Moses, Jesus and Mohammed." Many signs emphasize Islam's inclusive embrace of figures identified with Judeo-Christian religions, all of whom are honored by Islam. Such signs are also characteristics of the Muhurram procession in Canada and the Sufi processions in Britain described elsewhere in this volume (cf. Schubel, Werbner).

The domain in which the parade takes place is a prominent New York City public space: a march southward down Lexington Avenue heading from Thirty-third Street to Twenty-third Street, a route identified with South Asian food, travel, and sari stores. Thus, Muslim space on a New

Figure 38. The 1991 Muslim World Day Parade: Banners preceding the float of the Ka'ba. Photograph by Susan Slyomovics.

York City avenue can be temporarily created by combining two contrasting forms: the ephemeral structure and format of a civic parade and the monumentality of mosques on floats during the parade (Slyomovics 1995).

"STOREFRONT" MOSQUES

Muslim civic parades highlight issues relevant to a survey of some New York City storefront mosques: the use and nature of signs, the designated space in which to hear the call to prayer, the orientation toward Mecca, and the presentation of the Muslim self to the American public.

The Queens Muslim Center

The mosques that float down Lexington Avenue may be recognizably famous structures such as the Dome of the Rock or they may be prototypical mosques in high architectural style. However, the fourth mosque float in the Muslim World Day Parade in 1990 represented the future Queens Muslim Center. This float is the point of departure for my inquiry into the nature of storefront mosques (fig. 39). The float is the only currently realized form of that mosque, which otherwise exists only as a hole in the ground in Flushing in the Borough of Queens.

Figure 39. The 1991 Muslim World Day Parade: Float of the Queens Muslim Center, with sign of the *basmala* (In the name of Allah, the compassionate, the merciful). Photograph by Susan Slyomovics.

The Queens Muslim Center was founded in June 1975 by Hanafi Sunni immigrants from Bangladesh, Pakistan, and India, in a rented apartment on Forty-first Avenue in Queens. The center is situated in the well-to-do middle-class neighborhood of Flushing, where the other predominant ethnic group is the flourishing Chinese community, estimated at seventy thousand strong. In 1977, the center was incorporated as a nonprofit tax-exempt institution, and by 1979, members had purchased a one-family house for $75,000 in cash. The adjacent house was purchased shortly afterward, and the two structures were razed for the new building. Groundbreaking for the new building took place on May 21, 1989. Photographs of the event prominently feature the presence of the imam of the Ka'ba, Sheikh Saleh bin Abdullah bin Homaid of Saudi Arabia, flanked by then Mayor Edward Koch.

While awaiting the completion of their new structure, the members meet in a two-and-a-half story, gable-roofed house located around the corner at 137–63 Kalmiah Street. The temporary quarters of the Muslim Center has room for only two hundred members. The carved wooden door leads to an enclosed porch with shelves for storing shoes and a bulletin board for written notices. From the porch, a staircase leads to the upstairs women's section. The downstairs is completely opened up, except for the kitchen wall entrance. The interior is carpeted and strips of tape orient the worshipper to Mecca. A pulpit made from kitchen cabinets and two wooden steps surmounted by a simple flat, wooden domelike ornament creates a *minbar* (pulpit or seat). *Markaz* ("The Center"), the magazine published by the Queens Muslim Center, describes a new building with room for five hundred and fifty people to pray in the main mosque, outside halls with room for one thousand six hundred people, another community hall seating four hundred, a kitchen, an Islamic school, and a gymnasium offering lessons in martial arts and the Qur'an. When it is finished, the Muslim Center will be an instance of successful transition from rented apartment to purchased house (both of them makeshift "storefront" expedients) to architecturally purposeful mosque and community center complete with designed dome, crescent moon, and minaret, the kind of mosque now typically preferred in the diaspora (cf. Haider, this volume).

The Queens Muslim Center embodies the aspirations of many, although not all, Muslim communities in New York City. These are best articulated by Levent Akbarut in "The Role of Mosques in America," an article written for *The Minaret,* a widely circulating newspaper based in East Orange County, California, and excerpted in *Markaz* (1990). Akbarut argues that the American mosque, in contrast to mosques in the countries of origin, needs to be a school, because urban schools are substandard; a community center, because the streets are dangerous; and a locus of political activity, such as voter-registration drives, so that Muslims will have a say in the decision-making processes of this country (cf. Eade, this volume). Quoting a saying, or *hadith,* from Al-Bukhari, the author acknowledges that "a mosque within the confines of four walls and a ceiling is not a requirement for a Muslim community to offer prayer, because God has made the whole earth a sanctuary for worship." Why then, he asks, did the Prophet build a mosque during the Medinan era? The answer is that the mosque functioned as a center of Islamic affairs and organization and thereby nurtured and sustained the Islamic effort. This example should be kept in mind by Muslims seeking to establish Islam in America (Akbarut 1986: 10). What the author envisions is precisely what the Muslim Center in Queens hopes to achieve: not only a mosque, but a building that unmistakably declares what it is, as opposed to the unmarked Queens house that currently functions as a mosque.

Masjid Al-Falah, Corona, Queens

This same theme is evident in the building of a second Hanafi Sunni mosque located in Corona, Queens, a lower-middle-class neighborhood populated primarily by Spanish-speaking immigrants from Central and South America. Masjid Al-Falah, at 42–12 National Street, began as a rented storefront carved out of a three-story wooden house in 1976. (The storefront is now occupied by a Pakistani restaurant, the Mi'raj, whose proprietor is active in the mosque.) The mosque membership then purchased the lot across the street, where a single-story mosque structure was completed in 1982.

Masjid Al-Falah was given a building prize by the Borough of Queens. It holds approximately seven hundred and fifty people, but there are plans for two additional stories, a dome, and a forty-foot-high minaret. Only the base of the minaret has been laid out, because a forty-foot minaret is not certain to obtain a borough building permit. Although the Queens Muslim Center has received borough permission for minarets and domes, its muezzin and the sounds of the call to prayer must remain electronically unamplified, and out of deference to the secular authorities, the Corona mosque's imam likewise uses only the power of his voice to summon worshippers.

In this case, the architectural goals derive not from the membership but from the builder, William Park, a Korean construction engineer who was at one time chief engineer of Korean construction crews in Saudi Arabia and Iraq. (The architect named on the billboard outside the project, Jone Jonassen, is in fact a "front," since a valid architect's license is needed to file the plans.) Park says his designs are based on his own impressions of the composite mosque architecture that he saw and helped to construct in the Gulf states. Thus, the architectural tastes of the oil-rich countries, filtered through the sensibilities of a Korean crew working in Saudi Arabia, have also immigrated on a smaller scale to New York.

Al-Fatih Mosque, Brooklyn

A third example of transforming structures designed for other purposes into an acceptable mosque is the Turkish Al-Fatih mosque located in the multi-ethnic Sunset Park district of Brooklyn at 5911 Eighth Avenue. Serving some five hundred and fifty members, the building, purchased in 1979, provides space, not only for prayer but also for a school on weekends, a women's organization, youth clubs, and student cultural activities. The mosque is located on a block that houses a series of Turkish businesses whose storefronts fill half of the block, among them a *halal* grocery for Middle Eastern foods and a business that acts as a cultural and linguistic broker for the local Turkish-speaking community by providing income tax, realty, air travel, and translation services. Sunset Park's ethnic diversity is evident in the adjacent block, which houses a Japanese hairdresser, a Buddhist storefront temple, and a Chinese bookstore and restaurant.

The Turkish mosque was originally a movie theater, designed, as many American movie houses have been, as a Hollywood amalgam of Orientalist-

Moorish-Arabesque fantasies (cf. Haider, this volume, fig. 6). The conversion of the movie house into a mosque reclaims the Orientalist style, invests it with new meaning, and literally reorients the building. The exterior portals have been refashioned by a Turkish carpenter, Irfan Altinbasak, to form semicircular arches. New American-made plastic-based Turkish-styled tiles are being used to replace the original Iznik tiles, dislodged one by one by the inclement New York City weather, to redecorate the exterior.

As worshippers enter on the left, they encounter the former ticket booth area, now converted to a religious bookstore, while on the right-hand side, there is a wall decorated with beautiful Turkish tiles from Iznik. Although a donor's name might be calligraphically acknowledged on mosque walls in Islamic lands, it is a distinctly American touch to set up a wall of donors: eventually each tile will carry the name of a donor who contributed to the establishment of the mosque. What was once the lobby of the movie house is now divided into sections by a series of arcades layered with marble added by the Turkish carpenter, a genuine Oriental addition to the original Oriental decor. The arcades serve no structural purpose but provide a decorative and emotional tone. Once, the Oriental touches made the movie theater feel like a luxurious, privileged space, set off from ordinary life; what they do now is "to make the interior feel like a mosque," as the Turkish leaders informed me.

The main part of the praying area is the actual screening auditorium, the back wall of which serves as the *qibla,* with a wooden *minbar* and a tiled *mihrab.* The stage where the screen once was has become a cordoned-off women's section. The Turkish mosque is thus a very powerful reinscription of interior space: American moviegoers once faced in the opposite direction to present-day Muslim worshippers, who literally turn their backs on the space where sex goddesses were once displayed on the screen, which is instead now occupied by women screened off from view.

Curvilinear, draperylike forms overhang the stage and have been highlighted and emphasized by painted designs. The carpeted interior is bare, with the exception of two model mosques. One is used as a collection box, and the second, evoking the minaret skyline of Istanbul, is placed on a raised dais; no explanations were given to me for its presence. Amplification is only permitted in the interior of the mosque. The imam expressed a wish for an exterior dome and a minaret, but here, too, there had been difficulty in obtaining the necessary building permit.

Creating Mosques: The Bronx, Brooklyn, and Queens

Several other examples illustrate the transformation of buildings into mosques. The Islamic Sunnat-ul-Jamaat, a Hanafi Sunni mosque in the Bronx at 24 Mt. Hope Street was created by English-speaking Guyanese immigrants of Indian Muslim descent. Beginning in a basement on the Grand Concourse in 1978, they purchased a three-story single-family building in 1988 for $45,000 and now have 500 paying members, among them a minority of West Africans. They now plan to buy the adjacent building in order to be able to accommodate the three to four thousand worshippers they hope to have. They have marked the entrance to their mosque as sacred space by a sign in Arabic with English transliteration: "O God, open to me the doors of your mercy."

The interior staircase separates men praying on the first floor from women on the second. Interior walls and partitions have been gutted; as in other American mosques, masking-tape guide lines run the length of the first and second floors to orient worshippers toward Mecca. On Sunday, October 7, 1990, the Prophet's birthday (Mulid an-Nabi), a celebration was combined with the annual general meeting and election of mosque officers, thus complying with New York State rules for nonprofit organizations and combining ritual and business. The members videotaped the event, not only for themselves, but for their families back in Guyana, who could thus see the building and the celebration. The four-hour celebration ended with a homecooked meal of Indian, West Indian, and West African cuisine served upstairs to the women and outside to the men.

Two true storefronts in Brooklyn exemplify modest transformations to create appropriate mosques. The Masjid Ammar Bin Yasser, at Eighth Avenue and Forty-fourth Street in Brooklyn's Sunset Park, is a storefront of a building owned and inhabited by a Palestinian family from Ramallah. Most of the two hundred and fifty members are Palestinian, Lebanese, and Jordanian. The first-floor mosque and the basement school, named after Al-Aqsa Mosque in Jerusalem, have been operating since 1986. The interior space was transformed into a mosque by cutting two large semicircular arches into the wall that formerly divided the space in two and by turning the two interior doorways that once opened into the next building into mihrabs, one signaled by a carpet, and the second more elaborately by a carpet and tiling and by the installation of a minbar. On the outside, varnished wooden slats have replaced the storefront windows. Most poignantly, signs depicting a dome and minaret stand in for the absent, prohibited structures.

The second nearby storefront mosque, Masjid Moussa Bin Omaer, is situated on Fifth Avenue near Sixty-second street in Brooklyn, an area of three-story single-family homes whose bottom floors were converted to storefronts as the street became a commercial thoroughfare. The mosque has rented space since 1987, and its interior is protected by white-painted wooden planks, now covered with graffiti. The members of the mosque, mainly Egyptians and Palestinians, did not wish me to photograph the interior because they had just begun to build and felt, therefore, that this was not yet a real mosque and should not be documented.

Similarly, one of the members of the Masjid Al-Fatima in Woodside, Queens, interrupted my interior picture-taking. The Al-Fatima mosque occupies the basement, rent-free, of a commercial building and storefront owned by a Pakistani, who runs a fleet of taxis from the rest of his building. The downstairs uses alternating strips of colored carpet to orient the worshipper to Mecca. The minbar is a simple carpeted step. The entrance to the basement mosque is again signaled by a green-painted carved dome with a sign.

The Turkish-Cypriot mosque in Morris Park, the Bronx, is the former rectory of a Protestant church. The new owners put their imprint on the front of the building by appropriating decorative techniques of Italian-American grillwork on window frames for their latticelike, nonfigurative qualities and then transforming the side square windows with cardboard inserts, two visual display techniques suggesting Islamic not Gothic arches.

Mosques have also been created from suburban homes in Queens (for example, a one-year-old Afghan mosque marked only by its discreet sign); from a five-story commercial warehouse (Masjid Al-Farouq on Atlantic Avenue in Brooklyn); from a Brooklyn Heights townhouse (Masjid Daud, established in 1936); from a commercial warehouse (by Crimean Turks, who are located in the otherwise entirely Orthodox Jewish Hasidic neighborhood of Borough Park in Brooklyn); from a former dentist's office (in the Queens neighborhood of Jamaica); and from the basement of a storefront in the Bronx. This last example may be a first stage: the basement "storefront" mosque might expand upstairs to the actual storefront and eventually be replaced by a newly constructed mosque.

It should be emphasized that Muslims and mosques in the outer boroughs of New York City are regarded by non-Muslims as positive presences in a neighborhood, even in an insular Italian-American neighborhood like Morris Park. Dan Fasolino, the local Democratic district leader, a former New York City police officer turned realtor, tightly monitors neighborhood property sales. He claims to speak for the local community when he says that immigrant Muslims are hard-working, entrepreneurial, upwardly mobile new Americans. One does well to remember this, given that one storefront mosque acquired sudden prominence in the United States: the al-Salam mosque, currently occupying the third floor of a commercial building in Jersey City (*New York Times,* September 9, 1993). This is the mosque associated with Sheik Omar Abdel-Rahman, who is alleged to have been implicated in the bombing of the World Trade Center in 1993.

CONCLUSION

A song sung by the female students of the Sunnat-ul-Jamaat mosque in the Bronx on the occasion of the Prophet's birthday (fig. 40) suggests themes in Muslim self-representation in New York City shared by mosque architecture as well. The melody was a southern railroader's dirge made famous during the folk-song revival of the early 1960s by groups such as The Journeymen, The Kingston Trio, and Peter, Paul and Mary. It also became famous under the song title "Five Hundred Miles":

> If you miss the train I'm on
> You will know that I am gone
> You can hear the whistle blow 500 miles
> 500 miles, 500 miles
> Lord I'm 500 miles away from home
> Not a shirt on my back
> Not a penny to my name
> Lord I can't go back home this-a-way

The Peter, Paul and Mary version was a worldwide best-selling record, and clearly it must have been heard in Guyana. The original American verses speak of the adventure, the poverty, and the romance of the lonesome road that never reverts back home. The new Muslim lyrics make a different use of the metaphor of life as a road: "Do you know what Islam says / It says life's a big big chance / It says that life is a far road space / Return upon rest." The words of the chorus replace "This-a-way, Lord I can't go back home this-a-way" with "A way of life, Islam is a way of life, a complete way."

The melody, a kind of architectural framework, is given, but the content is new. Similarly, a pamphlet describing the Shi'ite mosque services, which was pressed into my hand by the Iraqi imam of the Brooklyn Shi'ite temple during the bombing of Baghdad by the United States and its allies in the Gulf War, bears this legend superimposed on a map of the United States: "This is our destiny, let us make it." Muslims express their culture in new ways within the space and institutions of their larger sociopolitical world.

The movement I am charting begins with interior space gutted, transformed, and even acoustically reconfigured to Muslim sacred space, then expands outward according to the increased membership and prosperity of the community, and finally triumphantly rewrites American locales, either transiently, as for the Muslim World Day Parade, or permanently, as in the case of the new Manhattan All-Muslim mosque on Third Avenue and Ninety-sixth Street, between the Upper East Side and Spanish Harlem, officially serving all of New York City (fig. 4, this volume). While Muslims would acknowledge that a mosque requires little more than a property or

Figure 40. Young students at the Sunnat-ul-Jamaat mosque in the Bronx.
Photograph by Susan Slyomovics.

rented space, many seek such impressive buildings. One of the members of the Guyanese Bronx mosque said to me that their mosque in the Bronx, the Sunnat-ul-Jamaat, was not a real mosque. The real mosque was a picture appliqued on her purse depicting a Saudi mosque. A real mosque, she said, had a minaret and a dome and was richly decorated inside and outside. Her description in fact resembled the official All-Muslim mosque.

We can never be sure, when using architecture or vernacular architecture to "read" contemporary ethnicity, whether a given reading accurately interprets what is being said. Even though architectural phenomena are hard and objective, their meanings are soft and ambiguous. Architecture represents social meaning. Physical space also affects its occupants. For example, do Turkish worshippers in a transformed Oriental-style movie house come to think of themselves as "Oriental"?

New York City is a center of cultural production, a process that has been more laissez faire in the United States than in Europe. Ritual prayer and creating spaces for that prayer have been central activities in Muslim community life. In the Muslim World Day parade—featuring, above all, mosque replicas—and the new mosques, Muslims are finding ways to create new communities while inserting themselves into this particular state and its larger society. This is a process that leaves both sides changed.

WORKS CITED

Akbarut, Levent. 1990. "The Role of Mosques in America." *Markaz: Journal of the Muslim Center of New York* (Groundbreaking Special Number) 12: 10–12. Reprinted from *The Minaret*, November–December 1986.

Hobsbawm, Eric, and Terence Ranger, eds. 1983. *The Invention of Tradition.* New York: Cambridge University Press.

Kasinitz, Philip, and Judith Friedenberg-Herbstein. 1987. "The Puerto Rican Parade and the West Indian Carnival." In *Caribbean Life in New York City: Sociocultural Dimensions,* ed. Constance R. Sutton and Elsa M. Chaney, pp. 327–50. New York Center for Migration Study.

Kelton, Jane Gladden. 1985. "The New York City St. Patrick Day's Parade: Invention of Contention and Consensus." *Drama Review,* no. 29: 93–105.

Kugelmass, Jack. 1991. "Wishes Come True: Designing the Greenwich Halloween Parade." *Journal of American Folklore* 104: 443–65.

Rudofsky, Bernard. 1964. *Architecture without Architects: A Short Introduction to Non-Pedigreed Architecture.* Albuquerque: University of New Mexico Press.

Slyomovics, Susan. 1995. "New York City's Muslim World Day Parade." In *Nation and Migration: The Politics of Space in the South Asian Diaspora,* ed. Peter van der Veer, pp. 157–76. Philadelphia: University of Pennsylvania Press.

TWELVE

Nationalism, Community, and the Islamization of Space in London

John Eade

The focus on Islam in certain London locales has been strengthened during the past five years by national and international events such as *The Satanic Verses* controversy and the Gulf War. The appearance of mosques and community centers has visibly reminded non-Muslims of the expansion of Muslim settlers in certain urban neighborhoods. The construction and use of these buildings has been part of a process of making new demands upon public space, a process that has become embroiled with non-Muslim concerns over a visible and audible Muslim presence. Although both sides have concentrated on religion as a basis for community identity, non-Muslims have sometimes referred to other notions of belonging that are, even if implicitly, racist through their construction of a British or English nation whose cultural heritage is threatened by Muslim "outsiders."

In the debates described below, the same Muslims who took sides over religious issues had previously united in other contexts around other symbols of identity—as Bangladeshis, for example (see Eade 1989, 1990, 1991, 1992). Although it is not surprising that a Muslim identity has been preeminent in conflicts over mosques and other Islamic spaces, that identity has, in general, been emphasized in recent years, rather than secular, nationalist identities. Non-Muslim opponents, meanwhile, have developed notions of belonging based on an urban, secular, national heritage sometimes linked to a "Christian tradition," a process Bloul refers to as dual ethnicization (cf. Bloul, this volume). These attempts to co-opt Christianity in an exclusive formulation of local and national belonging have, ironically, been repudiated by at least some representatives of the established church. The debate over the Muslim presence in London has operated across local, national, and international levels. The process has encouraged people on both sides to prioritize certain identities as authentic.

TOWER HAMLETS AND THE ESTABLISHMENT OF MOSQUES

The borough of Tower Hamlets adjoins the City of London, the famous square mile of international high finance. Tower Hamlets has until recently been a predominantly working-class area heavily dependent on the docks and associated industries, as well as the garment trade, brewing, paper manufacture, furniture, and other specialized crafts. The borough has been intimately associated with the settlement of overseas settlers—Calvinist Protestant Huguenot silk weavers during the seventeenth century; Irish Catholics during the eighteenth century and the first half of the nineteenth; Russian and Polish Jews, as well as Chinese, at the end of the nineteenth century. More recently, the area has attracted settlers from Malta, Cyprus, the Caribbean, Somalia, and, most significantly, Bangladesh. Today, Bangladeshis constitute by far the largest ethnic minority in Tower Hamlets—according to the 1991 Census, they comprised 22.9 percent of the population, or 36,900. In some western wards, the proportion of Bangladeshis ranges from 30 to over 75 percent.[1]

The establishment of mosques in the borough has been heavily influenced by these Sunni, Hanafi Bangladeshis. Not surprisingly, the well-established mosques are based in the western and central wards, which form the heartland of the "Muslim community." The first building to be used for congregational worship, the East London Mosque, was on the Commercial Road near the docks. The mosque served Bengali lascars who had jumped ship during the interwar years and stayed on in Britain, finding work in Midlands manufacturing, traveling as peddlers, setting up the first "Indian restaurants," and working in London's major hotels (see Adams 1987).

Like so many mosques across the country, the East London Mosque was initially based in private accommodation. However, during 1965 it moved to a purpose-built construction nearby on Whitechapel Road. The new center provided facilities for a large congregation, as well as a bookshop, school, administrative offices, shops, living accommodation, and funeral service (cf. Haider, Slyomovics, this volume). During the past five years, the mosque's prominent location and the diverse activities within its walls have enabled its leaders to gain a high profile, at least among non-Muslim outsiders such as central and local government officials, politicians, teachers, and welfare workers.

A second mosque, now known rather grandly as the London Great Mosque (Jamme Masjid), uses a building on Brick Lane, Spitalfields, that symbolizes the area's intimate association with overseas settlers. The building was constructed by the Huguenots for religious worship and opened in 1742. It was later used as a Methodist chapel, and in 1895 it was leased to an ultra-orthodox Jewish society, the Machkizei Hadtha, which worked among the rapidly expanding population of Russian and Polish Jews. During the 1970s, the no-longer-used synagogue was bought by a group of Bangladeshi businessmen to use for congregational prayers. Inside, the building was still recognizably an eighteenth-century Protestant chapel, with the original gallery and wall paneling intact, although in a poor state of repair.

The two mosques developed contrasting and competing styles, whose origins lay in divergences between religious leaders during the late nineteenth century in British India. The Brick Lane Mosque recruited mullahs aligned with what is known as the "Barelvi" orientation, which emphasized the role of custom and shrines. Religious leaders at the East London Mosque, on the other hand, were influenced by the rival "Deobandi" teachings, which fostered a more self-consciously reformist tradition and criticized devotions around Sufi shrines (Metcalf 1982).

The differences between the mosques were also deepened by political cleavages. The Brick Lane Mosque was closely associated with the Bangladesh government and the Bangladesh High Commission in central London—an association celebrated by official visits to the mosque by President Hussain Muhammad Ershad during the 1980s. The East London Mosque, with its more "scriptural" religious style, was more closely aligned with Arab states in the Middle East and with Pakistan. King Fahd of Saudi Arabia, for example, contributed £1,100,000 of the £2,000,000 total cost of building the new center, while ambassadors from Saudi Arabia and Egypt were members of the mosque's management committee.

Different strategies toward links with community organizations further sharpened the differences between the mosques. Religious leaders at the Brick Lane Mosque did not establish many ties with Bangladeshi community groups and non-Muslim outsiders partly because that role was performed by the Bangladesh Welfare Association (BWA). The offices of the BWA were in a neighboring building, and its business leaders played a key role in the establishment and the management of the mosque. The leaders of the East London Mosque, with no such community organization as ally, encouraged Muslim youth groups on the one hand and international organizations on the other. The East London Mosque established a close alliance with the Young Muslim Organization (YMO), for example, which rented offices in an adjoining street. The YMO was linked to the Da'wat ul Islam, a missionary organization based in Bangladesh and Pakistan but active across Britain. The East London Mosque's funeral director and one of its oldest members was involved in another missionary organization, the Tablighi Jama'at, which occupied a former synagogue in nearby St. Katharine's ward, while the secretary of the East London Mosque's management committee was a leading member of the Council of Mosques U.K. and Eire, a national pressure group supported by Saudi Arabia and located in central London.

The organizations and individuals associated with the East London Mosque gave the new purpose-built center a range of contacts at local and more global levels that were more cosmopolitan than the predominantly Bangladeshi ties established by the Brick Lane Mosque through the BWA. Furthermore, the East London Mosque encouraged a more literary approach toward Islam through its bookshop, which stocked devotional and educational books in English, Bengali, Urdu, and Arabic. The bookshop attracted the interest of non-Muslims from schools and colleges, who were also encouraged to visit the mosque. The custodians of the Brick Lane Mosque, in contrast, have made no effort to encourage non-Muslim visitors, although outsiders are welcome to come and go as they please. (The London Tablighi mosque, in further contrast, welcomes outsiders only once a week for the evening public meeting held in its building. See Metcalf, this volume.)

Although other mosques had emerged during the settlement of Bangladeshis in Tower Hamlets, the Brick Lane Great Mosque and the East London Mosque were the main focus of public debates about the presence of Islam in the borough during the 1980s. Those debates entailed factional struggles among Bangladeshi community leaders and organizations, as well as concerns of outsiders such as local government planners, politicians, businessmen, and residents.

THE BRICK LANE GREAT MOSQUE AND ARCHITECTURAL CONSERVATION

The Brick Lane Mosque occupies an eighteenth-century site, "listed as a building of architectural and historical interest" (fig. 41).[2] It is located in a conservation area that began to be "gentrified" during the 1980s—a process that entailed the "decanting" of Bangladeshi garment factories, shops, and residents and their replacement by well-heeled white owner-occupiers, City offices, and up-market shops. These changes, largely to the west of Brick Lane, rapidly transformed the character of the area known as Spitalfields. For some white outsiders, the mosque building was a physical expression of both a local English heritage and a gentrified, Georgian present. For the Muslim congregation, the mosque's main attraction lay in its proximity to their council estate homes. For the mosque management committee, the building, while convenient, was a source of concern because of its need for renovations consistent with Muslim ritual requirements.

The mosque committee did little to change or Islamize the exterior, merely posting a list of prayer times on its main door and a large notice in

Figure 41. Brick Lane Mosque, Spitalfields, London. Photograph by John Eade.

Bengali, Arabic, and English on the building adjoining the former chapel. The exterior was recently refurbished and still appears to the non-Muslim visitor to be a plainly decorated eighteenth-century chapel.

Internally, however, the committee undertook substantial modification, reasonable to mosque members but offensive to local conservationists. The changes were stimulated by the 1985 visit of President Ershad and subsequent contributions from the Bangladesh government to finance a new floor to accommodate an additional six hundred worshippers. The refurbishment entailed the elimination of the dilapidated gallery and wall panelling.

No planning permission was required from the local authority for these renovations. Conservationists, however, were quick to protest. The architectural historian Dan Cruickshank, features editor of *Architects' Journal,* a prestigious national weekly, and a leading member of the local conservation movement, was quoted in the local newspaper as saying: "What is so terrible is the way in which it was done. A lot of people are renovating houses in that area and they saw panelling being smashed. It was carried out brutally." The president of the mosque management committee, however, insisted that concerns for the historical character of the building were in fact taken into account: "We are taking out a gallery, but the historical things are not being touched, they are being preserved." Most important, he explained that the extra space provided by the refurbishment would alleviate a situation where "people are praying in the streets outside now" (*East London Advertiser,* October 17, 1986).

Both sides in this exchange appeared to agree on the importance of conservation of historical sites, but they differed over standards and procedures. Dan Cruickshank's protest expressed the concern of the locally influential Spitalfields Historic Buildings Trust, of which he was "an indefatigable member" (Girouard et al. 1989: x), which condemned changes of a sort that at an earlier period would have attracted little public comment. Internal modifications of the Brick Lane site by its Jewish occupants during the late nineteenth century, for instance, do not appear to have caused concern (see *Jewish Chronicle,* July 3, 1973). Now, however, the conservationist lobby clearly regards the Huguenot refugees' chapel as a vital expression of an indigenous urban culture and landscape. Whatever may have happened in the past, a wide constituency considers both the exterior and interior of the building as part of the local heritage.

The dispute highlights a fundamental problem at the heart of the conservationist project. What should be preserved as an authentic expression of England's urban heritage? Raphael Samuel, a social historian and local resident, has made a powerful critique of the Spitalfields conservation process:

> Is it a real historical past which provides the point of reference—or an imaginary one, of grandiose or gracious living? Where, if anywhere, is the line to be drawn between repair and reproduction, the authentically old and the contrived replica? . . . What alterations and additions are to be respected— the 1780s fanlight? the 1850s fireplace? the 1920s bracket lamp? the 1940s radiator?—and what removed as alien grafts? (Samuel in Girouard et al. 1989: 161)

The mosque management committee succeeded in solving the problem of the overcrowding during religious festivals while avoiding drawing further attention to the building's Islamic function. It thus deflected what would presumably have been an even stronger reaction from outsiders.

The changes taking place in Spitalfields call into question the continuing effectiveness of this low-key strategy. The movement of City businesses and wealthy owner-occupiers into the ward has been accompanied by the migration of Bangladeshi firms and residents from West Spitalfields as the garment trade has shifted its center toward the south and east of Brick Lane. Bangladeshis still dominate council estates in the central and eastern areas of the ward, but they have begun to search in larger numbers for employment outside Spitalfields. The industrial and commercial character of the ward is being radically changed by forces beyond Bangladeshi control (see Forman 1989; Samuel in Girouard et al. 1989). Indeed, Samuel even speaks of "a holocaust which is about to wipe out their [Bangladeshi] tracks": a transformation that conservationists have unwittingly encouraged and that now "threatens to engulf Spitalfields in a sea of Georgian fakes" (Samuel in Girouard et al. 1989: 170). Of course, the leaders of the mosque management committee may well believe that they can use this process to their material advantage by selling out and moving to an imposing, purpose-built center that might rival the East London Mosque. Through such a move, they would be able, perhaps, to escape the limitations of the present site and the debate about conservation and urban heritage. In the process, they might, of course, exchange one set of problems for another, as the experience of the East London Mosque in fact suggests.

Members of the mosque defended the Islamization of the site on the opponents' own terms, insisting on their respect for "historical things" and denying "brutality." The debate was, however, about more than wood panels. Architectural conservation is part of a more general, ongoing discussion about what it means to belong to the nation, whether defined as "England" or "Britain." This discussion incorporates questions about the plural character of that nation and the part played by "ethnic minorities" in shaping that plural character as Britain engages in a rapidly changing Europe. If the former Huguenot chapel needed to be carefully preserved as a particular expression of a national heritage, how did that "sacred" imperative relate to another sacred imperative, the desire of those from an ethnic minority to adapt the building for ritual purposes? Issues of cultural pluralism have been equally at stake at the rival East London Mosque, whose leaders adopted a strikingly different strategy toward representing their Islamic presence in the borough.

THE EAST LONDON MOSQUE, THE CALL TO PRAYER, AND URBAN "NOISE"

A London firm of architects designed the East London Mosque with Middle East models in mind. Its tall minaret is similar to those overlooking the "holy of holies," the black rock, or Ka'ba, in Mecca; its golden dome and high main entrance accord with popular concepts of what a mosque should look like (fig. 42). The mosque is intended to make a visual claim on "public space." The mosque committee was determined from the outset, moreover, to remind local people of the building's religious function as loudly as possible. As one of the few mosques in Britain permitted to broadcast calls to prayer (*azan*), the mosque soon found itself at the center of a public debate about "noise pollution" when local non-Muslim residents began to protest. The issue was eagerly taken up by the media at the national level, with reports in the *Daily Mail* (March 4, 1986) and the *Daily Star* (April 14, 1986). The controversy was fueled locally by an item in the

Figure 42. East London Mosque, Whitechapel Road, London. Photograph by John Eade.

weekly *East London Advertiser* that claimed that the mosque's leaders wanted to increase both the volume of calls to prayer and their frequency from two to five daily, including "one in the early morning" (May 2, 1986). According to the article, the mosque request was supported by local Muslims. A "devout Muslim" in a neighboring street, for example, was reported as claiming that he could not hear the azan. He also wanted the call to be made five times "like in other Muslim countries" (ibid).

The reference to "other Muslim countries" indicated that some local Muslims did not locate the issue within a debate concerning "noise pollution." Rather, they regarded it as an audible expression of their Islamic presence in the neighborhood, as well as of their links with the Muslim world at a more global level. Some felt, moreover, that opponents of the azan were in fact racist. Some letter writers to the *East London Advertiser* certainly expressed an intolerance associated with racial prejudice. Thus a writer, responding to a mosque representative, who mentioned the noise of local church bells, declared: "What bells? You hardly ever hear them these days. I'm sure I would sooner listen to the tolling of church bells than someone screaming out words I cannot understand and don't want to" (*East London Advertiser*, April 25, 1986). The reference to "screaming" supported derogatory images of Muslim fanaticism, while a clear distinction was made between acceptable and unacceptable noise. Church bells were preferable because they were an expression of "our" cultural tradition—a tradition audibly challenged by the broadcasting of alien formulae. As in the debate on conservation, the conflict provided an occasion for constructing a definition of what was authentically English.

Yet this highly exclusive presentation was rejected by those whose churches were the symbols of the English national heritage. A group of local Church of England clerics wrote to the *East London Advertiser* (April 25, 1986) in support of the azan: "We have no complaint against their 'calls to prayer' and given all the other sounds of traffic, sirens, bells, people, trains and life in general [we] think that two short periods each day . . . are entirely reasonable." The letter moved the discussion away from different types of noise to noise in general. Since the East London Mosque was located on a busy main road linking the City of London to the vast metropolitan eastern sprawl, the azan made only a brief, if novel, contribution to the buzz of inner city life. Of course, what the clergy considered "reasonable"—two calls to prayer during the working day—fell far short of the demand by the Muslim correspondent for the complete cycle of azan both day and night "like in other Muslim countries." The borough council, the source of permission to the East London Mosque, had not extended that right to the other mosques in Tower Hamlets. Now, in response to the public furor over the broadcasts, it proved unmoved by arguments favoring the azan and neither extended the right to the other mosques nor allowed the East London Mosque to implement the full daily sequence of calls to prayer.

The opening of the highly visible and unmistakably Islamic East London Mosque thus very quickly resulted in a dispute articulated as "noise pollution" in a crowded inner-city neighborhood and focused by local government officials on presumably "objective" criteria, such as an agreed level of acceptable noise. Again, however, other issues were at stake. The letter writer who criticized the broadcasting of azan as alien, yet accepted (while noting its virtual disappearance) the tolling of church bells, was motivated by cultural exclusivism. This exclusivism was ironic given the ethnic history of Tower Hamlets and doubly so since it made the church bell a symbol of indigenous culture for an area whose predominantly working-class population had been either indifferent to religion or Nonconformists, Roman Catholics, and Jews. The only non-Muslim religious defenders of azan to find a voice in the local press were Anglican clerics, who were evidently unmoved by the nostalgic appeal to a symbol associated with them.

The controversy about "noise pollution" entailed issues of what was culturally acceptable. The leaders of the East London Mosque wanted to establish the azan, and the Muslim settlers, as part of the local culture. To this end, they were far more willing to engage openly in local politics and media controversy than their co-religionists at the Brick Lane mosque. Yet local politicians largely ignored their interests in order to reassure critics of azan. There are clearly powerful external constraints on Muslim self-expression in Spitalfields, as well as in other neighborhoods within the borough.

Among Muslims themselves, one might note, the new East London Mosque stimulated another debate, in this case about the building's exotic design. (Some white residents may also have reacted to the new building on these grounds but there was no public debate.) K. Manzoor, features editor of a new journal, *MuslimWise,* argued that new mosques in general showed "little respect for the time-honored Muslim tradition of appreciating indigenous art forms in the attempt to 'Islamize' them . . . when the consummation of the 'Islamic' and the 'regional vernacular styles' took place it gave birth to new and exciting art forms that practically reflected the beauty of both." He proceeded to exonerate "indigenous non-Muslims who look in horror at the dome-capped buildings we are erecting as they are as alien to them as they are to Islam. A good example of such monstrosity is the East London Mosque in Whitechapel. It is a cold, characterless, and impractical 'wordprocessor,' which is neither aesthetically nor spiritually attractive" (*MuslimWise,* December 1989). Manzoor included the most imposing and celebrated Islamic center in London—the Islamic Cultural Centre in Regent's Park—in this charge.

Another Muslim critique questioned any concern with buildings at all. Indeed, according to Hajji Taslim Ali, the East London Mosque's funeral director, who also undertakes missionary work for the Tablighi Jama'at based in a former synagogue nearby, the attention paid to material objects such as mosques represents so much wasted effort. In his 1989 talk to a group of my students in the mosque's prayer hall, he claimed that it was not important to have a beautiful building to pray in—rather one had to be a Muslim "from the heart." As he showed us around the center, he drew attention, with a wry smile, to the building's various defects and the costs involved in correcting them.

This issue was articulated at the Aga Khan Awards for architecture— meant to identify buildings that utilize a Muslim tradition yet relate to their specific context—held in Cairo during October 1989. The distinguished Egyptian architect Abdel Wahed el-Wakil discussed the "principle of sacred architecture" in the context of Islamic architecture and the "growing spiritual lack and need in the West." At this point, a Moroccan economist, Professor M. Emandjara, "who had been swelling up with outrage finally blew up" and accused "El-Wakil of trying to transplant Western and Judaeo-Christian ideas about 'sacred art' into Islam. The whole point was that Islamic architecture was not sacred; the mosque was just a place for praying and teaching" (*Observer,* October 22, 1989). His, however, is a minority voice.

Mosques have clearly become places not only for prayer but for representation of the Muslim presence. The mosques in London's East End have, in this regard, stimulated a wide-ranging debate. The debate implicitly addresses the symbolic significance of Islamic buildings in a predominantly non-Muslim country. Whether Islamizing a historic building or using a purpose-built center, Muslims have found themselves severely constrained by local economic and political forces beyond their control. Yet they did succeed in creating mosque congregations and, in the East London Mosque, a site that physically and audibly asserts the Muslim presence. Muslims outside the core areas of settlement in London have, however, faced forces arrayed against the establishment of an Islamic presence that sometimes proved more formidable.

DAWOODI BOHRAS IN WEST LONDON: FINDING A HOME

The borough of Ealing possesses a much smaller Muslim population than its East End counterpart.[3] Most Muslim settlers reside in the Southall area and originally came from Indian Punjab, Pakistan, and East Africa. The Sunni majority established two mosques during the late 1960s and early 1970s in Old Southall, and, during the early 1980s, the small business community of Dawoodi Bohras (a Shiʿa sect whose heartland lies in Gujarat) took over a former Jewish youth club in neighboring Boston Manor for its religious and cultural activities. The Bohra activities triggered off a series of events that exposed the racist nature of some white residents' opposition to Muslim centers.

The Bohras' use of the former youth club, which they renamed Mohammedi Park, soon led to protests from white neighbors about noise and parking during religious celebrations. At informal meetings between senior Conservative and Labour councilors and planning officials, it was agreed that the Bohras could use the site for social and religious functions. This consensus was, however, destroyed by pressure from white residents, who were supported by their local councilor (the chief whip of the Conservative majority group).

A new Labour administration took over the case after the 1986 elections and offered to buy the Boston Manor site in exchange for a more appropriate location. The Dawoodi Bohras eventually chose a disused industrial site in Northolt, several miles north of the Southall area. The site had been derelict for over five years and was spacious enough to allay any objections about noise and parking. The Bohras proposed to build a center for religious, educational, and social functions, as well as a number of houses—once again an indication of the wide range of activities associated with Muslim religious buildings in the diaspora in contrast to most South Asian mosques.

The plan again met with fierce opposition from white residents, however, as well as from local businesses using the industrial estate, their employees, and at least one real estate agent. Protests by white people at public meetings were so intense that there were councilors, officials, and Bohra representatives who left feeling physically intimidated. Nonetheless, in December 1988, the Bohras were given planning permission to develop the site.

Local press coverage of the Northolt development dispute made clear the racism in the opposition. A garbled report titled "Islamic Ghetto Worries" referred to a planning committee report that described local objections "to the 'alien' nature of the plan" and described the local claims about the area's character: "Northolt is a 'garden suburb' and should not become another Southall. This is an alien development—an Islamic ghetto—and will lead to a racial imbalance. Integration, not separation, is required" (*Ealing Gazette,* November 25, 1988, p. 27).

The report sharply distinguished a green and pleasant Northolt and a ghettolike Southall. Northolt was purportedly at risk of becoming an alien "Islamic ghetto." The opponents saw themselves not as racist but as proponents of a racially balanced, integrated society. As in the debates concerning conservation and noise, opponents believed themselves to be taking the moral high ground.

Yet hostile local residents in fact sought a racial imbalance in Northolt to keep the area exclusively or at least predominantly white. A local real estate agency colluded in fears that nonwhite settlement in Northolt would lead to a fall in property values by displaying a poster exhorting people to sign a local petition against the plan. The National Front and other ultra-rightist groups long active in Northolt also encouraged white hostility to "alien" settlers, and their supporters attended the public meetings that experienced serious violence. White protesters made the familiar claim that they were the ones suffering discrimination. As one protester put it: "They [the council] have called us racist but we are the ones being discriminated against. The council has treated us as second-class citizens" (*Ealing Gazette,* December 2, 1988, p. 7).

The local Labour leader, accused of betrayal (*Ealing Gazette,* November 18, 1988, p. 4), insisted that the Bohra proposal be dealt with in the context of bureaucratic and legal procedures. Again, the Anglican minister of the church distanced himself from local opponents to the Bohra scheme, saying, "The proper Christian response is to make welcome those from different cultural and religious backgrounds coming into the area" (*Ealing Gazette,* November 25, 1988, p. 27)—despite the fact that the residential association fighting the proposal had used a view of the church in its logo. Many local white residents ignored this liberal plea for tolerance and have continued to fight the redevelopment of the Northolt site through letters of protest to politicians and the *Ealing Gazette* and public demonstrations, particularly after the Conservatives regained control of the borough council in May 1989. A typical argument was that the mosque was proposed "on a job site in an area of high unemployment." The Muslims were, moreover, outsiders, since "very few" Dawoodi Bohras "live locally and [they] have made it clear that they do not wish to be part of our close and friendly community" (*Ealing Gazette,* April 24, 1991).

Since I live very close to the Burhani Centre in Fulham, I have been able to observe local reactions to the Bohra presence in a different location. The center is close to a private housing estate in a predominantly white neighborhood, and judging by the odd broken window, it has not escaped damage in a relatively quiet locality. However, during the summers of 1989–92, when the Bohras used neighboring secondary schools for the kind of lengthy and lively celebration that caused so much hostility in Boston Manor, the events passed by without adverse local comment. Their presence in the Labour-controlled borough of Hammersmith and Fulham did not play a significant role in local politics, although it might well have done had they envisaged the kind of major redevelopment proposed in Northolt.

The position by early 1995 is that the development of the site is in full swing. Most of the main building has been constructed and the shells of the surrounding residential block are also complete. The High Court decision in November 1989 appears to have been decisive, and the Bohras' strategy of working through the planning and legal process has been successful. The public protests, the ministrations of Conservative councilors, and legal action by Gallaghers, a tobacco company, which used an adjacent site on Rowdell Road, delayed the scheme for several years, but the sect has eventually been allowed to go ahead with building what was advertised as an "Arabic Academy Campus Project."

Although local opposition has not prevented the Bohras from eventually developing the site, developments at a more global level have conspired to halt the completion of the project. Difficulties in collecting adequate resources have meant that there has been sufficient money available only to fund the completion of the foundations and the shell of the mosque. Work at the site ground to a halt during 1992, and the available money has been spent on the refurbishment of the Fulham Burhani Centre (fig. 43). In 1992, I met the leader of the Bohra community, who expressed satisfaction that at least the first stage of the Northolt development had been completed. The next step was to engage in a vigorous campaign among Bohras across the country to raise the millions of pounds needed to complete the grandiose Northolt scheme and to bring the Syedna, the leader of the Bohra community worldwide, from India to open the Arabic Academic Campus in full pomp and majesty. As of spring 1996, the site

Figure 43. The Burhani Centre in Fulham, London. Photograph by John Eade.

has not been completed, but its rose-pink domes and minarets are now visible; town houses have been built close by for community members; and the Prince of Wales, wearing cap and shawl, has planted a ceremonial tree (*Guardian*, March 20, 1996).

ISLAM AND DEFINITIONS OF COMMUNITY IN LOCAL POLITICAL ARENAS

The disputes described here represent a shift in the local politics of Tower Hamlets and Ealing. In the early 1980s, "white," "black" and Asian activists united to seek community needs defined in secular and class terms—housing, education, jobs, and amenities. Now we find leaders focused on a range of needs specific to Muslims and establishing Muslim ritual and community space. The defeat of the Labour Party in the 1986 borough election and the abolition of the Greater London Council and Inner London Education Authority were massive blows to the alliance between secular Bangladeshi activists and white radicals. Meanwhile, the growing shift to the deployment of an Islamic vocabulary in Bangladesh politics, particularly under Ershad, also fed into this new orientation.

In East London, debates in the local newspaper made Islam more visible to all. The debates strengthened the position of Bangladeshi activists who had criticized Bangladeshi Labour Party candidates in the 1986 borough elections for ignoring Islamic issues. Those claiming to represent "the Bangladeshi community" were under increasing pressure to declare at least a formal concern for the provision of Islamic facilities, as well as the championing of the rights of Bangladeshis in the areas of public houses, state education, jobs, and amenities.

In Ealing, the public debate about the use of space for Islamic purposes did not involve substantial numbers of local Muslim residents. The Dawoodi Bohras, a minute Shi'a sect, were scattered over the metropolis and possessed no local political power base. Throughout the controversy, they refused to be drawn into making any public statements and relied on the operation of legal and bureaucratic structures and their informal links with powerful local councilors. It was therefore white activists rather than Muslims who used Islam, describing it as an alien invasion of local space and calling on Labour and Conservative political leaders to respond to what the activists claimed were the interests of local (white) residents.

Despite the differences between the social and political dynamics in two London boroughs, the media debates revealed a common theme—Islam as an alien threat to an indigenous, non-Muslim urban community and culture. The theme could be defined in terms of architectural heritage, the design of a building, or the call to prayer, and could engage both well-heeled gentrifiers and working-class "Cockneys" in a defense of "tradition."

With the appearance of more purpose-built mosques and the articulation of "Islamic" needs in London and other urban areas, the kinds of issues described in this chapter may well become more common, and "Islam as alien threat" may well play a more significant role in local urban politics. The Islamization of local urban space is only one element in the public debate in Britain's media about Islam, which *The Satanic Verses* controversy raised to a national level. Yet as the intensity of the feelings raised by the publication of Salman Rushdie's book fades and Iran tentatively approaches Western powers, the public, physical manifestation of Islam at a local level continues to remind the non-Muslim majority in London and elsewhere of the Muslim presence and to provoke among some members of that majority at least a conscious reflection on local community and culture—a reflection linked to the articulation of identity, community, and culture at other levels, in particular to what it means to be "English" or "British" at the national level. As Bloul (this volume) suggests in the French case, there has been a process of double ethnicization here, of "Englishness" on the one side and "Islam" on the other.

Two points must be stressed: (1) the process is partial, and many people do not share in it, and (2) Islamic identity expresses itself in ways that are new, using new arguments (whether those of conservation or of British legal processes) and creating new kinds of institutions, such as centers. The mosque itself takes on new meanings, thanks in part to the political debates around its establishment and use in London. Outsiders unwittingly encourage those Muslims who wish to give the mosque, in Emandjara's view, "a significance it shouldn't have." The local political arena therefore plays a key role in the construction of a range of meanings associated with being "Muslim" in London today—meanings that engage ethnicity, "race," class, and national ideology, as well as Islam.

NOTES

This essay is partly based on an earlier paper of mine, "The Political Articulation of Community and the Islamisation of Space," in *Religion and Ethnicity: Minorities and Social Change in the Metropolis,* ed. R. Barot (Kampen, Netherlands: Kok Pharos, 1993).

1. The Census confirms earlier estimates showing the rapid increase of the Bangladeshi population during the 1980s and its concentration in the western wards (*Census Update,* October 1992). See, e.g., Tower Hamlets 1987; Rhodes and Nabi 1992.

2. See the *East London Advertiser,* November 27, 1970. The newspaper noted then that the alteration of the interior was already an issue. The reporter claimed that the "Pakistanis wanted to pull down the three inner galleries and Tuscan columns to provide the open space needed for their services." However, it was also noted that the Greater London Council was "unlikely to favour this alteration to such an historic building." Significantly, perhaps, the refurbishment took place after the demise of the Greater London Council.

3. Local estimates claimed that of approximately 40,000 South Asian / East African settlers in a borough of over a quarter of a million residents, only about 5,000 were Muslims. Two mosques had been established in Old Southall, one of which has recently been refurbished and expanded in a more demonstrably Islamic mode.

WORKS CITED

Adams, Caroline, ed. 1987. *Across Seven Seas and Thirteen Rivers: Life Stories of Pioneer Sylhetti Settlers in Britain.* London: THAP Books.

Budd, Leslie, and Sam Whimster, eds. 1992. *Global Finance and Urban Living: A Study of Metropolitan Change.* London: Routledge.

Census Update. 1992. Research and Strategy Group, Tower Hamlets.

Eade, John. 1989. *The Politics of Community: The Bangladeshi Community in East London.* Aldershot: Avebury.

———. 1990. "Nationalism and the Quest for Authenticity." *New Community* 16, 4: 493–503.

———. 1991. "The Political Construction of Class and Community: Bangladeshi Political Leadership in Tower Hamlets." In *Black and Ethnic Leaderships: The Cultural Dimensions of Political Action,* ed. Pnina Werbner and Muhammad Anwar. London: Routledge.

————. 1992. "Quests for Belonging." In *Where You Belong: Government and Black Culture,* ed. Alrick Cambridge and Stefan Feuchtwang. Aldershot: Avebury.

Forman, Charlie. 1989. *Spitalfields: A Battle for Land.* London: Hilary Shipman.

Game, Anne. 1991. *Undoing the Social: Towards a Deconstructive Sociology.* Milton Keynes: Open University Press.

Girouard, Mark, Dan Cruickshank, and Samuel Raphael. 1989. *The Saving of Spitalfields.* London: Spitalfields Historic Buildings Trust.

Metcalf, Barbara. 1982. *Islamic Revival in British India: Deoband, 1860–1900.* Princeton, N.J.: Princeton University Press.

Rhodes, Chris, and Nurun Nabi. 1992. "Brick Lane: A Village Economy in the Shadow of the City?" In *Global Finance and Urban Living: A Study of Metropolitan Change,* ed. Leslie Budd and Sam Whimster. London: Routledge.

Rushdie, Salman. 1989. *The Satanic Verses.* New York: Viking.

Shields, Rob. 1990. *Places on the Margin: Alternative Geographies of Modernity.* London: Routledge.

Short, John Rennie. 1991. *Imagined Country: Environment, Culture and Society.* London: Routledge.

Tower Hamlets. 1987. *Tower Hamlets Health Inquiry Report.* London: Tower Hamlets Community Health Council.

Werbner, Pnina, and Muhammad Anwar, eds. 1991. *Black and Ethnic Leaderships: The Cultural Dimensions of Political Action.* London: Routledge.

THIRTEEN

Engendering Muslim Identities

Deterritorialization and the Ethnicization Process in France

Rachel Bloul

Thanks to the massive postcolonial immigration that has taken place in recent years, France is today a state in which people are increasingly concerned with their collective identities as either "Maghrebi"/"Muslim" or "French." It is important to see that this creation of politicized ethnic identities exists on both sides, not just that of the minorities. The process of "ethnicization" involves linking a specific population to distinctive cultural characterisics. The collective control of female behavior and the use of feminine representations is central to this process. In this regard, both French and Maghrebi men have contrasted the image of veiled Muslim women with that of presumed-emancipated second-generation "Beurettes" (the daughters of Maghrebi immigrants, called "Beurs"), notably in recent controversies over the right of Muslim schoolgirls to wear hair coverings in class. Some Maghrebi men have used this contrast to assert the need to protect Muslim interests, while some French have used the same images to arouse fears of the Muslim population. These issues have then become involved in contests for control over the public sphere.

The focus in this chapter is deliberately on men. Although women, and most notably Beurettes, have been involved in Maghrebi collective action in France,[1] they have been relatively invisible in contrast to men, who create a Muslim collective identity as generically male. Moreover, Frenchwomen are heard from but rarely in most public controversies. Men monopolized the earlier (1989–90) debate over the "veil."[2] This situation is not unique, since it is possible to argue that cultural communities are generally "communities of males" (Appadurai 1990: 19). In the case of the Maghrebis/Muslims, this process of "engendering" ethnicity can be seen as an understandably intense response to the situation of a population no longer defined by their identification with a particular territorially defined entity.

A frequently heard comment, and self-definition, of Maghrebi men goes like this: "We are Muslims: our women don't [go out alone, wear lipstick, etc.], unlike Frenchwomen, who do." Frenchmen contribute to this claim to distinctiveness by making exactly the same distinctions about Muslim women. Maghrebi men who make such arguments are more likely to be involved in Muslim organizations with international connections and to disapprove of French government attempts to encourage a "French Islam." They are thus more directly involved in an arena that makes issues of gender central in building a collective identity. As Helie-Lucas (1994) argues, there, too, men not only turn women into markers of collective identity but also make them the very stakes of cultural competition. In so doing, they claim to be able to speak for Islam (Bloul, forthcoming).

What is the relationship of Maghrebi "deterritorialization" to this use of "sexual politics"? As Arjun Appadurai (1990) argues, the increasingly integrated economic world-system and the dominance of Western media may not in the end be creating worldwide homogenization. "Global culture flows" may well create differences and an intensified sense of criticism or attachment to home politics in displaced populations. In this context, migrant communities, assaulted by the desires and fantasies depicted by the mass media, strive "to reproduce the family-as-microcosm of culture." In these circumstances, "the honor of women becomes not just an armature of stable systems of cultural reproduction" but also increasingly "a surrogate for the identity of embattled communities of males" (Appadurai 1990: 19). This may produce violence against women, who become victims of men's sense of displaced identity.[3]

DIVERSITY AMONG MUSLIMS IN FRANCE

The self-understanding of Maghrebi migrants and second-generation Beur men is varied and complex, even if all see themselves primarily as Muslim actors in a "Christian" (Nasrani), or white (Gauri) country. It is critical to recognize this complexity before generalizing about the transition to gendered (and twin) ethnic identities that has taken place in recent years in France.

My arguments are based on local fieldwork in 1986–87, with a return visit in 1991, coupled with an analysis of the so-called "affair of the head scarves" over the right of Muslim schoolgirls to cover their heads. I worked in Mulhouse, a middle-sized industrial town in the northeast of France. Mulhouse has a high proportion of predominantly Maghrebi migrants, who are concentrated in the poorest surrounding suburbs, typical of the semi-ghettoized enclaves of postcolonial immigration in Europe (Belbahri 1987; Berger and Mohr 1982; Castles 1984, 1986; Jourjon 1980; Miles 1982). The distinguishing characteristics of Qsarheim, the neighborhood in which I primarily worked, was its grassroots association of household heads, formed on the initiative of one local Tunisian man in 1984, under the tutelage of various French officials and "personalities," including the local mayor and the head of a housing company. Interestingly, a similar initiative was taken in the nearest Maghrebi neighborhood, Qsarstadt,[4] but there the association soon lost its impetus and became inoperative in less than a year. The French officials involved explained this in terms of Qsar-heim's "dynamism" and "will to effect changes," in contrast to Qsarstadt's "instability," "population turnover," "local rivalries," and "lack of leader-ship."

Maghrebis themselves had a different interpretation. They argued that Qsarstadt had a number (about a dozen at the time) of young, educated Maghrebi migrants, who came to Mulhouse to study in the local university and research center, and often participated in the Association des musul-mans d'Alsace et de Lorraine, a Muslim organization known by its acro-nym, AMAL. AMAL is identified in the minds of many with the Muslim Brotherhood, an Islamist movement based in Egypt. By contrast, the Qsar-heim leaders were older, more settled, much less educated, and often be-longed to mainstream Maghrebi associations organized along national lines: the Association des Algériens en Europe (AAE), the Association des travaiileurs et commerçants marocains (ATCM), and the Association franco-tunisienne (AFT). Rumor attributed the collapse of Qsarstadt's lo-cal association to infiltration by AMAL.

Each association wanted to build a leisure center under French govern-ment patronage, with the necessary funds being raised from a variety of contributors, including the town council; the housing estate; the Fonds d'action sociale (FAS) and Comité pour le logement des travailleurs immi-grés (COTRAMI), specialized national agencies of migrant welfare; and local donations. In 1987, the Qsarstadt center had been built, but it soon passed under the control of COTRAMI. AMAL, referred to by both Magh-rebis and French as the "Muslim Brothers," took the lead in expressing resentment at the takeover. This did nothing to improve Qsarstadt's repu-tation as an inhospitable politicized ghetto. By contrast, in spite of consid-erable internal difficulties (Bloul 1992), Qsarheim's association survived. Qsarheim men were quite proud of the visible improvements in the neigh-borhood, although disaffection among the local youth drastically limited their ability to effect change, especially after a leadership crisis reduced their association to near paralysis.

Nonetheless, by 1991, not only had Qsarheim been prettified, but there was also a general feeling of more prosperity. There were fewer children playing in the streets, since, I was told, parents now sent their children to the various activities organized by the town council, "even if they had to pay." More children of both sexes were encouraged in their studies and sent to university. To help with the costs, almost all mothers now worked,

mostly part-time. This last bit of news was most surprising. Four years earlier, only four married women had worked (out of eighty-four Maghrebi
families): they had tended to be younger and better educated than most,
and they were subjected to not a little criticism. All the other women stayed
at home and generally abided by the customary restrictions. In 1987, a
married woman going out alone to shop at the local market too regularly
used to raise censorious eyebrows. What had happened?

When I commented on these various changes and remarked that Qsarheim was getting to be quite undistinguishable from its French surroundings, people beamed at me and said that six or seven families had even
quit the neighborhood to build their own homes in better suburbs. Their
example had stimulated the remaining families. The generally more affluent feel was attributed to the fact that in most families, the father's salary
was now complemented by the earnings of the mother and one or two
elder siblings.

The various changes suggested quite a shift in family strategies. There
was little mention of the "dream to return," of the house to build in the
Maghreb. Instead, each family's communal effort centered on improving
their chances in France. What seemed most remarkable was the effect of
this changed perspective on women's positions. Over and over, people
drew my attention to married women's employment. Finally, they explicitly
contrasted this with the fate of Qsarstadt, which, they told me, had become
"quite fundamentalist": most Qsarstadt women now "wore a veil" and their
Leisure Center had "become a mosque." Muslim proselytizers, some of my
informants confirmed, had tried to "impose the veil here," but without
much success. When I inquired about the reasons for such "failure," my
female informants were categorical: husbands, they said, did not insist on
the "veil" being worn, hence the "failure." My observations confirmed this.

Qsarstadt women wore a bewildering array of costumes: some were in
traditional Maghrebi dress, some in modest Western clothes with an "Islamic scarf," and a few in the remarkable Egyptian fashion of the full, black
neguab, in which only the eyes are uncovered. If the Leisure Center had
not quite "become a mosque," it nonetheless now housed a prayer room,
and use of its facilities was sex segregated.

Meanwhile, Qsarheim's center was mostly used by children and youth.
Qsarheim's association, almost moribund when I left in 1987, had divided
into a renters' association, composed of older Maghrebi men (all former
members), and the association "Animation et cultures," whose directing
committee now included a few French social workers and educationists
and two Beur youths. Although women were still excluded, the inclusion
of two sons was an extraordinary concession on the part of older men
jealous of their patriarchal privileges (Bloul 1992). It had been a battle,
one son told me, but the older men were now reconciled to the change.
The very different evolutions of two such similar neighborhoods should

discourage easy generalizations about "the Muslim and/or Maghrebi presence" in France. The "affair of the veil," in spite of the facile characterizations in some of the media, offered another such lesson.

The affair started as an incident involving three Maghrebi girls who refused to take off their head scarves in class in spite of the headmaster's demands, and were henceforth refused entrance to the classrooms. This soon became a national controversy, which at its peak figured daily and prominently in all national media for two months until mid December 1989. Nor was "the affair" resolved then. Rather, it was abruptly silenced when the effects of its political exploitation became dramatically obvious: local elections in November 1989 registered a marked increase in support for the right-wing National Front (FN), which led the FN leader to make outrageous demands in its bid for power. This furious debate over females' proper attire was dominated, almost monopolized, by men, both French and/or Muslims.

Women's opinions were hardly ever heard. Mme Mitterand took a position in favor of the "veil" in the name of individual rights, a stance widely criticized as a political embarrassment to her husband. Some French feminists and female politicians belatedly opposed the veil, and their opinion was duly registered and forgotten (*Le Monde*, October 25, p. 14). Although the positions of a few well-known Muslim women (Mme Sebbar, Mme Tazdait) and of Beurettes' associations were reported (ibid.; *L'Express*, November 3, p. 10), their arguments were not on the whole publicized and even less debated. Pride of place was given to prominent men's views: French and Muslim male intellectuals, politicians, and religious representatives heatedly argued the vexed question of republican secularity as an ethnically neutral space. In addition, some Frenchmen delighted in defending Muslim women's rights. In particular, the Freemasons, not particularly noted for their practice of gender equality, were the first to raise this issue.

Blurring the usual distinctions between Left and Right,[5] however, the question of women's rights was quickly downplayed. The debate centered resolutely on secularity, the problems of immigration, the possible birth of a "French" (i.e., "democratic, secular, and privatized") version of Islam, and the consequences of all this for French identity. What is most important, and has been little commented on, is that both French and Muslim professional opinion-makers took various positions for and against the veil in the name of the same values—that is, secularity and individual rights. For those in favor of the veil, secularity was a matter of "ensuring that everybody has a right to their own opinion, and to express it freely and safely. This right is only limited by the respect of the right of the other" (Cheikh Haddam, head, Paris Great Mosque, quoted in *Le Monde*, October 24, 1989, p. 16). For those opposing the veil, secularity meant the deliberate avoidance of any particularistic, symbolic inscription of institutional (republican) space, understood to be the only guarantee for tolerance and individual freedom. Thus, in a typical argument: "Displaying one's minority group symbols against each [symbol] of the other groups [denotes] a logic...of intolerance and of ethnic exclusion, precisely the logic that the spirit of true secularity fights" (Cocq 1989: 2).

Opinion polls showed that French and Muslim public opinions in general coincided with the parameters set by the media debate. French people, for example, were not so much opposed to the veil per se (32 percent only opposed the wearing of the veil in the street) as to the veil as an ethnic marker in republican institutional space such as schools (75 percent against the veil in school). Second-generation Beurs showed the whole gamut of public positions for and against the veil in the name of secular values and individual rights, a result congruent with a marked gallicization of norms among Beurs (Bloul 1992). Among Muslims in general, women (49 percent) and older people (66.7 percent) were more opposed to the veil in school than men (42 percent) and youth (43.6 percent) (*Le Monde*, November 30, 1989, p. 14). Most Beurs defending the veil did so in the name of a specific understanding of secularity and individual rights as respect of differences, while older Maghrebis opposed it in the name of discretion.

Thus, the divisions among Muslims in France, although downplayed in general by the French media, were as great as among the native French population. In addition, most Muslims, whatever their positions, appealed to the same values (freedom and individual rights) that French opponents of the veil in school invoked, and that form the core of the dominant French public discourse on morality. Finally, one must add that in spite of the scale of the debate, no resolution emerged. Whether the "veil" was or was not to be allowed in school was deemed a question to be answered in each specific circumstance. In this case, the girls involved removed their scarves the following January (1990) after the king of Morocco demanded it of their father, to the embarrassment of a French government whose relations with King Hassan II were already strained.[6]

NOTES TOWARD A GENDERED APPROACH

The data above show the determining importance of male social actors. Whether French or Maghrebi, men used female attire and behavior as markers of a distinctive collective Islamic presence and identity—or as a way to blur distinctions. They also illustrate the divisions among Muslim/Maghrebi men. Finally, this account shows the appropriation of the dominant French moral vocabulary of freedom, secularity, and human rights to legitimate all the actors' strategies, however different they might be. These common elements do not adequately describe whatever dynamic processes underlie the mutability of Muslim and Maghrebi realities in France, but they do offer a start.

Obviously, the different fates of Qsarheim and Qsarstadt are related to the different roles and circumstances of their leading men. Men in Qsarheim have come to believe that they can recreate a male social life for themselves through their association. In it, they have found, or believe they have found, some access to French public life and public recognition. They meet with the local mayor and "important" people, and the local newspapers write about them. These are significant and frequently cited signs of collective prestige. The men are also proud of the neighborhood renovations they have achieved.

These are men who came to France before the 1970s in hopes of bettering their socioeconomic status. They had no driving political or cultural goals, and for a long time they dreamed of return. They had throughout strong ties with the Maghreb, and most were members of the more traditional migrants' associations, organized along national lines. When they slowly abandoned hope of making an economically successful return to the countries of their birth, taking into account the economic and political troubles in the Maghreb and their children's gallicization, they focused on succeeding in France. All this spurred them to redirect family strategies toward integration, which involved women working to pay for their children's studies. A few Qsarheim families had built their own houses in France rather than in the Maghreb, and this was a stimulus to others to attempt their own escape from the "Arab quarter."

The Qsarstadt "leaders," if not the bulk of the Qsarstadt population, differ in that they are younger men who came to Mulhouse primarily to study. They belong to Islamic associations whose programs include political reform in the Maghreb, as well as proselytizing among Muslims, and even to some extent among the ethnic French. They also maintain strong cultural and social ties to the Maghreb, and they have not necessarily ruled out the possibility of return; they perceive themselves as Muslims first and have a very strong sense of belonging to a transnational, not to say universal, Islamic space. Unlike the older migrants in Qsarheim, who often split into opposed parties along national divides, Qsarstadt leaders form friendships and alliances across national lines on the basis of their Muslim allegiance.

For the Qsarstadt leaders, no participation in French public space can occur at the expense of their Islamic identity. Unlike Qsarheim men, they make their Islamic distinctiveness a central component of their recognized identity. To that end, and in line with their mastery of the moral vocabulary of freedom and individual rights, they mobilize Islam, within the limited sphere of the French public scene, following the logic of minorities' ethnic politics of "cultural difference." This is a language familiar to them as students and semiprofessionals with a Westernized formal education.

Figure 44. "Are you for or against the veil [*le voile*] at school?" *Le Monde*, November 7, 1989.

Figure 45. "Here are the ayatollah, the headmaster, and the prefect back again to find out what you are wearing today!" *Le Monde*, November 7, 1989, p. 1.

This is not to say that this particular type of mobilization of Islam is their only, or preferred, strategy in other domains. It is simply that in their fight for self-recognition in France, Qsarstadt leaders, unlike Qsarheim men, have chosen to stress their Islamic distinctiveness, emphasizing an Islamic allegiance (over mere national ones) and identifying themselves as members of an educated transnational Muslim elite. And one of the ways in which they mark their collective difference is through their women's distinctive appearance in public, which is all the more remarkable in that few of these men themselves display any distinctive signs of their Muslim allegiance. Few wear beards, and they dress more in track suits, jeans, leather jackets, and casual Western attire than in white robes, which I have seen only the imam wearing. They are not alone in using women as markers of collective identity: as noted above, a common Maghrebi self-definition asserts: "We are Muslims, our women behave/look this way."

Maghrebi women have some autonomy, but their individual freedom of choice, their margins of action, are severely limited precisely because they are in the position of individuals facing collective social might, whether French or Maghrebi. The three schoolgirls of the veil affair illustrate this most pertinently. They were presented by supporters of the veil as independent moral actors, but by detractors as the puppets of either patriarchal tyranny or religious militants. Two cartoons illustrate the pressure presumed to impinge on them from a father in one case (fig. 44) and from a trio of powerful French and Muslim males—the "ayatollah," the headmaster, and the prefect—in the second (fig. 45). Ironically, the monopolization of the debate by men, whether French or Maghrebi, questions their autonomy just as much as their abandonment of the scarf after Hassan II's intervention with their father. The acrimony of this male political debate over female attire clearly points to the collective stake at the heart of this particular bout of sexual politics, namely, the role and use of women in the constitution, and public display, of collective identities. Why else would three scarves threaten French identity and values or assert Muslim ones? Control over women is also a brutal affirmation of the genderization of such collective identities, whether French or Maghrebi, as generically male.

THE GENDERED POLITICS OF REPRESENTATION IN A MULTICULTURAL CONTEXT

Feminists have long argued that collective identities are androcentric. Julia Kristeva (1989), for example, argues that collective identities are produced along a logic of masculine identity formation that includes rejection of some "other" and stresses the control, if not the suppression, of differences within.[7] As far as Western cultures are concerned, many feminist analysts have expressed their suspicion of "substitutionalist universalism," inasmuch as they detect male, middle-class, white men profiled behind the equal individual of democratic discourse (Benhabib 1986; Fraser 1989;

Love 1991). Similarly, the case for the androcentric mold of the Islamic *ummah* has been made repeatedly by Muslim feminist scholars (Abrous 1989; Ait Sabbah 1986; Jowkar 1986; Lazreg 1988; Mernissi 1983, 1987). This argument is at the core of my understanding of the gendered politics of representation as illustrated in the male public debate about female attire.

In this case, deterritorialization brought about by Maghrebi postcolonial immigration raises the problems of the cultural reproduction of identity and values, not only for Maghrebis facing possible gallicization, but also, I would argue, for the French, whose territory now contains "strange foreigners," to paraphrase Kristeva (1989: 274–77). Because of the gendered dynamics of collective identity, deterritorialization has specific consequences for both French and Maghrebi men, as male vehemence during the affair of the veil so aptly demonstrates.

The affair challenged patriarchal and fratriarchal understandings of gender roles and identities. In this particular instance, Maghrebi fathers and religious hierarchies were joined by Catholic and Jewish clerics who demonstrated unreserved support for the veil. Together they opposed the free circulation of women in the fraternal and secular French Republic. Those among the second-generation Beurs hoping to join the French fraternity (such as Arezki Dahmani of France-Plus), however, supported a strict interpretation of secularity. Others, less confident of their place in France or more involved in a process of ethnicization, defensively supported the veil and their right to "difference" in protecting "their women." For them, Islam has become the main resource and guarantor of a marginalized and ethnicized androcentric collective identity (Bloul 1992), and Muslim women have become the privileged site for the affirmation and display of such identity, quite apart from any individual decision women may make. Frenchmen's responses betray their understanding of this collective use of women. As Qsarstadt and Qsarheim men are also well aware, the existence of "veiled women" in the French public space—whatever the motive—is perceived by Frenchmen as a Muslim male challenge to their own control of French republican fraternal space.

In this regard, the disruptions of masculinity brought about by deterritorialization are aptly captured, for the French side, by the particularly polysemic caricature shown in figure 46. The ugly, old, neutered Catholic nun is an obvious reference to the convergence of views of religious leaders of all denominations in favor of the veil. The nun stands for the old religious and patriarchal orders as seen from a modern French male point of view: denying access to women in the name of the old orders is out. The glamorization of the Muslim student is counterfactual, as a photograph of the students suggests (fig. 47). But it reveals what the unconscious stakes are: the unsupportable presence of forbidden women on the collective male

Figure 46. "Give them this . . . they want this!" *Le Canard enchaîné,*
October 25, 1989.

territory of republican institutions. This is an old theme in the history of
French/Maghrebi colonial relations, here given a new postcolonial twist.

The presentation of both the nun and the sexy Muslim student as active
agents is also counterfactual. While the caricatured nun is a classic example of scapegoating (the victim as oppressor), such presentation of the
hypersexualized young Muslim woman as an autonomous actor is more
complex. The cartoon is obviously addressed to the French viewer as para-
digmatically male. It is also a deliberate attempt to enlist the sympathy of
young Beurettes, quite congruent with the "chivalrous" position taken by
most Frenchmen in the debate, who suddenly became champions of wom-
en's rights. By fantasizing young Muslim women as autonomous actors
(while denouncing their subjection!), it establishes with them an imagined
alliance in the ridiculing of the old, repressive patriarchal orders represented by a nun (rather than an imam). Thus the French male viewer can
fantasize complicity with a forbidden postcolonial object of desire. Finally,
this fantastic seduction is staged without compromising a remarkably per-

Figure 47. Two students at the Collège Gabriel-Havez de Creil, Oise.

sistent misogyny, quite congruent with the more habitual exclusion of women from French republican fraternal space.

THE GALLICIZATION OF MAGHREBI VALUES AND THE ETHNICIZATION OF ISLAM

As noted above, every (male) participant in the debate over the "Islamic scarves," whatever his origins or opinions, invoked freedom, secularity, and individual rights as supportive arguments for or against the veil. The preeminence of this particular moral vocabulary, however French or indigenized its widely different interpretations might be, is an extremely interesting, if often ignored, fact. Nor is that moral vocabulary limited to the various Maghrebi, Muslim, and French social commentators with access to the media. Qsarstadt men defend their right to cultural difference and often make Islam part of their ethnic Muslim identity in the name of their inalienable rights as equal individuals. Cheikh Haddam's argument, quoted above, in favor of veiling because "secularity is about ensuring that everybody has a right to their own opinion, and to express it freely and safely" articulates a very similar position. This comment effectively reduces Islam to the mere "opinion" of atomized individuals. This is a peculiarly ironic product of the global cultural flow. It has produced the Qsarstadt leaders as an embryonic transnational Muslim elite, yet has fostered the gallicization/Westernization of Maghrebi children in France.

Qsarheim men also use this vocabulary, although they are more skeptical. For them, freedom and individual rights are specific French values (as opposed to Maghrebi practices), which Maghrebi men in France can and should use to their advantage. But such reasoned application is characteristically specific and contextualized. "We are in France now. We must do things in the correct democratic way," a Qsarheim association president said to restore procedural order to a committee discussion that had become personal and heated. "There is freedom here . . . freedom is dangerous for those not used to it. Moroccans in France tend to abuse their [newfound] freedom and go bad," a Moroccan father said. The same reasoning was applied by men to Maghrebi women: they couldn't have the same freedom as Frenchwomen because, not being used to it, they would "exaggerate" if not under the firm restraint of Maghrebi men.

As for the younger Beurs, they characteristically show a marked gallicization of their moral understanding and practices, albeit quite limited and circumscribed in relation to the status of Maghrebi women and of Islam as guarantor of an androcentric Beur collective identity (Bloul 1992). This preeminence of the moral vocabulary of freedom and individual rights permeates the whole discussion of the modernization of Islam in France. Just as even the most gallicized Beurs affirm their allegiance to Islam (Bloul 1992), very few, if any, Maghrebi men's understanding of their faith is uninfluenced by the (French) public moral discourse of universal individual rights, although such influence does not extend to the discriminatory consequences of sexual politics, as has been documented above. But then, as feminist critiques of substitutionalist universalism show (see above), Frenchwomen also must bear the effects of similarly discriminatory sexual politics. Thus, siding with some French proposals about a "French Islam," Beurs sometimes propose a model of gallicized Islam characterized as democratic, secular, and privatized (Kaltenbach 1991). Relevant to this also are a number of government initiatives, most notably the establishment of a consultative Islamic body, the Conseil de réflexion sur l'Islam en France (also noted in Diop and Michalak, this volume). Others argue that a fundamental rereading of Islam would purify it of historical misconceptions, since Islam is in fact compatible with the key democratic concepts of equality and solidarity. Many have more nuanced positions and consider the basic texts of Islam, not as absolute guidelines for modern everyday life, but as requiring sophisticated exegesis (Arkoun 1986). Such developments characterize the central paradox of Islamic renewal in France as it simultaneously engages globalization (or is it gallicization?) and ethnicization.

CONCLUSION: ON ETHNIC REVIVALS AND ANDROCENTRIC CULTURAL PROCESSES

Qsarstadt leaders, and others, ethnicize Islam as a Maghrebi attribute in France, while simultaneously proselytizing for Islam as an alternative universalism. This localized strategy, like those revealed by the debate on "difference" generated around the affair of the veil, appears to be the ironic by-product of the deterritorialization resulting from global cultural flows—in this case, the transnational migration of Maghrebi Muslims and their adoption of the key French politico-moral concepts of equality, freedom, and secularity. The French also contribute to such processes. Such processes and strategies operate within the parameters set by the gendered politics of representation according to which women are both markers and stakes for androcentric collective identities. Not only in France but in many instances of conflict between Muslims and non-Muslims, a similar paradox between the globalization of the Islamic ecumene and the ethnicization of the relevant Islamic communities exists and is also to be understood in the context of the gendered politics of identity.

The final ironic result of the gendered politics of representation in a multicultural context is the effect on the host population. In this particular case, French perceptions of "an internal Islamic threat" have led to another ethnicization process—namely, the ethnicization of French identity, most crudely and powerfully expressed in the demagogic discourses of the National Front, which raises as a symbol a singular collage of Gaulish Christianity. The anxious interrogations of French identity and cultural values that have multiplied recently in France are another symptom of the push toward this dual ethnicization process. The affair of the veil acted as a catalyst for such discussions. The range of these discussions, from affirmations of ethnocentrism to a revisitation of universalist ideals, allows one a slender hope that such twin processes of ethnicization might be counteracted. This cannot be done successfully, however, if the gendered nature of the processes of cultural reproduction is not understood.

NOTES

1. Beur collective action made its first national impact in 1983 when several hundred Beurs and Beurettes marched through France to Paris to protest against racist incidents (Bouzid 1984; Jazouli 1986). Beurettes played an important role,

although relatively few in number, and some have been politically active ever since. One, Mme Djida Tazdait, has been elected to the European Parliament.

2. The situation has somewhat changed since the resurgence of the debate in 1994, when the then minister for education, François Bayrou, expressly forbade the wearing of "conspicuous symbols" of group identity in the republican institutional space of the schools. When a number of adolescent females protested against what they perceived as discrimination, French media depicted them as "manipulated by extremist groups" and "blind" to the Islamist danger to themselves as women and to the advantages of liberal French gender arrangements. I have argued elsewhere that this contemporary French defense of Muslim women's rights echoes the French colonial "sexual politics" of penetration in Algeria (Bloul 1995).

3. Appadurai's use of gender shows how unreflectively he associates gender and women: he mentions gender only in relation to women as victims of (increased) male violence resulting from certain deterritorialization effects. This derivative use robs the concept of gender of much of its analytical potential vis-à-vis "the cultural politics of deterritorialization."

4. Both names are pseudonyms.

5. The rightist opposition delighted in taking an unusual position for women's rights. The parties of the Left and the usual antidiscrimination associations, as traditional supporters of women's rights (in lieu of France's very weak feminist organizations) and of minorities, were in an ambiguous situation, which produced belated attempts to diffuse the question as much as possible.

6. Hassan II of Morocco opposed François Mitterrand's vague desire to give immigrants the right to vote. He had also been considerably offended by the publication in France of a book and various articles denouncing Moroccan human rights failures.

7. Another version of this argument (Bloul 1992) is partly inspired by the works of Chodorow (1978, 1989), Fox-Keller (1984), and Pateman (1988).

WORKS CITED

Abrous, Dahbia. 1989. *L'Honneur et le travail des femmes en Algérie*. Paris: L'Harmattan.

Ait Sabbah, Fatna. 1986. *La Femme dans l'inconscient musulman*. Paris: Albin Michel.

Appadurai, Arjun. 1990. "Disjuncture and Difference in the Global Cultural Economy." *Public Culture* 2, 2: 1–24.

Arkoun, Mohammed. 1986. *L'Islam: Morale et politique*. Paris: Desclée de Brouwer.

Bailey, Frederick George. 1971. "Gifts and Poison." In *The Politics of Reputation*. Oxford: Blackwell.

Belbahri, Abdelkader. 1987. *Immigration et situations postcoloniales: Le Cas des Maghrébins en France*. Paris: CIEMI / L'Harmattan.

Benhabib, Seyla. 1986. "The Generalized and the Concrete Other: The Kohlberg-Gilligan Controversy and Feminist Theory." *Praxis International* 5, 4: 401–29.

Berger, John, and Jean Mohr. 1982. *A Seventh Man*. London: Writers and Readers Pub. Col.

Bloul, Rachel. 1992. "Compromising Masculinities: The Engendering of Morality among Maghrebis in France." Ph.D. thesis, Macquarie University.

———. 1995. "Victims or Offenders? 'Other' Women in French Sexual Politics." Paper written for the conference "Women, Colonialisms, Imperialisms and Nationalisms through the Ages," Montreal, Canada, August 27–September 3.

———. Forthcoming. "Gender and the Globalization of Islamic Discourses." In *Beyond Nationalism and Ethnicity: Southeast Asian Identities in a Postcolonial Age*, ed. Joel Kahn. Honolulu: University of Hawaii Press.

Bouzid. 1984. *La Marche: Traversée de la France profonde*. Paris: Sindbad.

Castles, Stephen. 1984. "Here for Good." In Stephen Castles, Heather Booth, and Tina Wallace, *Here for Good: Western Europe's New Ethnic Minorities*. London: Pluto Press.

———. 1986. "The Guest-Worker in Western Europe: An Obituary." *International Migration Review* 20, 4: 761–77.

Chodorow, Nancy. 1978. *The Reproduction of Mothering: Psychoanalysis and the Sociology of Gender*. Berkeley: University of California Press.

———. 1989. *Feminism and Psychoanalytic Theory*. New Haven, Conn.: Yale University Press.

Cocq, Guy. 1989. "Espace laïque." *Le Monde*, October 24, p. 2.

Fox-Keller, Evelyn. 1984. *Reflections on Gender and Science*. New Haven, Conn.: Yale University Press.

Fraser, Nancy. 1989. *Unruly Practices: Power, Discourse and Gender in Contemporary Social Theory*. Minneapolis: University of Minnesota Press.

Humphrey, Michael. 1990. "Religion and Cultural Politics in Australia." *Islam and Christian Muslim Relations* 1, 2: 208–32.

Helie-Lucas, Marie-Aimee. 1994. "The Preferential Symbol for Islamic Identity: Women in Muslim Personal Laws." In *Identity Politics and Women: Cultural Reassertions and Feminisms in International Perspective*, ed. Valentine Moghadam. Boulder, Colo.: Westview Press.

Jazouli, Adil. 1986. *L'Action collective des jeunes maghrébins en France*. Paris: L'Harmattan.

Jourjon, Pierre. 1980. *L'Emigré, oú fleurira ton soleil?* Paris: Le Centurion.

Jowkar, Forouz. 1986. "Honor and Shame: A Feminist View from Within." *Feminist Issues*, Spring, pp. 45–65.

Kaltenbach, Jeanne, and Pierre Kaltenbach. 1991. *La France, une chance pour l'Islam*. Paris: Editions du Felin.

Kristeva, Julia. 1989. *Etrangers à nous-mêmes*. Paris: Fayard.

Lazreg, Marnia. 1988. "Feminism and Difference: The Perils of Writing as a Woman on Women in Algeria." *Feminist Studies*, Spring, pp. 81–107.

Love, Nancy. 1991. "Ideal Speech and Feminist Discourse: Habermas Re-visioned." *Women and Politics* 11, 3: 101–21.

Mernissi, Fatima. 1983. *Sexe, idéologie, Islam*. Paris: Tierce.

———. 1987. *Le Harem politique: Le Prophète et les femmes*. Paris: Albin Michel.

Miles, Robert. 1982. *Racism and Migrant Labour*. London: Routledge and Kegan Paul.

Pateman, Carole. 1988. *The Sexual Contract.* Stanford: Stanford University Press.

Rollat, Alain. 1989. "Les Francs-Maçons sonnent la charge contre les intégrismes religieux." *Le Monde,* October 24, p. 17.

Solé, Robert, and Hervé Tincq. 1989. "Le Rejet de l'Islam et l'attrait de la France." *Le Monde,* November 30, pp. 1, 14.

Tazdait, Djida. 1989. "C'est le voile de l'obscurantisme." *L'Express,* November 3, p. 10.

Tincq, Hervé. 1989. "Un Entretien avec Cheikh Tedjini Haddam, recteur de la Mosquée de Paris." *Le Monde,* October 24, p. 16.

NOTES ON CONTRIBUTORS

Rachel Bloul received her Ph.D. from the University of New South Wales and currently teaches sociology at the Australian National University.

Robert Dannin received his Ph.D. in anthropology and ethno-linguistics from the Ecoles des hautes études en sciences sociales (Paris) and currently teaches in New York University's Metropolitan Studies Program. He is the co-author, with Jolie Stahl, of *Black Pilgrimage to Islam* (forthcoming).

Moustapha Diop received his Ph.D. in sociology in 1981 from the Ecoles des hautes études en sciences sociales (Paris). He is currently a Maître de conférences at the Institut national des langues et civilisations orientales (Paris). His publications include *Le Mouvement associatif islamique en Ile-de-France,* on voluntary Islamic associations in Ile-de-France (1990), and *Structuration d'un tabligh,* on structuring the Jama'at Tabligh network (1994). Dr. Diop is currently doing research on Islamic brotherhoods in France and on the transmission of culture among immigrant populations in France.

John Eade is a principal lecturer in the Department of Sociology and Social Policy, Roehampton Institute, London, where he teaches anthropology and sociology at undergraduate and postgraduate levels. He has undertaken research in Calcutta and the East End of London on issues of identity and political representation. His publications include *The Politics of Community* (1989) and, with co-editor Michael J. Sallnow, *Contesting the Sacred: The Anthropology of Christian Pilgrimage* (1991). He is currently editing a book on globalization in London and planning another edited volume on ethnic violence in Europe.

Victoria Ebin has a Ph.D. in anthropology from Cambridge University and a master's degree in journalism from Columbia University. She is currently working as an editor at the Population Reference Bureau in Washington, D.C., and is a research associate at the American Museum of Natural History. She carried out research for several years at ORSTOM (Institut français de recherche et developpement en coopération) in Senegal and France.

Gulzar Haider is Professor of Architecture at Carleton University, Ottawa, Canada. He has been involved over the past three decades in the theory and practice of the design of mosques in North America. He is a member of the International Commission for the Preservation of Islamic Cultural Heritage and has written and lectured extensively on the questions of tradition and modernity in Islamic architecture.

Aminah Beverly McCloud, an assistant professor in religious studies at De-Paul University, specializes in Islamic studies. She is the author of *African-American Islam* (1995).

Ruth Mandel received her Ph.D. from the University of Chicago and teaches anthropology at University College, London. She has recently undertaken research in Kazakhstan.

Barbara Daly Metcalf, a historian, is dean of the Division of Social Sciences at the University of California at Davis. She is the author of *Islamic Revival in British India: Deoband, 1860–1900* (1982), the editor of *Moral Conduct and Authority: The Place of Adab in South Asian Islam* (1984), and the translator of *Perfecting Women: Maulana Ashraf 'Ali Thanawi's Bihisti Zewar* (1990).

Laurence Michalak received his Ph.D. in cultural anthropology in 1983 from the University of California at Berkeley, where he is currently vice chair of the Center for Middle Eastern Studies. He is the co-editor of *Social Legislation in the Contemporary Middle East* (1986) and of a volume in preparation on the effects of international labor migration on North Africa.

Regula Burckhardt Qureshi was trained in anthropology and music; she is a professor of ethnomusicology as well as an adjunct professor of anthropology and religious studies at the University of Alberta. Her research centers on sonic performance traditions, with an ethnographic focus on Muslim cultures in India, Pakistan, and Canada. She is the author of *Sufi Music of India and Pakistan: Sound, Context and Meaning in Qawwali* (1986) and co-editor of *The Muslim Community in North America* (1983) and *Muslim Families in North America* (1991).

Vernon James Schubel is chair of the Department of Religion at Kenyon College, where he teaches courses on Islam, Hinduism, and the History of Religions. He is the author of *Religious Performance in Contemporary Islam:*

Shi'i Devotional Rituals in Pakistan (1993). His current research focuses on Uzbekistan.

Susan Slyomovics teaches in the Department of Comparative Literature at Brown University. She is the author of *The Merchant of Art: An Egyptian Hilali Oral Epic Poet in Performance* (1988) and a member of the editorial committee of MERIP/Middle East Report.

Jolie Stahl is a photographer with a fine arts background. Her pictures are part of a visual anthropology of American Muslims and were taken during field research for the ethnography entitled *Black Pilgrimage to Islam.*

Pnina Werbner is a senior lecturer in Social Anthropology at Keele University and research administrator of the International Centre for Contemporary Cultural Research, Manchester and Keele. Her publications include *The Migration Process: Capital, Gifts and Offerings among British Pakistanis* (1990) and she has co-edited *Black and Ethnic Leaderships in Britain: The Cultural Dimensions of Political Action* (1991) and *Economy and Culture in Pakistan: Migrants and Cities in a Muslim Society* (1991). She is currently directing a major project on South Asian Popular Culture: Gender, Generation and Identity, funded by the Economic and Social Research Council (UK).

INDEX

In the index, as in the text, we have not attempted to impose consistency in the transliteration of Arabic, Persian, and Urdu names and terms. (See "Toward Islamic English?" on pages xv–xix of this volume.) Where appropriate, cross-references to alternate spellings used in this book are given.

Compositor: Maple-Vail Manufacturing Group
Text: 10/12 New Baskerville
Display: New Baskerville
Printer and Binder: Maple-Vail Manufacturing Group